A GUIDE TO
WRITING AND PUBLISHING
in the
Social and Behavioral Sciences

A GUIDE TO
WRITING AND PUBLISHING
in the
Social and Behavioral Sciences

CAROLYN J. MULLINS
Editorial Consultant
Institute of Social Research
Indiana University

A WILEY-INTERSCIENCE PUBLICATION
JOHN WILEY & SONS, New York • London • Sydney • Toronto

Published by John Wiley & Sons, Inc.
Copyright © 1977 by Carolyn J. Mullins

Library of Congress Cataloging in Publication Data
Mullins, Carolyn J.
   A guide to writing and publishing in the
social and behavioral sciences.

   "A Wiley-Interscience publication."
   Bibliography: p.
   Includes index.
   1. Social sciences—Authorship. 2. English
language—Technical English. I. Title.
H91.M8   808'.066'3   77-1153
ISBN 0-471-62420-9
ISBN 0-471-02708-1 pbk.

Printed in the United States of America

10 9 8 7 6 5 4 3 2 1

To Nick,

and to our children:

Nick   Rob   Nancy

Preface

I wrote this book primarily for students and professionals in the social and behavioral sciences, but also for their typists, editors, and publishers. I hope the book will help authors to write better and more easily. I also hope it will reduce the antagonism that often touches relationships between authors and their critics, editors, and publishers.

In Chapters 10 to 17 I sometimes offer statements of fact with no documentation. An explanation is in order. Some of my research consisted of interviews with persons involved in different kinds of publishing. Most of the information I received was given with the understanding that I would not specifically attribute it. The interviewees have read my chapters to assure that I broke no confidences.

Some readers may feel that some instructions are obvious. Unfortunately, among my critics different readers felt that way about different instructions. Skip any that you find unnecessary. However, you may find even the obvious instructions useful when you assign some of your work, such as typing and checking documentation, to others. Appendix D and the photo-reproduced examples in Chapter 8 will be especially helpful to your typists.

Some of the discussion in Chapters 6, 7, 10, and 11 was originally published as parts of two editorials in *The Sociological Quarterly:* "Where Can I Get This Paper Published?" **15** (4, 1974), pp. 466, 599–600; and "Critics and Criticism," **16** (1, 1975), pp. 2, 140–142; both by Carolyn J. Mullins. The discussion is presented here by permission of *The Sociological Quarterly.* Figure 8.4 is reprinted with the permission of Phillips Cutright and of the American Sociological Association. Walter Hirsch, Andrew M. Kulley, and Ronald T. Efron gave permission to cite (in Chapter 9) their unpublished manuscript, "The Gatekeeping Process in Scientific Communication: Norms, Practices, and Content of Book Reviews in Professional Journals," Working Paper #83, Institute for the Study of Social Change, Department of Sociology and Anthropology, Purdue University (1974, mimeo). Nicholas C. Mullins gave permission for me to print his unpublished prospectus for *Power, Social Structure, and Advice in American Science* as Appendix C.

For help with the research I want to thank Herbert Addison, Thomas Begner, Nancy Bergman, George Bohrnstedt, C. William Brown, Jerome Chertkoff, Stanley J. Evans, John Gallman, Pokey Gardner, Helen Gilbart, Polly S. Grimshaw, Robert Heinich, Terry Hoover, David Knoke, Bernard Perry, Pam Rockwell, Susan Shuster, Eric Valentine, and Evelyn Wilde.

For their critical reviews of various chapters I want to thank Michael Armer, Marjory Bankson, Stanley J. Evans, Elizabeth M. Fink, Allen D. Grimshaw, Linda S. Hunkins, James L. McCartney, James F. Short, Jr., Norman W. Storer, Sandra M. Turner, Eric Valentine, and Jim Vincent. For reading and criticizing the entire manuscript I am particularly grateful to Corydon T. Johns, Marilyn Lester, Nicholas C. Mullins, and Whitney Pope. Any errors that remain are my responsibility. Linnea McIntosh helped to design Tables 1.1 and 7.1.

For help with the typing I want to thank Debby Adams, Kathy Carpenter, Sue Hussey, Bob Hutchinson, Janice Kennedy, Linnea McIntosh, and Marcie Wenzler. I am particularly grateful to Bob, who typed most of the manuscript, for his consistently fine typing and skill at correcting my inconsistencies. Julie Gray and Cecily Weisstein helped with proofreading.

Important in many ways has been the support given by George Bohrnstedt and Doris M. Weeks of Indiana University's Institute of Social Research. Also important has been the encouragement of my clients, who welcomed with enthusiasm the chance to edit *my* writing. Most important has been the encouragement of my family.

CAROLYN J. MULLINS

Bloomington, Indiana
February 1977

Contents

List of Illustrations

List of Tables

CHAPTER ONE

Why Use This Book?

INTRODUCTION

1.1 Scientists are frequently criticized for writing poorly. Some of this criticism reflects the misunderstanding of persons who expect all good writing to be imaginative and colorful. In fact, the task of scientific writing is the careful, objective reporting of research findings, methodology or theory, and this task is often best served by standard outlines and neutral words (discussed in Sections 2.21 to 2.23). Often, though, the criticism is well deserved. As critics, scientists shake their heads in amazement at manuscripts that are poorly written and improperly prepared for submission to publishers. Nonscientific writers object to unjustified technical language. As Edwin Newman (1974, p. 146) remarked, much "social scientific practice consists of taking clear ideas and making them opaque."

1.2 Journal editors and book publishers also despair as they wade through manuscripts that are verbose, grammatically sloppy, or inappropriate for their journals. Often this distress reaches the authors in the form of rejections. In sociology one response to this problem has been *The Sociological Quarterly*'s editorial series on problems in writing for scholarly publication (McCartney 1972, p. 430).

THE DILEMMA

No Systematic Information on Writing and Publishing

1.3 Most scientists are acutely aware of the criticism, but do not know how to correct their shortcomings. Most graduate students are not taught how to write for publication—a task that is often quite unlike writing to fulfill class or dissertation requirements. They are also not taught how to find appropriate publishers for their manuscripts. Some students learn these skills informally, perhaps by coauthoring a manuscript with a supervising professor. Others learn them accidentally, as when they notice that some articles are alike in specific ways. Still others never learn. The sad fact is that almost all who learn do so inefficiently, by trial and error. Only those who learn become successful scientists—insofar as success is measured by number and quality of publications (see Cole and Cole 1973). The rest waste their attempts to write, thereby advancing neither their careers nor scientific knowledge.

The Need for Systematic Information

1.4 Most scientists want to write effectively and to publish. They know what George Orwell (1950, pp. 77–78) knew: The English language "becomes ugly and inaccurate because our thoughts are foolish, but the slovenliness of our language makes it easier for us to have foolish thoughts. . . . Written English is full of bad habits. . . . If one gets rid of these habits one can think more clearly." They also know that effective writing improves research. It prevents misunderstanding while permitting the exchange of ideas and the replication and verification of findings. Effective communication—published and unpublished—also prevents duplication of prior research. The nature of published scientific communication is well known to scientists. For a description of unpublished communication, see Garvey, Lin, and Nelson (1970).

1.5 The author of either a scientific report or a textbook is in a unique position. The intended audience is not a supervisor, who is required to read employees' reports regardless of their quality, but rather peers or students. Before either audience can be reached through publication, the manuscript's substance and clarity must convince referees and editors to recommend it as a quality product (Zuckerman and Merton 1971, p. 66).

1.6 Most scientists find that publication is necessary to professional advancement. Since the late 1960s the supply of scientists with doctoral degrees has been at least equal to the demand (McCartney 1973a, p. 450), and the result has been a cruel rise in the pressure to publish. This pressure has gradually increased because the number of available pages in journals and books has not increased in proportion to the number of new, aspiring authors (Sections 10.3, 14.1). In addition, production costs have forced publishers to require a higher quality of writing from authors submitting manuscripts.

1.7 Some scientists want to reach and influence important groups of readers who lack specialized scientific training. For example, students are an important audience for authors of textbooks. Government policymakers designing family-planning programs may be an important audience to researchers studying topics such as fertility, family planning, and spontaneous fetal loss. Researchers in education, linguistics, psychology, and sociology often make discoveries that can be used by teachers, school administrators, guidance counselors, and social workers. Thus descriptions of a new technique for inservice teacher training, for example, should be written not only for a professional journal but also for a journal read largely by teachers and school administrators. The factual content of the two manuscripts might be similar, but organization and emphases would differ. In the first article the author might concentrate on validating the research; in the second, on how to use the technique. Most scholars find it harder to write for people who lack specialized training.

THE SOLUTION

1.8 The effective writing and reasonably speedy publication of good scientific work should not depend, even in part, on serendipidous learning about writing and publishing. All other things being equal (e.g., quality of research), all scientists should have an equal chance to publish. Part of the solution to the dilemma is a well-organized handbook on writing and publishing.

Effective Writing

1.9 Effective writing is clear and efficient; thus it can be published with little copy editing. An effective author writing for scientific peers states a problem, describes and validates the evidence and methods used to find a solution, interprets the solution, and discusses its implications and uses—all within a limited number of pages. Effective textbook writing is didactic; the author teaches a specified amount of substance, theory, or methodology, or all three. Effective writing of either type uses an outline and a style appropriate to both the topic and the intended audience. The outline and style, in turn, affect the ordering of sentences and paragraphs, the connecting words, and the choice of language. For example, authors writing for peers usually use formal English and standard outlines.

1.10 Effective writing is not necessarily excellent writing. Excellent writing requires more than reasonable proficiency. An excellent manuscript contains no unnecessary words. Its organization and language usually present its topic not only effectively but in an aesthetically pleasing writing style that is often unique to the author, though common in all of his or her writings. Long after achieving an effective draft, the excellent writer continues revising for style—changing one word for another, playing with word combinations, looking for literary allusions to emphasize points, and so forth.

1.11 Not every scientist has the potential to become an excellent writer. In contrast, effectiveness is possible for any writer willing to follow specific guidelines for organizing, writing, and revising. Of those scientists who might become excellent writers, many prefer to settle for effective writing and spend the extra time doing research. Moreover, some argue that for most scientists excellent writing is neither a realistic nor a necessarily desirable goal (American Psychological Association—APA 1974, p. 28).

Reasonably Speedy Publication

1.12 Publication of a manuscript is most likely if its author knows which publishers are most appropriate for it. An astonishing number of articles are submitted to inappropriate journals. Similarly, many monographs are submitted to publishers who specialize in textbooks. It is not surprising, then, that of the hundreds of thousands of scientific articles and books written every year only a few are published immediately. Others of equal scientific merit circulate in unpublished form for long periods of time before publication, and still others are never published. There are many reasons for such delays, and each reason should receive systematic attention from authors who want to write and publish as well and efficiently as possible.

The Purpose of This Book

1.13 Many tasks—such as outlining, preparing tables, and selecting an appropriate publisher—stand between an aspiring author and a published manuscript. These tasks vary with the kind of manuscript—for example journal article, book review, textbook, monograph. This book suggests efficient and effective ways to perform the tasks. The information in the book is not necessarily new, though some is, or surprising; I have no magic formulas. The information is basic, practical, timesaving, and systematized. My purpose is to help authors to avoid problems, and to resolve efficiently those that they cannot avoid. This book also explains little-known details of publishing that directly affect authors, thereby decreasing the expenses to publishers caused by authors' ignorance of proper ways to prepare and submit manuscripts.

The Book's Organization

1.14   In Part I of this book I discuss general problems in scientific writing and ways to correct them. Because there are already many good books on excellent writing, effective writing in general, and effective writing in the natural and physical sciences, I concentrate on scientific writing in the social and behavioral sciences. Such writing must be effective if the writers and the scientific community are to benefit fully from the ideas that motivated the writing.

1.15   Parts II, III, and IV deal with choosing appropriate journals for scientific articles, preparing articles for submission to journals, and working with journal editors; writing books; and choosing appropriate book publishers, writing prospectuses, negotiating contracts, and working with publishers. If you want help with a specific task on a given manuscript, perhaps with contract negotiations on a textbook,

○ Consult Table 1.1, which cross-classifies types of manuscript by tasks, listed in approximately the temporal order in which authors encounter them.

The intersection of the column "Contracts" with the row "Monographs, textbooks" shows that the relevant information is in Chapters 13 and 16.

Table 1.1 Where to Find Information in This Book

	Getting Started; First Drafts	Outlines, Organization	Revisions	Collegial and Editorial Assistance; Criticism	Tables, Illustrations, Documentation, Appendixes, Indexes, Bibliographies	Evaluation of Journal Editors and Book Publishers	Preparing and Submitting a Manuscript to a Publisher	Authors' Dealings with Journal Editors and Book Publishers	Prospectuses	Contracts	Marketing Questionnaires
Articles	4	2	5,6	6,11	3,8	7,A	8,11,D	10,11		11	
Research notes	4	2,9	5,6	6,11	3,8	7,A	8,9,11,D	10,11			
Brief reports	4	2,9	5,6	6,11	3,8	7,A	8,9,11,D	10,11			
Comments, responses, debates	4	2,9	5,6	6,11	3,8	7,A	8,9,11,D	10,11			
Review articles	4	2,9	5,6	6,11	3,8	7,A	8,9,11,D	10,11			
Book reviews	4	2,9	5	6,11	3,8	7,A	8,9,11,D	10,11			
Monographs, textbooks	4,13	2,13	5,17	6,17	3,8,12	14,16	8,11,12,17,D	14,17	15,C	13,16	17
Edited collections, bibliographies	4,13	2,13	5,17	6,17	3,8,12	14,16	8,11,12,17,D	14,17	15,C	13,16	17
Dissertations, class papers, grant applications, reports, oral presentations	4	2,B	5,B	6,B	B						

Note. Blank cells show that the intersecting row and column are mutually inapplicable.

1.16   This book was prepared for writers in the social and behavioral sciences. Thus my examples are taken from social- and behavioral-science manuscripts, and Table 7.1 reports data only on journals in the social and behavioral sciences. In every other respect this book is equally useful to other scholars.

1.17   Because most authors are too busy to spend much time hunting for instructions, each chapter begins with an outline and ends with a summary. In many sections I list cross-references to related descriptions, explanations, and instructions that may be useful to some readers. There is also an index. Many of the instructions are indicated by circles, as in Section 1.15. Very important points are indicated by squares. Cautions and exceptions to general rules are preceded by CAUTION or EXCEPTION. To avoid bias in use of pronouns, I follow the guidelines in Sections 5.47 and 5.48.

1.18   Some aspects of writing and publishing are sufficiently complex that they cannot be reduced to simple rules. Instead, authors need to understand the important factors in each situation and then apply them to individual cases. Accordingly some chapters—for example, Chapters 10, 11, 13, and 14—contain several pages of discussion with no instructions.

SUMMARY

1.19   Many scientists write poorly or not at all. Of those who write, many have trouble getting their manuscripts published (Sections 1.1 to 1.7). This book gives organized practical information on scientific writing, on preparing and publishing journal articles, and on writing and publishing books (1.8 to 1.18). Table 1.1 lists topics and the chapters in which each is discussed. The book was written for social and behavioral scientists, but most of it is equally useful to other scholars (1.16).

Part One

OUTLINES, FIRST DRAFTS, REVISIONS, AND RESOURCES

CHAPTER TWO

Outlines

GENERAL FUNCTIONS

2.1 Use outlines to provide:

○ A plan for writing.
○ An internal order, or skeleton, for your manuscript.

All effective authors use internal order well. Not all use outlines as planning devices. Sometimes, especially when an author

11

uses a standard outline, the internal order of the completed manuscript closely resembles the plan for writing.

2.2 Specialists in writing often give primary consideration to grammatical correctness, smooth flow, and style. These matters are important, but no more so than organization. When beginning a manuscript,

○ Establish internal order before spending much time on correctness, flow, and style.

OUTLINE MECHANICS

Expression of Topics

2.3 Figure 2.1 shows how to express the importance of topics in an outline. The basic principles are:

○ Order topics by decreasing importance.

I. The first major topic   First level of importance
 A. A subtopic of *I*   Second level of importance
  1. A subtopic of *A*   Third level of importance
  2. A subtopic of *A*
  3. A subtopic of *A*
 B. A subtopic of *I*   Second level of importance
  1. A subtopic of *B*   Third level of importance
  2. A subtopic of *B*
   a. A subtopic of *2*   Fourth level of importance
   b. A subtopic of *2*
    (1) A subtopic of *b* Fifth level of importance
    (2) A subtopic of *b*
     (a) A subtopic of (2) Sixth level of importance
     (b) A subtopic of (2)

II. The second major topic   First level of importance
 A. A subtopic of *II*   Second level of importance
 B. A subtopic of *II*

Figure 2.1 Levels of importance in an outline.

○ If you make any entries at any level of importance in any part of an outline, make at least two entries. For example, in Figure 2.1, *I* has *A* and *B* as subtopics. *IB1* has no subtopics, but *IB2* has two subtopics.

In general, for manuscripts of fewer than 40 pages, such as many articles and most research proposals,

○ Use only four levels of importance.
○ Use the first three levels as the basis for topically expressed headings and subheadings in the manuscript's text. See Section 5.6 for help in writing headings. Sections 8.31 to 8.34 show how to prepare headings in different editorial styles.[1]

Kinds of Outline

2.4   Topic Outlines. These outlines are made up of clauses and phrases. Sections 2.9, 2.14, and 2.31 show topic outlines with open punctuation (no punctuation at ends of topics).

☐ Advantage: you can express ideas briefly.
☐ Disadvantage: brevity can leave your meaning unclear.

2.5   Sentence Outlines. These outlines are made up of complete sentences. The sentences may be punctuated at the end (closed punctuation) or not. The only requirement is that punctuation be consistent. The following example is a sentence outline with closed punctuation (for a longer example, see Section 9.23).

I. I found three strong correlations.   [1].
   A. I found a correlation between age and education.
   B. I found a correlation between education and job status.
   C. I found a correlation between job status and income.

Advantages:

☐ Ideas and the relationships between them are clearer than in a topic outline.
☐ Many sentences are ready for use in drafts.

Disadvantage:

☐ Some of the writing may ultimately prove unnecessary. For
example, an author using outline [1] might reduce it to one
sentence in the text: I found strong correlations between age
and education, education and job status, and job status and
income.

2.6 Combination Outlines.

○ Use sentences for major topics.
○ Use clauses, phrases, or words for subtopics.
○ Use combination punctuation: periods, question marks, or
exclamation points after sentences; no punctuation after topics.

For example, a combination outline of [1] might look like [2]:

I. I found three strong correlations.   [2]
   A. Between age and education
   B. Between education and job status
   C. Between job status and income

2.7 A combination outline has the advantages of both sen-
tence- and topic-outline forms while minimizing the disadvantages. However,

○ Pay special attention to parallel, grammatical construction of
entries if the outline is to be used by anyone except you—
perhaps by a coauthor or a book publisher evaluating outlines for chapters in a proposed book. For example, items *A*,
B, and *C* in [2] all begin with prepositions. In [3] below,
items *1* to *5* begin with infinitives. Items *a* to *d* are nouns.

PERCEIVING AND EXPRESSING ORDER

2.8 Useful outlines result from clear thinking about both topic
structure and context.

Topic Structure

2.9   Outline [3] is for part of Chapter 1:

I. B. The need for systematic information   [3]
   1. To clarify thinking
   2. To improve research
   3. To attract readers
   4. To advance professionally
   5. To influence audiences without specialized scientific training, for example,
      a. Students
      b. Government policymakers
      c. School administrators and teachers
      d. Social workers and guidance counselors

Time sequence determines order of items at the third level of importance. Clear thinking precedes writing that will improve research and attract readers. Only if a manuscript has attracted readers, particularly referees, and received their approval can an author communicate research findings through publication and thus advance professionally. Communication with readers other than scientific peers does not necessarily follow professional advancement, but often high professional standing is a prerequisite for such communication. Items *a* to *d* are examples.

2.10   A writer who misunderstood the structure of topic *IB* might write outline [3], from *4* on, like outline [4]:

   4. To advance professionally   [4]
   5. To influence students
   6. To influence government policymakers
   7. To influence school administrators and teachers
   8. To influence social workers and guidance counselors

This order violates the structure of the topic. Order of time does not determine the sequence of the last four items. Also, this order implies that items *5* to *8* are as important as items *1* to *4* when, in fact, the last four are merely examples. Both violations would mislead readers. For another example and its rationale see Section 9.15.

Context of Topic

2.11   A proper context:

☐ Enhances readers' ability to understand your writing because they have the proper background in mind.
☐ Aids the cumulation of theory and findings.
☐ Helps foundation directors, journal editors, and book publishers to select appropriate referees for research proposals, articles, and book manuscripts.

When outlining context, you are not usually trying to discern the one perfect outline for your topic. Rather, you are choosing among several possibilities: some better, some worse, and some that are similar in their effects.

○ Choose on the basis of your topic's intellectual roots, your intended readers, and the best way to present the topic to them.

2.12   Establish intellectual roots in the introduction. See Sections 2.25 to 2.28 for guidelines and an example. Then choose an outline to fit your readers' needs and background.

> For example, for persons with limited reading time, such as administrators of governmental agencies, discuss the most important topics first. Place a brief abstract and a summary of conclusions at the beginning of a manuscript that is otherwise organized in order of increasing importance (Section 2.18).

2.13   For all readers, cite appropriate background documents. For example, the introduction to a psychological study of effects of the Vietnamese war might refer to the songs, speeches, and writings of Joan Baez, Eugene McCarthy, and Jane Fonda. If the author is writing for radically oriented readers, those references might be appropriate. However, an article written for scientific peers might more appropriately refer to documents that report related research by other scholars. For example, psychiatric studies of men who had been drafted and then classified as conscientious objectors might give valuable background material.

2.14 For professional publications,

○ Cite only documents bearing directly on the topic.

For example, an economist studying the Vietnamese war's effect on America's inflation and balance of payments would probably not discuss psychiatric studies. Similarly, discussion of effects on Vietnam's economy probably would also be inappropriate. Instead, he or she would establish a context within the literature on America's problems with inflation and balance of payments. Some of that literature might be substantive—the economist's figures on inflation might differ from someone else's. Some might be methodological—he might have measured inflation and balance of payments using techniques different from those of past researchers. And some might be theoretical. The result could be an introduction following outline [5]:

I. Introduction   [5]
   A. Substantive findings of past researchers
      1. On inflation
      2. On balance of payments
   B. Past methods and measurements
      1. On inflation
      2. On balance of payments
   C. Theory
      1. On inflation
      2. On balance of payments

Different Organizational Patterns

2.15 The following discussion is partly based on Tichy (1966, pp. 67–83).

2.16 Order of Time (Chronological Order). Order of time, sometimes used by historians and political scientists, has several advantages:

- [ ] The date of an event automatically establishes its place in an outline.
- [ ] Time sequence suggests natural transition words such as *after, then, before.* For others, see Section 5.33.
- [ ] Readers can easily locate specific information.

Chronology also has disadvantages:

- [ ] It can bury important topics, because the order of an event is not determined by its importance.
- [ ] It can become monotonous.

Section 2.9 shows an example.

2.17   Order of Place.   Geographical order, sometimes used by anthropologists, political scientists, and comparative sociologists, has advantages similar to those of time order.

- [ ] A topic's place in an outline is determined by where it occurred. For example, a political scientist comparing the voting patterns in three states might organize the data by states.
- [ ] Geographical order suggests natural transition words such as *where, directly north.* For others, see Section 5.33.

Geographical order also has disadvantages similar to those of time order:

- [ ] It may bury important topics and bore readers.

2.18   Order of Increasing Importance.   Scientists often write research articles by arranging topics in order of increasing importance. See Sections 2.21 to 2.42 for detailed discussion.

2.19 Order of Decreasing Importance. Authors sometimes arrange topics in order of decreasing importance if their intended readers have limited reading time. The major disadvantage is that having read the most important material first, readers may subsequently lose interest.

2.20 Order of Emphasis by Position. At its best, order of emphasis by position has the advantages, while eliminating the disadvantages, of outlines based on increasing or decreasing order of importance. To use this order,

○ Begin with a short summary.
○ Then present topics in order of increasing importance.

This order is typical of manuscripts that begin with an abstract.

STANDARD OUTLINES

The Value of Standard Outlines

2.21 Standard outlines draw many complaints, and I agree with some of them. Such outlines *are* unoriginal, and I, too, sometimes tire of seeing all manuscripts divided into the same four or five parts. Nevertheless, most scholarly articles in the social and behavioral sciences—particularly those by psychologists, sociologists, and educators—conform to one of the standard outlines.

2.22 These outlines serve many purposes. First, the goal of scientific writing is to convey information without bias, and not necessarily to give aesthetic pleasure. This fact severely limits the amount of imagination a scientist may use in organizing and writing. As Pirsig (1974, p. 101) put it, "If you . . . [romanticize] scientific information, giving it a flourish here and there, Nature will soon make a complete fool out of you. . . . One logical slip and an entire scientific edifice comes tumbling down." Also, scientists usually need to find information rapidly. When a research article follows a standard outline, readers can always find the results in approximately the same place in every article—about halfway through. Finally, referees can easily find the information they need and may thus complete more rapidly their reports to journal editors and book publishers.

2.23 I am not saying that scientific writing lacks either originality or style. The organization may lack originality, but if effectively written a manuscript will have "a classic esthetic which romantics often miss because of its subtlety. The classic style is straightforward, unadorned, unemotional, economical and carefully proportioned. Its purpose is . . . to bring order out of chaos. . . . It is esthetically restrained. Everything is under control. Its value is measured in terms of the skill with which this control is maintained" (Pirsig 1974, p. 67). Furthermore, originality is important to the research that precedes the writing. Judge a scientist's originality by the problems he or she chooses to study, the research designs he creates to solve problems that have baffled previous researchers, the ways in which he controls for persistent sources of bias, and the use he makes of analytical tools.

Data-Analysis Outline

2.24 The data-analysis outline has many other names—for example, the APA (American Psychological Association) format. Scientists use it to organize their reports of research done in accordance with the scientific method. Though sometimes used in books (Section 13.5) and in research proposals (Section B.4), this outline is most commonly found in research articles. The examples below are based on articles.

2.25 Problem Statement. The problem statement establishes context by reviewing previous research and theory specifically related to the problem. Sometimes this section is titled *Introduction* or *Background*, but unless it constitutes more than 15 percent of an article, leave it untitled. The position indicates its purpose. In the problem statement,

○ Present specific questions, or issues.
○ Show why they are important.
○ State what is known about these questions, and who has done significant work on them.
○ Cite only the most pertinent documents.

One sentence for each issue, supported by one or more references to pertinent literature, is often adequate. Sometimes you can summarize very briefly but cite several supporting documents. It is unnecessary, except in some class papers and doctoral dissertations (see Section B.2), to cite all the relevant literature on a question.

2.26 In the final paragraph of the problem statement, briefly and clearly present:

○ The article's single focus.
○ The research method.
○ The central hypotheses.
○ The major finding (optional, but common).

If this paragraph does not focus the problem clearly, the reader may never finish—or not properly understand—the remainder of the article. Reading a problem statement should be like looking through a microscope and gradually fine-tuning it until, in the concluding paragraph, the problem and your approach to it are completely clear.

2.27 Emphasize issues on the basis of factors such as:

○ The hypotheses.
○ The results of the research.
○ The subjects.
○ The preferences of the journal in which you wish to publish the article. See Sections 7.8 to 7.17 for help in choosing a journal.
○ Overall, move from general issues to the specific problem.

2.28   For example, Jeanne Smith, reporting her research on the causes and resolution of conflicts within small groups of students, might first discuss relevant aspects of small-group research and theory in general. Next, she might discuss related research and theory from topical areas such as peace research, conflict resolution, and the sociology and psychology of education and teacher education. If writing for teachers who want to learn how to resolve conflict within small groups of students, she might use outline [6] for the introduction.

I. Problem statement   [6]
  A. Prior research and theory
    1. On small-group conflict generally   [General]
    2. On resolving conflict   [Less general]
    3. On resolving conflict within small groups   [Specific]
    4. On resolving conflict within classroom groups   [More specific]
  B. Summary paragraph
    1. Specific problem: conflict in classroom groups arises when . . .
    2. Central hypothesis: teachers can resolve conflict by . . .
    3. Method used for study
    4. Major finding

2.29   Method.   The method section describes items such as study design, subjects, sampling procedure, equipment used, procedures for data gathering, controls, nature of data, and analytic technique. Some scientists put details in footnotes. Psychologists usually do not. If the method is new,

○ Give enough detail to permit replication.

If the method has been published before,

○ Cite the document describing it but do not summarize it.
○ Or cite the document and summarize. Different journals have different preferences. For example, APA journals prefer the latter (APA 1974, pp. 16–18).

2.30   There are several possible outlines for the method section.

○ Choose an outline that fits your research design, data-gathering procedure, data, and analytical techniques.

○ If using one of the sample outlines, delete items irrelevant to your research. Add others as needed. Miller (1970, pp. 3–4) lists other items.

2.31   Outline for Experimental Designs.   Psychologists and social psychologists using experimental designs in laboratory settings often choose outline [7].

II. Method   [7]
   A. Subjects (human and animal)
      1. Demographic characteristics (give sex, age, race, etc.; for animals, add physiological condition)
      2. Total number of subjects, and number assigned to each experimental condition (including how many in each category did not complete the experiment, and for what reasons)
      3. Selection (e.g., selection and assignment procedures, payments, promises made, general geographical location, type of institution used)
   B. Setting and equipment (e.g., research laboratory with one-way mirrors, stop watches, tape recorders, questionnaires)
   C. Procedures for data gathering
      1. Instructions to participants (usually summarized or paraphrased)
      2. Formation of groups (e.g., experimental and control groups, random assignment)
      3. Manipulations (what they were, how applied)
      4. Controls (e.g., randomization)
      5. Nature of data (e.g., observations of play, responses to questionnaires before and after application of stimulus)
      6. Analysis: data reduction
         a. Statistical description (e.g., percentages)
         b. Statistical inference (e.g., analysis of variance)

Alternatively, psychologists sometimes add entries C5 and 6 to the discussion of results.

2.32   Outlines for Case Study, Survey, and Other Nonexperimental Designs.   In outlines [8], [9], and [10] descriptions of data and analytic techniques are nearly always in the method section and are usually fairly substantial. The reason for this difference from outline [7] may be the differences in research design. Because experimental designs rule out many sources of bias, the design and the data-gathering method are the chief topics of interest. In contrast, scientists using other designs must often compensate for biases in the data. Thus description and inference are often affected by control procedures such as subclassification, norming, and standardization (Labovitz and Hagedorn 1971, pp. 80–82). As a result, the analytic techniques may be at least as important as the data-gathering procedure.

2.33   Scientists using nonexperimental designs and gathering at least some of their data from human populations sometimes choose an outline like [8] (based partly on Selltiz, Jahoda, Deutsch, and Cook 1961; Labovitz and Hagedorn 1971). For still other outlines and items, see Miller (1970, pp. 4–5). If the journal's policy permits (see Section 2.29), minimize discussion of items that have been previously published.

II. Method   [8]
   A. Type and design of study (e.g., cross-sectional survey at one point in time, panel study using questionnaire)
   B. Site (e.g., general geographical area, urban or rural setting)
   C. Time of year (if the data might be affected by events at that time, as would data on political attitudes gathered at election time)
   D. Subjects
      1. Number of subjects, total and in each demographic category (e.g., age, race, sex)
      2. Sampling procedure (e.g., all persons who crossed Main Street between 4:00 and 5:00 p.m. on August 15, 1975)
      3. Time of selection (e.g., August 15, 1975)

E. Procedures for gathering data
1. Data sources (e.g., questionnaire responses, observer reports, historical records)
2. Instruments used (e.g., questionnaires, informal interviews)
3. Administration: when and by whom (e.g., by white females aged 20–30, in August 1975, to housewives in their livingrooms)
4. Instructions to respondents (e.g., answer *yes* or *no* to all questions)
5. Controls (e.g., randomization)
6. Recording of data (e.g., on sheets precoded for keypunching)
F. Analysis: data reduction
1. Statistical description (e.g., percentages)
2. Statistical inference (e.g., analysis of variance)

2.34 Scientists using sources other than human subjects sometimes choose an outline like [9] (see also Section 2.29).

II. Data and method [9]
A. Type and design of study
B. Description (e.g., all vacancies in organizational positions, plus information on prior and subsequent positions of persons who have held those positions)
C. Sources (e.g., organizational records)
D. Sample size and procedure (if all available data are not used)
E. Data collection: how, when, for what period of time (e.g., in August 1975, by hand, for period from 1900 to 1960)
F. Controls
G. Limitations in the data
H. Analysis: data reduction
1. Description (e.g., units)
2. Inference (e.g., from algebraic patterns)

2.35 Finally, some scientists, particularly demographers and economists, use data sets that have been gathered by other scientists or agencies. Demographers use census data.

Economists use government statistics on employment. These scientists often minimize discussion of the data-gathering procedure and emphasize descriptions of the data and analysis. They use an outline like [10]. If descriptions have already been published, use only a sentence or two and cite the published documents (see Section 2.29).

II. Method   [10]
  A. Data used
    1. Nature of data (e.g., survey results)
    2. Sources (e.g., heads of households, sampled randomly)
    3. Data collection: where, when, and how gathered
    4. Controls used
    5. Limitations in the data
  B. Variables
    1. First variable (description and coding)
    2. Second variable (treated like first variable)
    3. Third variable (and so forth)
  C. Analysis: data reduction
    1. Statistical description, with attention to statistical controls
    2. Statistical inference

2.36 Results (Findings) and Discussion of Implications. In general,

○ Never present raw data.
○ Give all the data needed to test the hypotheses stated in the introduction, but no more.

There are three ways to organize results and discussion.

○ (1) Present the results in one section, using only tables, brief textual mention of general trends, and brief explanations. Then write a separate discussion section.

This way is most efficient when you can discuss the theoretical implications and generalizations most clearly in an order different from the order in which you stated the findings. Separation permits you to make a theoretical point once, refer briefly to the findings that confirm or disconfirm it, and then move to the next point. Often you can take the outline for the discussion directly from the introduction. Your outline might look like [11].

III. Results   [11]
  A. Summary of data and analytic technique, if not given in method section (see Section 2.29)
  B. First finding (stated in text as a pattern in the data, accompanied by tables; if no tables, list the findings)
  C. Second finding (stated as in *B*)
  D. Third finding (stated as in *B*)
IV. Discussion of implications
  A. For hypotheses
    1. First hypothesis; discussion of data that confirm or disconfirm
      a. What was expected
      b. What happened
      c. Explanation of results
    2. Second hypothesis (treated as in *1*)
    3. Third hypothesis (treated as in *1*)
  B. For general theory (or theories) from which hypotheses were derived
  C. For future research
  D. For policy or other applications, if any

2.37 If you wish to relate results to hypotheses immediately,

○ (2) Present results and discussion together, in which case you might title the whole section either *Results and Discussion* or *Analysis.*

A typical outline might look like [12].

III. Results and discussion (analysis)   [12]
  A. Summary of data and analytic technique (see Section 2.29)
  B. Findings pertaining to hypothesis #1

  1. Results (using tables if necessary)
  2. Discussion of data that confirm or reject the hypothesis
  3. Explanations of results
  4. Implications
      a. For the theory or theories from which the hypothesis was derived
      b. For future research
      c. For policy or other applications, if any
C. Findings pertaining to hypothesis #2 (discussed as in *B*)
D. Findings pertaining to hypothesis #3 (discussed as in *B*)

2.38 If you need a mixture of the first two options,

○ (3) Present results and discussion of specific hypotheses together, and then write a separate discussion of general implications.

APA journals often publish articles that follow this option. A typical outline might look like [13].

III. Results and discussion of hypotheses   [13]
    A. Hypothesis #1
        1. Results
        2. Discussion
        3. Explanation
    B. Hypothesis #2
        1. Results
        2. Discussion
        3. Explanation
    C. Hypothesis #3 (and so forth)

IV. Implications
    A. For general theory
    B. For policy and other applications, if any
    C. For future research

2.39 Whichever approach you choose, state clearly your decisions

○ To accept, reject, or modify the hypotheses, and the reasons for those decisions.
○ To accept, reject, or modify the general theory or theories from which the hypotheses were drawn, and the reasons for those decisions.

2.40 Summary. Summaries are brief. A basic principle is:

○ Leave the reader with your strongest point.

The summary paragraph to Jeanne Smith's article (see Section 2.28) might follow outline [14].

V. Summary[2] [14]
   A. Problem: conflict in classroom groups arises when . . .
   B. Major finding: teachers can reduce conflict by . . .
   C. Major implication: students will learn more if . . .

Outlines to Present New Theories and Methods

2.41 Major Version. Authors presenting a new theory or a new method often use a standard outline that orders topics by increasing importance. The guiding principle for the summary is the same as with the data-analysis outline: leave the reader with your strongest point. A sample outline might look like [15].

I. Problem statement [15]
   A. Context in prior theory or methodology
   B. The specific problem
   C. Summary paragraph
      1. The problem
      2. Description of new theory or method
      3. Major implications or uses
II. Exposition of new theory or method

III. Discussion
    A. Improvements over past theories or methods
    B. Implications for future work
IV. Summary

2.42 Modification for Demonstrating Method. When presenting a new method, you may want to show how the method works on data.

○ Present the same data description as in a research article, but make the description much briefer because interest is in the method.
○ In subsequent discussion, mention substance only to make a methodological point.

When demonstrating a method with data, make the following alteration in the second section of outline [15]:

II. Exposition   [16]
    A. Description of method
    B. Description of data
    C. Demonstration

NONSTANDARD OUTLINES

2.43 Some manuscripts, especially for books, fit no standard outline. In such cases the author might use several different outlines in succession as devices to keep the writing moving forward. Section 2.44 suggests additional resources for those who need help with nonstandard outlines.

SUMMARY AND SUGGESTED RESOURCES

2.44 Use outlines as devices to order writing and as skeletons to provide internal order. In this chapter I first discuss the mechanics of using outlines (Sections 2.3 to 2.7), the expression of a topic's structure and context (2.8 to 2.14), and different organizational patterns (2.15 to 2.20). I then examine sections of standard outlines and possible modifications of each section (2.21 to 2.42). I give example outlines for each modification. Outlines for comments, debates, and book reviews are in Chapter 9. Outlines for book prospectuses are in Chapter 15. For more information on outlines, see Tichy (1966, Chapter 6) and Perrin (1972, pp. 213–217, 414–417, 429–431). Students might also want to read Bart and Frankel (1971, Chapter 2: The Sociology Paper).

NOTES TO CHAPTER 2

1. The numbering system shown in Figure 2.1 is appropriate only for outlines. Do not use it for numbering headings in a manuscript or lists in text.

2. If you are following option (2), Section 2.37, the roman numeral will be *IV*.

CHAPTER THREE

Drafting Titles, Tables, Illustrations, Appendixes, Documentation, and Bibliographies

INTRODUCTION

3.1 Drafting titles, tables, illustrations, appendixes, documentation, and bibliographies can be as important as drafting text. Sometimes these parts are drafted before text. This chapter discusses the function of these parts, requirements for proper drafting, and ways to draft efficiently. Chapter 8 gives details on editorial styles. Information in this chapter is based on Menzel, Jones, and Boyd (1961), Davis and Jacobs (1968), University of Chicago Press (1969), Linton (1972), and APA (1974).

TITLES

Uses of Titles

3.2 Many scientists will not read documents whose titles do not show clearly that the topic is related to the readers' interests. Also, abstracting services and automated information-retrieval systems catalog documents by mechanical searching of titles to locate key concepts. Too often, a clever title has double and triple meanings only for those who have read the document. If not properly cataloged, articles with undescriptive titles are likely to be used only by readers who own copies of the journals in which the articles are published.

Qualities of a Good Title

3.3 A good title is an "ultrabrief abstract" (Linton 1972, p. 41). In a title,

○ Summarize your topic briefly and simply.
○ Use no abbreviations.
○ Mention important variables, measurement techniques, or theoretical perspectives.

Such a title will communicate clearly and compress easily into a running head (for publication; see Section 8.19). For example,

"Sex and the Process of Status Attainment: A Comparison of Working Women and Men" shows that Treiman and Terrell (1975) studied the effects of working persons' sex on status attainment. The title contains no abbreviations. It gives the important dependent (status attainment) and independent (sex) variables, and compresses easily into "Sex and Status Attainment." Sections 8.18 to 8.23 and 12.23 explain how to prepare title pages on manuscripts intended for publication.

TABLES

Definition and General Rules for Table Construction

3.4 Tables are systematic arrays of numbers or words, presented in rows and columns. Use a table if:

○ You have more than eight entries, and the data will be clearer in a table than in text.
○ Relationships will show up more clearly.
○ Use of a table will reduce the amount of discussion needed.

For example, if the data in a table show a trend clearly, in text note only the trend. Do not cite each supporting entry.

3.5 When drafting,

○ Arrange tables so that readers may both see and test inferences.
○ Make each table's meaning clear without reference to text. Use notes to give sources and explain abbreviations. If possible, do not mix different kinds of information in the same column.
○ Arrange data for easy comparison within and among tables.
○ Construct in similar format tables that use similar data and analyses, perhaps with different variables. Use the same terminology in headings. For example, avoid using "job status" in one table, and "occupational status" in another as

headings for columns that show the same type of data on occupations.

○ In general, do not present tables showing raw data or analyses of variance (although, for analysis of variance you may want to include error mean squares in your text; Linton 1972, pp. 104–106 shows how to present such statistics).

○ In text, discuss every table presented. Omit any that you do not discuss. For more details on discussion, see Sections 2.36 to 2.38.

○ See Sections 8.15 to 8.17 and 8.60 to 8.68 for instructions on preparing and typing tables in manuscripts intended for publication. See Section B.3 for suggestions on typing tables for class papers and dissertations.

Formats for Tables

3.6 Formats for cross-tabulation, analysis of variance, regression and other types of table are shown in many textbooks on methodology and statistics, and in some style manuals. Zeisel (1968, Chapter 9) shows many ways to present cross-tabulations, and explains the logic behind cross-tabulation. Davis and Jacobs (1968) show many ways to arrange tables of percentages. Linton (1972, pp. 112–119) and APA (1974, pp. 43–50) show examples of tables that are commonly used by psychologists.

3.7 If you have difficulty creating a format for a particular table, and you find no help in textbooks or style manuals,

○ Consult articles on topics similar to yours in recent issues of leading journals.

Scientists who have studied similar problems and used similar data have often met similar obstacles in constructing their tables. The most helpful examples are usually in the most widely read journals. (You may also find bad examples—formats that are ineffective and should be avoided.)

Parts of a Table

3.8 Tables have different parts. Each part is illustrated in Figure 3.1. Some parts, such as the double rule, are not used in all types of manuscript.

3.9 Number. Table numbers permit easy identification and reference.

○ In general, use sequential arabic numerals (1, 2, 3, etc.) throughout a manuscript.

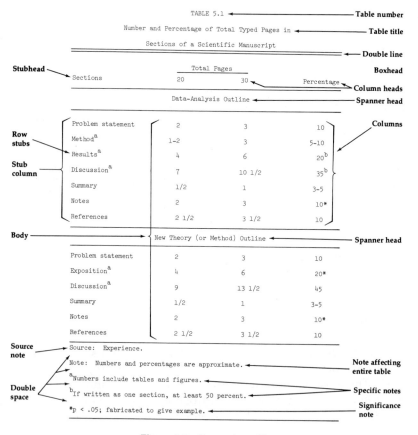

Figure 3.1 Parts of a table.

EXCEPTION. For book chapters, use sequential numbers preceded by the chapter number and a decimal point. For example, note the numbering of tables in Chapter 5.

○ In text, refer to tables by number and not by title.

3.10 Title. The table title should indicate a table's subject clearly and briefly, but should not be telegraphic. In general,

○ Omit from the title information that is contained in row and column heads, and in "spanner heads" (described in Section 3.18).

For example, "Outlines and Number of Pages" would be too brief a title for the table shown in Figure 3.1. However, "Data-Analysis and New Theory or Method Outlines: Number and Percentage of Total Typed Pages for Problem Statement, . . . and Reference Sections" would give too much detail. The types of outline are shown in the spanner heads, and the sections are listed as row stubs, so repetition in the title is unnecessary. For guidelines on capitalization, see Section 8.63.

3.11 Body. The body is the entries in a table. Construct it according to the following general principles.

○ Use as few entries as possible without eliminating vital information. See also Section 8.61, note 9.
○ Within each table, use the same rules for retaining decimals and for rounding.
○ Arrange entries so that the most important comparisons are between adjacent numbers.
○ To prevent confusion of percentages and numbers, place a "%" sign after the first number in a column of percentages that add up to 100 percent. Also use "Percentage" in the column heading (described in Section 3.17).
○ If a column head does not apply to an item in a row stub, leave the cell (intersection) blank. For example, see Table 1.1. Use three or more dots (leaders) if you have no data for a given cell. If the quantity in a cell is zero, enter 0.

○ If rounding prevents the sum of percentages in an additive column from being 100 percent, say so in a footnote.

○ Minimize horizontal and vertical lines. See Section 8.64.

○ Do not use intersecting lines to connect items in different columns.

3.12   Stub.   Stubs, or names of rows, are in the far left column. The names should be as short as clarity will permit. Within each table, they should also be grammatically parallel and conceptually equivalent. For example, use "Intelligent" and "Aggressive," not "Intelligent" and "Aggression" (see also Section 2.7). For psychologists, the stubs often name major independent variables (APA 1974, p. 45). For sociologists, the stubs often name dependent variables. However, these generalizations are often violated if following them would produce an aesthetically displeasing table, such as one with many more columns than rows. Abbreviations are often useful, for example: f = female, m = male. If you use the same abbreviations in several tables,

○ Use an explanatory footnote in the first table.

○ In subsequent tables used after a gap of several pages or chapters, add a note referring the reader to the table that contains the explanation.

For guidelines on capitalization, see Section 8.65.

3.13   Stub Column.   The stub column is the column of row stubs, or of row stubs and their subcategories. For example, "Method," "Data," and "Demonstration" (Section 2.42) are possible subcategories of the second row stub under the second spanner in Figure 3.1.

○ Indent subcategories at least one space from the margin, to distinguish them from the row stub they subdivide. Within a category, make subcategories grammatically parallel and conceptually equivalent (see Section 3.12). For example, use "Method," "Data," and "Demonstration," not "How I did it," "Data," and "Demonstration."

3.14 Stubhead. The stubhead is the title of the stub column. In Figure 3.1, "Sections" is a stubhead. For guidelines on capitalization, see Section 8.65.

3.15 Boxhead. The boxhead, a heading at the top of the body, may name just one column (and thus be a column head; see Section 3.17), or it may be a title for several columns, as is "Total Pages" in Figure 3.1. Use a boxhead over several columns if doing so will allow you to avoid repeating several words in each of several column titles. Guidelines for capitalization are in Section 8.65.

3.16 Column. Columns are vertical collections of entries. In general,

○ Omit columns that can be calculated from other columns. For example, I would ordinarily omit either the first two columns in Figure 3.1 or the last. I included all three only to make the table easier to use.

3.17 Column Head. The column head names the column. As with row stubs, column headings should be grammatically parallel and conceptually equivalent (see Section 3.12). For abbreviations and repetition of abbreviations, follow the instructions given in Section 3.12. Guidelines for capitalization are in Section 8.65. For psychologists, column heads often name the dependent variables in an experiment. For sociologists, column heads often name the independent variables. However, note exceptions stated in Section 3.12.

3.18 Spanner Head. A spanner head spans the entire width of a table, thus permitting further divisions in a table or the combination of two or more similar tables. For example, Table 5.1 was originally two tables: one for data-analysis outlines and one for new theory or method outlines. Guidelines for capitalization are in Section 8.65. Table 5.1 shows a style for spanners that is more common in books than the style illustrated in Figure 3.1.

3.19 Notes. Tables may have three types of notes: source notes, general notes, and notes to specific entries. Figure 3.1 shows examples of all three types.

○ Use source notes to show the sources of all data that do not originate in the research being reported.

○ Use general notes for information that pertains to the entire table. For example, you may want to report the exact question used to elicit certain data, or describe an index that is not well known.

○ Use specific notes only for specific entries. Sometimes you may want to designate notes of statistical significance with one or more asterisks. Designate all other specific notes by using superscript a, b, c, and so forth.[1] For guidelines on order of notes, capitalization, identation, and superscription, see Section 8.66.

ILLUSTRATIONS: USE AND GUIDELINES

3.20 Use illustrations to state points more clearly and efficiently than you can in words. As with tables (see Section 3.4), use illustrations to supplement rather than duplicate text. Illustrations include bar graphs, curves, drawings, causal models, diagrams of conversation flow, schematic representations of villages, and photographs.

○ For help with the basic organization of any illustration, consult journals for recent articles on topics similar to yours that use similar illustrations. See Sections 3.6 to 3.7.

○ Number illustrations with sequential arabic numerals, beginning with 1. In text, refer to them by number.

○ For detailed instructions on preparation, see Sections 8.15 to 8.17, and 8.70 and 8.71. If you are writing a class paper or a dissertation, see Section B.3.

3.21 When designing graphs,

○ Place the independent variable on the horizontal axis and the dependent variable on the vertical.

○ On both axes use scales that will permit curves or lines to reach across the entire figure.

○ Label the horizontal axis from left to right; the vertical axis, from bottom to top.

○ If you omit part of a scale, indicate the omission by using a double hatch mark between zero and the number at which you begin.

APPENDIXES: USE AND GUIDELINES

3.22   Use appendixes for material that is not essential, such as charts and tables that might interest only a few readers. For example, see Table A.1 in this book. Use appendixes also for explanations and elaborations that are necessary but are too long for footnotes. For example, Appendix B lists guidelines that are important, but only for authors of manuscripts *not* intended for publication. Some authors also use appendixes to reproduce questionnaires and explain methodological procedures. In most respects treat appendixes as you do chapters in a book or sections in an article. However,

○ Designate each appendix with either sequential numerals (beginning with 1 or I) or capital letters (beginning with A, as is done in this book).

○ In general, place appendixes at the end of a manuscript unless told to do otherwise. See Sections 8.15 to 8.17.

   EXCEPTION.   If you are writing a book, see Section 12.31.

○ For guidelines on numbering appendix tables and illustrations, see Sections 8.63 and 8.70.

DOCUMENTATION

Guidelines for Citing Documents

3.23   To acknowledge intellectual debts and to avoid any appearance of plagiarism,

○ Document all facts and ideas that are not common knowledge and that are not original with you.

Even the appearance alone can damage your reputation and cost you valued friendships. An author with an excellent memory sometimes begins work on a manuscript that seems to "write itself," and only later discovers that it (or some part of it) so closely resembles a prior document as to be almost indistinguishable from it. Authors who have had such an experience are usually genuinely surprised and acutely embarrassed at the result (see Houghton Mifflin Company 1974, p. 7).

3.24   To prevent unintentional plagiarism,

○ Carefully check related, prior writing on your topic. Check the periodicals indexes and abstract services and the card catalog in your library. Also check Table 7.1 for all journals likely to publish articles on your topic. Check the journals' annual indexes for articles, and the reference lists of the articles for additional articles and books.
○ In recent journals, check the lists of "Books Received for Review" and the American Bibliographic Service's *Quarterly Checklists* in various disciplines.
○ "Use quotation marks around any material that you quote directly *and* note the source, even if you mean to recast the material in a later draft. . . .
○ "Rephrase notes—lecture and otherwise—that you use as a resource for manuscript" (Houghton Mifflin Company 1974, p. 7; emphasis in original).

Authors whose writing is not based on research data, as is the case with some theorists, are particularly vulnerable to inadvertent plagiarism.

3.25   Unpublished work sometimes poses special problems. As most active researchers know, scientists working in the same specialty frequently share their findings informally. Indeed, many research findings are well circulated through in-

formal communication networks long before they reach published form (Price 1964, p. 655). Such work circulates with a
note, on the title page, such as: "Preliminary findings; do not
cite or quote without permission of the author" or "Draft; do
not cite or quote." If you want to cite unpublished work,

○ Always request permission first.[2] See Sections 12.43 to 12.50
for instructions.
○ For an article, indicate receipt of permission either in reference notes (8.72 to 8.73) or in an acknowledgment note (8.56
to 8.59).
○ For a book, indicate receipt of permission either in the front
matter (12.28) or in a note (12.49).

3.26   For all direct quotations, whether from published or unpublished documents,

○ Indicate clearly the source of all emphasis and all omissions
from, changes in, and additions to the original. For an
example, see Section 3.24. Section 8.37 gives instructions.
○ Type following the guidelines in Sections 8.35 to 8.37.
○ If quotations from a single source add up to more than 50
words, see Sections 12.45 and 12.46.

Guidelines for Collecting Facts of Publication

3.27   For all documents cited,

○ Give complete, accurate bibliographic information.
○ Collect the information when you first use a document. Put-
ting off that task only forces you to retrace your steps later.
○ Use one 3 × 5 file card per document.
○ Always take facts of publication from the title page of the
original source. Do not trust the facts on cards in your library's card catalog. Do not even trust an author's references
to his or her own prior publications (Blanchard 1974).
○ If you always publish in journals or with book companies

that use the same editorial style, record all bibliographic information in that style. See Sections 8.41 to 8.52 and 8.76 to 8.81 (articles) and 12.6 to 12.9 (books) for help.

○ If you are a student, record information in the style required by your teachers (often that described in Turabian 1973).

○ If you do not know where a manuscript will be published, record information in the style that is most common in your discipline. For example, if you are a sociologist, use ASA style; if a psychologist, use APA style. For help see Tables 7.1 and 8.1 and Sections 8.41 to 8.52 and 8.76 to 8.81.

○ If necessary, prepare a second set of cards in the style required by a specific journal or book publisher. Often a typist or a research assistant can transpose information from one style to another, thus saving you time.

3.28 Book. For a book, record:

○ Author's or authors' names; may also be editor's or institution's name.

○ Full title, including subtitle.

○ Series (if any).

○ Volume (if there is more than one volume).

○ Edition (if not the original).

○ Translator (if any).

○ City of publication (and sometimes the state or state's initials, if the city is not well known).

○ Publisher's name (sometimes in abbreviated form).

○ Date of publication.

For a book that is written and in production but not yet published, substitute "forthcoming" for the date. See Section 8.41. For a book that is written but not accepted for publication, give only author's name, book's title, and "unpublished manuscript."

CAUTION. Some journals forbid citation of unpublished documents or require that they be listed separately (Sections

8.72 and 8.73). Figures 8.9 to 8.13 and the notes to Chapter 8 give examples of this information in different editorial styles.

3.29   Chapter.   For a chapter in a book, record:

○ Author's or authors' names.
○ Full title, including subtitle.
○ Names of the book's author or authors.
○ The remaining eight items listed for books (3.28).
○ Inclusive pages of the chapter.

For examples in different styles, see Figures 8.9 to 8.13 and the notes to Chapter 8.

3.30   Article.   For an article in a journal, record:

○ Author's name.
○ Article's title (sometimes omitted in scientific bibliographies).
○ Name of the journal (sometimes abbreviated according to a standard list).
○ Volume number, date, or both.
○ Issue number, month, or season.
○ Inclusive pages.

For an article that has been accepted for publication but is not yet published, substitute "in press" for the volume or issue numbers, date, and pages. For an article that has not been accepted for publication, record only author's name, article's title, and "unpublished manuscript." For your own convenience but not for inclusion in a reference list, also record the date of the draft.

CAUTION. Some journals forbid citation of unpublished documents, or require that they be listed separately. See Sections 8.72 and 8.73. For examples of documentation in different styles, see Figures 8.9 to 8.13 and the notes to Chapter 8.

3.31   Paper.   For a paper presented at a meeting, record:

○ Author's name.
○ Full title.
○ "Paper presented at the meeting of the [association's name]."
○ City.
○ Month.
○ Year.

For examples in different styles, see Figures 8.8 to 8.13.

3.32   Dissertation.   For a dissertation, record:

○ Author's name.
○ Full title.
○ The words "Doctoral dissertation."
○ University.
○ Date.
○ University Microfilm number (if available).

For examples in different styles, see Figures 8.9 to 8.13.

3.33   Government Documents.   For government documents record, at minimum:

○ Author's name (often an institution or committee).
○ Title.
○ Technical report number (if available).
○ City.
○ Publisher (often, the agency sponsoring the research).
○ Month, year.
○ National Technical Information Service (NTIS) number, Government Printing Office (GPO) order number, or National Clearinghouse order number.

Across styles, for government documents there is less agreement on appropriate information and ways to present it than exists with regard to any other class of documents. Good examples are given in APA (1974, pp. 66, 129) and University of Chicago Press (1969, Chapter 17). However, when writing for publication in a journal, always follow examples in the journal. When writing a book follow the instructions in Sections 12.6 to 12.9.

Guidelines for Organizing Reference Cards

3.34   As you collect references, file the cards in a box.

○ File cards alphabetically, by author's last name.
○ Alphabetize word by word rather than letter by letter. Thus "Smyth" always precedes "Smythe" without regard for initials or coauthors' names. Alphabetize corporate authors by the first significant word in the name.
○ If you use more than one document by an author, order the cards by date. See Section 8.45 for further instructions.
○ If you use two or more documents by the same author with the same date, order them alphabetically by first letter of first word in the title that is not *a*, *an*, or *the*.
○ File single references by an author ahead of works that he or she coauthored with others and of which he is the first author.
○ For articles with the same first author, alphabetize by last name of second author, and place two-authored articles ahead of three-authored pieces with the same first two authors. Follow the same principle for organizing cards on documents with the same first three, four, and so on, authors.

Guidelines for Collecting Information in the Documents

3.35   When you collect information and quotations from documents,

○ Use 4 × 6 cards. They give more space than 3 × 5 cards and the difference in size will prevent you from mixing them up with the reference cards.

○ Also record the author's name, the publication date, and a page number, following name (date) citation style. See Sections 8.43 to 8.45 for instructions. This system permits easy retrieval of complete bibliographic information from the reference cards.

○ If you need permission to quote from a document or if you have received permission, note that fact on the card. The card acts as a reminder when you write the manuscript.

BIBLIOGRAPHIES

3.36 A bibliography may include uncited documents such as those that give additional background on a topic or are good outside reading for classes.

○ Prepare the bibliography from the reference cards. If necessary, rearrange the information. The most frequent difference is in order of authors' names. Section 8.81 lists other possible differences.

○ For each document, include the items listed in Sections 3.28 to 3.33. Then follow the instructions on editorial style in Sections 8.76 to 8.81. Figure 3.2 shows a common style for bibliographies.

○ Organize the cards either alphabetically by author, following Section 3.34, or alphabetically by author within categories such as type of document (e.g., books, articles, and unpublished documents) or subject matter (e.g., occupational mobility, stratification, urban anthropology).

○ Add descriptive notes if you plan an annotated bibliography. See Sections 12.33 and 13.39 for instructions.

Bibliography

Author, A. Tenured. A Monograph. City:. Publisher, 1974.

_____ , ed. A Second Book. Rev. ed. City: Publisher, 1974.

Research, A. Contract. A Report. City: Agency, 1974.

Student, A. Graduate. American Dissertation. University Name, 1974.

Student, Paul A., Research, A. G., and Smith, A. B. "A Chapter." In

   The Book, edited by Collector P. Excellence, pp. 199-213. City:

   Publisher, 1974.

Student, Susie K., and Coauthor, Samuel P. "An Article." A Journal

   32 (1974):341-349.

Figure 3.2 A common style for bibliographies.

SUMMARY

3.37   In this chapter I give descriptions of, and instructions for preparing, titles (Sections 3.2 and 3.3), tables (3.4 to 3.19), illustrations (3.20 and 3.21), appendixes (3.22), documentation (3.23 to 3.35), and bibliographies (3.36).

NOTES TO CHAPTER 3

1.   The exception to the a, b, c style is tables using either words or abbreviations, as for chemical elements (the letters used for notes are easily confused with the letters used in the body). In such cases, use a sequence of asterisks, daggers, double daggers, section marks, and so forth. See University of Chicago Press (1969, p. 287) for details.

2.   Some authors believe that unauthorized, unattributed use of unpublished documents cannot be detected. However, the active researchers in a specialty usually know who has written about what, because unpublished documents are often widely circulated.

CHAPTER FOUR

Getting Started:
The First Draft

INTRODUCTION

4.1 For some scientists the hardest part of writing is preparing a complete first draft. This chapter describes the various procedures that have helped authors write complete first drafts. On these matters one man's meat is often another man's poison.

What works well for you may seem outlandish—sometimes even immoral—to someone else. Therefore,

○ If you dislike one suggestion, skip it and read the next one.

Eventually you will find ideas that suit both your tastes and your needs.

INTELLECTUAL STARTERS

Writing from Beginning to End

4.2   Outline Used as Planning Device.   Some scientists outline a manuscript in detail and then draft it from beginning to end, following the outline in every detail. These scientists are often experienced authors, skilled at perceiving and expressing internal order and context. Years of disciplined practice usually precede completely successful use of this technique. However,

○ If you are an extremely well organized thinker, try outlining your manuscripts in detail and writing from beginning to end. For help with outlining, see Chapter 2.

4.3   Long the traditional approach to writing, this technique has a major disadvantage:

☐ Many scientists are *not* well-organized thinkers. Forcing them to work this way can prevent them from beginning to write. If they eventually produce outlines, requiring them to write from start to finish may prevent completion of drafts.

The chief advantage of this technique:

☐ It is the most efficient way to write a first draft. Thus scientists who do not think this way naturally often train themselves to do so.

4.4   No Formal Outline Used.   Some authors prefer to write from beginning to end, but with no formal outline and only a rough idea of major sections. One author, who described this procedure as "letting it all hang out," listed several advantages:

☐ He starts thinking about all aspects of his topic.
☐ Writing down ideas reduces his fear of losing them. He is then free to think about aspects that he did not include in the draft.
☐ Having a rough draft permits him to devise a formal outline to shape his next draft. The outline shows him where he has too much or too little information, or where the scope is too broad for his topic. Sections 5.7 to 5.11 discuss scope.
☐ He never worries about the inadequacy of his introduction. Having a complete draft always helps him improve the introduction to the second draft.

Writing in Blocks

4.5   The Procedure.   Some scientists use outlines as planning devices but prefer not to write continuously from beginning to end. To use this procedure,

○ Write the easiest part first.
○ Write the second easiest part next, and so forth.
○ Write the hardest part last.
○ When all parts have been completed, prepare a detailed outline from the parts.
○ Then prepare a complete first draft following the detailed outline (see Section 4.23).

4.6   This procedure has several disadvantages:

☐ The first draft usually includes repetitious material, and is therefore somewhat inefficient.
☐ The writing style may vary from one part to the next.
☐ The increasing difficulty of each succeeding section may

eventually present the author with a part that seems too difficult to write.

However, this procedure also has many advantages:

☐ Beginning with what they know best helps many scientists over the biggest hurdle of all: getting words on paper. For these writers, the ability to put words on paper compensates for any loss of efficiency.

☐ Each succeeding part is often made less difficult by the previously written parts. See the examples in Sections 4.9 and 4.10.

☐ Many writers who follow this procedure eventually find that they can outline and write from beginning to end, because their thinking and writing have become more systematic.

4.7 A few writers use a variant of this procedure that avoids some of the disadvantages. They write a section and then set it aside. Later they rewrite it and write the next section. They repeat this procedure several times, sometimes reediting previously edited sections. As a result, when they have written the last sentence of the last section of the first draft, the manuscript is completely finished (process described in Menzel, Jones, and Boyd 1961, p. 8).

4.8 Equipment. To prevent loss of parts and disorganization,

○ If you write on paper, use a notebook with dividers or a large folder with several pockets to hold your writing.

○ If you write on 5 × 8 file cards, use a large file box and dividers.

○ Write the title for each part on a divider.

4.9 Example. This example is based on the data-analysis outline (see Sections 2.24 to 2.40). Ann Jones has analyzed data from a 1973 survey, using personal interviews, of American wives' political beliefs. She is now writing major sections of an article in the following order:

☐ Method, results, discussion, problem statement, summary.

She first takes out the method section that she drafted while designing the research and adds more details. She next considers her results. What are the most significant findings? To display them, she constructs tables. She then drafts two pages that describe general trends.

4.10 As she does so, some implications of the research become clear. For example, some of the findings contradict findings from research done in 1970, but those findings came from a telephone survey. Because telephone surveys often produce less valid results than do personal interviews, Dr. Jones decides that we should accept her findings over those from the 1970 study. Eventually she joins these and other such notes into a discussion of findings and implications. With pieces of the method, results, and discussion sections done, she finds the limits of her article becoming clear, so she drafts a problem statement (see Sections 2.13, 2.14, and 2.25 to 2.28). After that she needs only a brief summary. Then she can prepare a detailed outline and put together a complete first draft.

4.11 Some scientists, particularly those whose analytic methods are as important as their data-gathering method (see Section 2.32), draft results first. Other differences in writing order are a matter of personal preference. Some authors draft results, method, and then discussion. Others prefer results, discussion, method. However, all three sections are usually written before the problem statement and the summary, either of which can be written before the other.

4.12 The parallel order for drafting purely theoretical or methodological articles (see Sections 2.41 and 2.42) is: exposition, discussion, problem statement, summary.

Writing in Bits and Pieces

4.13 Procedure and Equipment. Some scientists—even some who use outlines as planning devices—dislike writing in any formally organized way. Others, particularly those who have done little writing, find internal order and context (Sections 2.8 to 2.14) difficult to perceive when they start a manuscript. If you are one of these,

○ Begin with what you know best and write in bits and pieces.
○ Use the equipment listed in Section 4.8 and tape, paste, or a stapler.

4.14 With an Outline. Try using this technique if you have an incomplete outline, but enough detail to establish topics at the first level of importance (defined in Figure 2.1):

○ Label one divider for each major section.
○ Place completed pages or cards in the proper section of the notebook, folder, or file box.
○ Gradually, a detailed outline of each section will emerge, and you will find yourself working more and more like the author who writes in blocks.

4.15 A variation on this idea is:

○ Using 5 × 7 cards, write one idea per card.
○ From time to time, sort and organize the cards.
○ Label a set of dividers with topics at the first level of importance, such as *problem statement* or *method*; also label dividers with topics at the second level of importance. For example, *subjects, setting,* and *procedure* might be subtopics of *method*.
○ Arrange the dividers and then file the cards with ideas behind the appropriate dividers.
○ Write a first draft from beginning to end.

Done in this way, an article almost writes itself.

4.16 For example, when drafting tables John Smith writes a page on differences between his analyses and those of prior researchers, and files it in his problem-statement section. Then, remembering that his research design was quite different from the designs of earlier researchers, he writes about that difference (for his method section) and about its effects (for his discussion). While writing, he remembers controls that he used, both in data gathering and in analysis, so he drafts descriptions of them for the method section. A few days later he recalls that he had begun the research with a theory quite different from the theories of previous researchers. Noting with satisfaction that the findings support his hypotheses and seeing clearly where other researchers erred, he writes down these thoughts for the discussion section. Then he writes a page for the problem statement to prepare readers for his later discussion of theory. After writing each page, he clips it into his notebook in the proper section and then proceeds with the analysis. From time to time he organizes the material, and eventually unified sections emerge.

4.17 With No Outline. If you are using this procedure with no outline,

○ Write on any part of your topic that comes to mind and then place the pages or cards in an undivided folder or file box.

For example, if you are studying the relationship between Spencer's sociology and contemporary social theory, you might begin by writing about the implications that first made you realize that the topic was worth writing about. This procedure often works well with manuscripts that are not based on research data. The writing usually takes months. Periodically,

○ Sort and organize the material.
○ As major sections emerge, use labeled dividers to separate them.
○ From time to time, sort and organize the writing in each section. Eventually, a detailed outline will emerge.

For authors who use this method, manuscripts are like jigsaw puzzles: put together the recognizable parts, and eventually all the blue sky and green grass will fit, because there are fewer pieces, specified limits, and diminishing space into which the pieces can fit.

4.18 Disadvantages and Advantages. This procedure has disadvantages.

☐ It is inefficient.
☐ Repetition is likely.
☐ The writing style may be uneven.
☐ The prose may be very colloquial.
☐ Taped, pasted, and stapled sections can make a draft hard to read.

Nevertheless, if you write this way, you are working more efficiently than colleagues who share your inability to write by outline but who are still trying to begin at the beginning:

☐ By working first on what you knew best, you solved the problem of getting started.
☐ You have produced the pieces of a first draft.
☐ Also, you may eventually learn what internal order is by watching it emerge in your own work.
☐ Eventually, you may also learn how to perceive internal order *before* you begin to write.

4.19 This procedure has produced too many valuable manuscripts to be discarded simply because it appears disorganized and unconventional. The potential for self-teaching is also valuable. Aspiring authors who cannot write from outlines must find some way to get started before they can learn how to become efficient writers. Often, too, they need to be frustrated by inefficiency before they become willing to spend time learning how to be more efficient.

Implications of Different Starters

4.20 Scientists think in different ways. *Some scientists' thought processes seem to resemble a formal outline*. Each thought gives rise to subthoughts in rational segments. Only when one major topic has been completely thought through does the next major topic come to mind. Using a formal outline comes naturally to these authors. *Other authors think in clusters*. Each thought sparks others in a pattern rather like the spokes in a wheel. The related thoughts can be either subthoughts or major topics. These authors need writing procedures that retain all major thoughts and subthoughts, and the connections among them. For these authors, writing in blocks or in bits and pieces is natural. *Still other authors think both ways*. They begin at the beginning of their outlines, but from time to time their thinking shifts back and forth between major thoughts. These authors work largely from beginning to end, but they sometimes work in blocks.

4.21 Also, not all topics are alike.

☐ Manuscripts that report research findings, new theories, or new methods are easier to write by outline than are other manuscripts because standard outlines exist.

☐ Familiarity with topic may also affect the method chosen for drafting.

One author who normally drafts from a complete, formal outline finds this technique almost impossible when he has not previously written something that is related to his present topic. For him, drafting in blocks or in bits and pieces is the best way to begin writing on an unfamiliar topic.

4.22 There is nothing sacred about any of these starters. What matters is that you find a way to begin, and then to continue, working satisfactorily.

○ For each manuscript, choose a method for drafting that suits your tastes, your skills, and your topic.

MECHANICAL PROCEDURES

4.23 Eventually you will produce a detailed, clearly focused outline, and be ready to prepare a complete first draft. If you have drafted in blocks or in bits and pieces, preparing a first draft will seem more like "prerevision" than like writing. Now consider some techniques that may help you continue to work effectively.

Setting for Writing

4.24 Authors often have strong feelings about where and under what conditions they write. Some like an easy chair, some a desk. Some like to write at home, others in the office. Some like to write in the early morning hours, others prefer nighttime. Therefore,

○ Experiment with physical surroundings and time of day.

A particularly important aspect of setting is how you handle interruptions.

4.25 Drafting Without Interruptions. The most efficient way to draft is without interruptions. To avoid telephone calls, students, administrative responsibilities, and so forth, some scientists maintain a home office. Some obtain a library carrel or a second office. Outside interruptions, however, are by no means the central problem. Far more insidious and time-consuming is the urge to correct the tense of a verb, to complete a reference, to polish a sentence, or to devise a transition. Moreover, the author may well delete material in a subsequent revision and thus lose the time put into editing it. For efficiency's sake, then,

○ Draft without interruptions.
○ Do not edit while writing a first draft.

When you make an error continue writing, just as you would continue lecturing to a class. You might restate a sentence and then go on, but you would not stop the lecture. The chief advantage of this procedure is rapid completion of a draft. The chief disadvantage is the amount of subsequent editing that is needed.

4.26 Drafting with Interruptions. Some writers—particularly experienced authors—prefer to edit as they draft (see Section 4.7). Uncorrected grammar and incomplete references distract them sufficiently that they cannot think about substance until they have made corrections. As a result, the finished first draft usually needs less revision than do drafts written without editing. Unfortunately, though, drafting takes longer. Inexperienced writers often become discouraged by the amount of time needed to produce just one draft, and they lose some of that time if they later delete a sentence or a section. Also, editing done without the benefit of "cooling" (described in Section 4.36) is usually not the author's best.

4.27 The advantages of the procedures discussed below assume the value of writing without interruptions.

Multiple Copies

4.28 If you ask colleagues and other professional peers to criticize your writing (see Sections 6.4 to 6.6), you will need multiple copies of drafts.

- For five or fewer copies, use carbons or photocopies.
- For more than five, type the draft on a master, such as mimeograph (see Section 8.7 if you are writing for publication), and then reproduce the number of copies needed. If you do your own typing, ask your department secretary for instructions.
- For each draft, produce one copy for each critic, at least one copy on which to make revisions, and at least one copy for your files.
- Retain one copy each of all drafts until the manuscript has been published, graded, or approved in whatever way is necessary.

Codes for Drafts

4.29   On each draft,

○ Type a draft number and date in the upper, left-hand corner of each page; for example, "1, 5/75."

Some authors use different colors of paper for each draft—perhaps yellow for the first, pink for the second, and so forth. Unfortunately, some colors—particularly reds, blues, and greens—photocopy poorly on some systems. Therefore, if you use color coding,

○ Avoid photoreproduction.
○ Type on masters and reproduce on colored paper.
○ Type a draft number and a date in the upper left-hand corner of pages.

Physical Methods of Writing

4.30   Scientists write first drafts in many different ways. Also, they sometimes use different techniques on different drafts. Some dictate only first drafts; others dictate all but the last. Simply changing physical methods can make writing easier. Even changing from double- to triple-spacing between lines can make writing easier. My emphasis here is on first drafts. However,

○ Try different techniques on all drafts.

4.31   Handwriting.   Handwriting is slow, and the draft is sometimes hard to read. If you handwrite drafts,

○ Use lined paper in a notebook or attached to a pad.
○ Leave at least one space between written lines.
○ If you are using bits and pieces, work at a desk or table on which the pieces may remain, even if you must leave.

Handwriting is reasonably efficient if you have previously drafted either whole blocks or bits and pieces of a manuscript. Then you are largely drafting connections followed by taped-in sections. However, you cannot write at thinking speed, and you are tempted to edit because the pen or pencil is in your hand.

4.32 Typing. Many authors type their first drafts. Normal typing speed more closely matches thinking speed than does handwriting. Typed drafts are more legible than handwritten drafts. Also, you are less tempted to edit as you write. If you type drafts,

○ Use double- or triple-spacing. If you prefer triple-spacing, use legal-size paper ($8\frac{1}{2} \times 14$ inches) instead of letter-size ($8\frac{1}{2} \times 11$ inches). Legal-size paper shows paragraph length better and does not need to be changed as often. Or try typing on a "scroll" of white shelf paper, which you can later cut into 11-inch lengths.

○ If you are drafting with bits and pieces, either leave space on pages to insert pieces or retype them.

4.33 Dictating. Some authors dictate their first drafts, using either a dictating machine or a tape recorder with transcribing equipment. The major disadvantages:

☐ Dictation is cheap and efficient only for those with access to free, speedy, and literate typing help.

☐ Some authors feel self-conscious about talking to a machine.

The major advantages:

☐ Most authors can think and talk faster than they can handwrite or type.

☐ Dictation is exceptionally efficient if you draft from a detailed outline (Section 4.2) or from prewritten pieces.

☐ The typed transcript is clean and neat.

The gain in efficiency is sufficient that you should try this method at least once if you have both the equipment and secretarial help.[1]

CAUTION: The sheer joy of having a complete first draft, together with the beauty of a professional typing job, may lull you into thinking that revision is unnecessary. In truth, though, dictated drafts usually need more editing than do typewritten drafts.

4.34 Lecturing. Some scientists draft by lecturing if they happen to be discussing the manuscript's topic with a class.[2] To use this method:

○ Prepare the lecture with extra care.
○ Obtain a recorder with transcribing equipment and running time of at least 30 minutes without a change.
○ Test the recorder in the classroom and adjust the volume and other controls.
○ To prevent interruptions in your lecture, ask a student to turn and change the cassettes or tapes.

You cannot talk in a formal writing style, and the examples appropriate for a class are sometimes inappropriate for a manuscript. However, some scientists discuss the same topic far more clearly with a class than with an audience of professional peers. Lack of clarity is often pointed out by students' questions. Also, you will continue lecturing even if you stumble over a word or two.

☐ This technique is particularly useful when you are writing manuscripts for nonspecialized audiences.

THE RESULT

4.35 One or more of these techniques should work for you. When the substance is publishable, a potentially publishable manuscript eventually emerges because you are not trying to write in ways that do not match your abilities. Also, the message in the manuscripts is usually organized even if the sentences and paragraphs need revising and editing. If the manuscript is messy, type a clean copy. Then set it aside.

COOLING

4.36   Delay revision until you can see the manuscript as others see it. The length of time required for "cooling" (Tichy's term; see 1966, p. 10) varies from person to person and from manuscript to manuscript. Anywhere from a day or two to a year or two is possible, although over two months is uncommon.

○ Wait until you find yourself wondering how you could ever have said X, or what you meant by Y. Then begin revising.

Then you may sometimes discover, to your pleasure, that you had done a better job than you remembered.

SUMMARY

4.37   For many authors the most difficult step in writing is preparing a first draft. This chapter describes ways to get started (Sections 4.2 to 4.22). All have the same goal—a complete, organized first draft—but not all begin with a formal outline. This chapter also discusses several mechanical techniques that make writing easier (4.23 to 4.34). Treat this chapter like a smorgasbord.

○ Look over the selections offered.
○ Sample them.
○ Choose what fits your tastes, your skills, your manuscript, and your manuscript's state of completion.

NOTES TO CHAPTER 4

1.   Handwriting, typing, and dictating are discussed in more detail in Tichy (1966, Chapter 3), on which some of this discussion is based. Most of her suggestions are more appropriate for writers in businesses, but some may prompt you to think of useful variants.

2.   One of the original reasons for requiring scholars to do research and to publish was that those who did so usually brought fresh thinking to their teaching.

CHAPTER FIVE

Revision of Text: Home Remedies for Prosaic Problems

INTRODUCTION

5.1   It is harder to revise than to draft. When revising consider, in turn, organization and content, clarity, grammatical correctness, brevity, and writing style. Skipping one of these steps will leave a manuscript poorer than it might otherwise be. Considering them in a different order will make revision less efficient. Information in this chapter is taken partly from Strunk and White (1959), Menzel, Jones and Boyd (1961), Bernstein (1965), Tichy (1966), Gunning (1968), Perrin (1972), and APA (1974).

ORGANIZATION AND CONTENT

5.2   Organization and content are almost inseparable. I separate them here only to emphasize specific aspects of each.

Checking Organization

5.3   Checking the Outline.   Flaws in overall organization are more frequent in writing that does not follow a standard outline (described in Sections 2.21 to 2.42) than in writing that does. To evaluate organization,

○ Set aside outlines used to order your writing.

○ Using the written draft, prepare a formal topic outline through the fourth level of importance. If your manuscript exceeds 40 pages in length, consider using six levels of importance. See Sections 2.3 to 2.7 for help.

○ Check the outline for logical order. For each topic at each level of importance, ask whether all of its subtopics are relevant, understandable in context, and of equal importance relative to each other. Either unexplained or extraneous material can divert or bore a reader, causing him to miss important points. See Sections 2.9, 2.10, and 2.15 to 2.20 for help.

○ Ask whether the reason for the order is clear. For example, the reason for using a standard outline is clear without explanation. In contrast, a critique of a book might follow the book's outline and thus be enhanced by a statement such as: "I examine arguments in their order of appearance in Smith's book."

○ Check the outline's appropriateness for your audience. See Sections 2.11 and 2.12.

○ Ask whether the outline is the most efficient one possible.

5.4 For example, Pope (1973), criticizing Parsons's (1949; first published in 1937) interpretation of Durkheim, followed Parsons's outline. Pope could also have used a data-analysis outline. The data would have been Parsons's arguments and their documentation. The analysis would have discussed (1) which of Parsons's arguments were wrong and why, (2) statements of Durkheim's to which Parsons should have given more emphasis, and (3) the specific effects of Pope's analysis on interpretations of Durkheim's social theory. Pope used the first outline because an article based on it was clearer and shorter.

5.5 Correcting Errors in Organization.   If you find errors in organization,

○ Correct them by cutting out sections, changing their order, and taping them together in the new order.

○ Prepare a draft for each possible reorganization.

○ Prepare each revision from a fresh copy of your old draft.

○ Evaluate each revision using the criteria in Section 5.3 and choose one.

5.6 Preparing Headings and Checking Transitions. When you are satisfied with the organization of topics at each level of importance,

○ Insert headings and subheadings to show where each topic begins. Headings help readers to find topics quickly and to understand organization.

○ In general, prepare headings and subheadings only for topics at the first three levels of importance (explained in Section 2.3). Make them topical, grammatically parallel, and no longer than half a line. See Section 2.7 for an explanation and examples of parallelism. Sections 8.31 to 8.34 show how to prepare headings and subheadings in different editorial styles.

○ Also check the transitions between sections that you moved from one place in the manuscript to another. See Section 5.33 for help.

Checking Content

5.7 Overall Content. To check overall content,

○ Examine the manuscript's central focus.

Books often contain more than one major idea, but a central theme unites them. Most successful scholarly articles present only a single major idea. To test unity,

○ For a book manuscript, examine the introductory and concluding chapters for a central theme. You should find one and only one. Other ideas should be subordinate.

○ For an article, examine the summary paragraph of the introduction, the concluding paragraph, and the abstract for the number of major ideas involved. You should find one and only one. All other ideas should be subideas.

More than one usually means that your scope is too wide. None usually means that the manuscript lacks a focus. Both usually indicate that your thinking is not completely clear. If you have difficulty making repairs,

○ Consult with colleagues (see Sections 6.4 and 6.5). They have the advantage of distance from your topic.

5.8 Unity is easier to demonstrate than to explain. The following example, taken from the problem-statement section of a research article (Knoke 1974, p. 93), states clearly a major idea, in the first two lines, and three subideas.

> This paper bridges the gap between [sociological and psychological models of voting behavior] (1) by specifying a causal model of voting behavior, . . . (2) by providing quantitative measurement of causal relationships among variables, . . . and (3) by comparing parameters of the model over time.

5.9 Clarifying a single idea can be more difficult for the author who is synthesizing two or more topics rather than reporting the analysis of a single phenomenon. Synthesis is often the goal of authors whose manuscripts are not based on empirical research. For example, Pope (1973) disputed Parsons's (1949) claim that Durkheim was a positivist. To do this, Pope had to state concisely the essentials of Durkheim's theory, the essentials of Parsons's interpretation, and the discrepancies. A single idea united the paper: "Durkheim was never a positivist [because] Durkheim's thought does not undergo the changes identified by Parsons" (Pope 1973, p. 400).

5.10 In another article, Denzin (1969) proposed a synthesis between symbolic interactionism and ethnomethodology, two theoretical perspectives within sociology that most sociologists had perceived as two different ways of thinking about society.

Denzin stated his central idea as follows: With regard to the problem areas of "social organization, methodology, socialization, deviance, social control, face-to-face interaction, and the analysis of science as a social enterprise," there are sufficient similarities in the theoretical and methodological assumptions of symbolic interactionism and ethnomethodology that a synthesis of the two may be proposed (Denzin 1969, p. 922).

5.11   To synthesize,

○ Subordinate the theories, analyses, or topics on which you are writing.
○ Unite them by focusing on the similarities, differences, or other common factors that originally made you want to write a manuscript.

5.12   Content of Each Section.   Next, check the content in each individual section for relevance, coherence, and understandability. For help with the introduction, use the guidelines in Sections 2.13 and 2.14.

5.13   If you are following a data-analysis outline,

○ *Check the problem statement* with the guidelines in Sections 2.25 to 2.27.
○ *Check the method section* with the guidelines in Sections 2.29 to 2.35.
○ *Check the results and discussion* with the guidelines in Sections 2.36 to 2.39. Be certain the problem statement contains adequate preparation for the discussion of results. Conversely, check the problem statement for hypotheses you may have failed to discuss. Express conclusions unambiguously. If writing for a scholarly journal, assume that your readers have a professional knowledge of statistical procedures.
○ *Check the summary* against the guidelines in Section 2.40. For a 30-page manuscript, use no more than a paragraph or two. The content of a summary should match closely the content

of an abstract (described in Section 8.25). Write the summary so that it can be understood by persons who have not read the manuscript.

5.14 Topics of Paragraphs. Next, check the topics of paragraphs.

☐ Each paragraph should contain only a single thought that is described in a topic sentence, either at the beginning or at the end of the paragraph.

Checking Length of Each Section

5.15 After revising for organization and content,

○ Examine the amount of space given to subtopics relative to major topics. In general, the lower the level of importance, the less space you should give for discussion.
○ To measure, count words, sentences, paragraphs, and pages.

Expect some imbalance. However, if many of your presumably major topics take less space than one or two subtopics in other major sections, reexamine your outline and your intentions. You may have focused the manuscript improperly.

5.16 Also check the lengths of major sections.

☐ In general, introductions should constitute no more than 10 percent of a manuscript. Discussion should constitute half or more.

Table 5.1 shows guidelines for allocating space to topics at the first level of importance in manuscripts using standard outlines.

☐ These guidelines are approximate. Do not use them rigidly.

However, if your problem statement is over 15 percent, reevaluate it, particularly if the manuscript is taken from your

Table 5.1 Number and Percentage of Total Typed Pages in Sections of a Scientific Manuscript

Sections	Total Pages		Percentage
	20	30	
Data-Analysis Outline			
Problem statement	2	3	10%
Method[a]	1–2	3	5–10
Results[a]	4	6	20[b]
Discussion[a]	7	10½	35[b]
Summary	½	1	3–5
Notes	2	3	10
References	2½	3½	10
New Theory or Method Outline			
Problem statement	2	3	10
Exposition[a]	4	6	20
Discussion[a]	9	13½	45
Summary	½	1	3–5
Notes	2	3	10
References	2½	3½	10

Note. Numbers and percentages are approximate. Numbers are based on 250 words per page of text.
[a]Numbers include tables and figures.
[b]If written as one section, at least 50 percent.

doctoral dissertation (see Section 13.6 for help). Similarly, reevaluate if the percentages for discussion and results are more than 15 percent below those suggested. In such cases the relative size of sections may imply that the results matter little theoretically, methodologically, or empirically. You may want to do further analysis.

Typing a Clean Draft

5.17 After revising for organization and content,

○ Type a clean draft, or have it typed for you. See Section 4.28 for help.

○ Title, date, and number or color-code it. See Section 4.29 for help.

○ Put your name and address on the cover sheet with the words: "Draft; do not cite or quote without permission."

CLARITY

Checking Verbal Clarity

5.18　General Language.

○ Choose language appropriate for your intended audience.

Scholarly articles and monographs have a formal style. Their authors often use technical language. They usually avoid imaginative writing and informal grammatical constructions such as contractions. For example, the terms used to title major sections of a data-analysis article—method, results, discussion—are unimaginative.[1] In contrast, textbooks and trade books are written in general English. Technical language is minimized and usually explained. Imaginative writing is usually helpful. Slang expressions are sometimes used to make specific points.

5.19　Technical Language.　Properly used, technical language enhances clarity. Improperly used, it becomes jargon. Choice of technical language can also place a scientist's work squarely within—or in sharp contrast to—a recognized intellectual tradition. For example, use of *indexicality* implies that the writer is an ethnomethodologist.

☐ Appropriately used, technical terms act like idioms and clichés in general English: they say a lot in very few words.

It is ironic, then, that misused technical language almost invariably lengthens and muddles a manuscript—a result that is satirized in Manning's (1975) "Thurble's Fabulous Word Machine."

5.20 Follow these general rules for using technical language.

○ Use technical terms only when you cannot find a common English equivalent.

For example, do not use *configuration* when *pattern* would do, *conceptualization* in place of *thinking*, or *hypothesis* for *hunch* or *speculation*.

○ Use sparingly technical terms that belong to a discipline or specialty other than your own.

For example, use *parameter* only in its mathematical sense. Do not use it as a synonym for *boundary* or *limit*.

○ Do not create new technical language when an old term, either by itself or in combination with an ordinary English modifier, would serve as well.[2]

For example, scientists sometimes use *operationalize* or *operationalization* to describe the process of assigning variables to concepts to make concepts testable. Other scientists use it to describe the process of starting a program or project. Still others use it in other ways. Unfortunately, neither word is in the dictionary. As a result, only the writers know exactly what they mean. Using ordinary English would take up a bit more space but contribute immensely to clarity.

○ In the same manuscript, do not vary your prose by using two or more technical terms that have the same meaning. Readers cannot tell whether you intended the same or slightly different meanings.

For example, the effect of one variable when all others have been *controlled for* or *taken into account* and the effect of one variable *net of all other variables* refer to the same kind of analytic result. *Arithmetic average* and *mean* refer to the same descriptive statistic. *Normative influence* and *normative socialization* refer to the same social process. A *2 × 2 table*, a *fourfold table*, and a *dichotomous cross-classification* describe a table with two rows and two columns. When choosing one term from among those in such sets,

○ Choose the one that is best known. For example, *average* is a more familiar word than *mean*.

○ Also, do not use the same word in both an ordinary-language and a technical sense.

For example, if you use *employ* (or related words such as *employment* or *employee*) in the technical sense of *to provide with a job*, then do not also use *employ* as a synonym for *use* (e.g., I *employed* three measures).

5.21 When writing for peers in your specialty,

○ Do not explain technical language that is common in the specialty.

○ With the first use of less common terms, add quotation marks to the term and cite the source of a definition.

When writing for general readers,

○ Eliminate technical language. If you retain any such terms, define or explain them. For example, few nonscientists know what a chi-square test is. If you want to use the term, either define it (sometimes within parentheses or in a footnote) or substitute an explanation that does not mention the term.

5.22 Unnecessary Long Words. Some long words are necessary. However,

○ Question words over three syllables in length before leaving them in a draft.

Those that must remain will be more effective for being fewer in number, and will not make the manuscript unnecessarily stuffy.

5.23 Indecisiveness. Words such as "seem," "apparently," and "appear to," particularly when they refer to what others have said (as the author interprets it) or to findings, are indecisive.

○ Do not use indecisive words to indicate modesty (usually false) or to mask an insecurity with data or conclusions.

For example, simply state "X *is* [not *seems to be*] more important than Y." The fact that an interpretation is yours, or that a conclusion is based on the data shown, is assumed unless you give another source.

○ If genuine doubt exists, use them and give an explanation.

For example, "Smith said X on page 1, but he said Y on page 331, and there is no apparent reason for the shift." Or, "The data apparently show that the President is well liked, but they should be interpreted with caution because they also show a strong acquiescent response bias." There are also other legitimate uses for these words—to show sarcasm, for example—and some writers use them well. However, misuse is common.

○ Before using indecisive words, examine your purposes carefully.

5.24 Author Self-Reference. Traditionally, scientists have been forbidden to use first-person singular pronouns in scholarly articles. However, that taboo is passing. "I found . . ." is shorter, clearer, and more direct than "the researcher found . . ." or "the result of the analysis was . . . ." As Price (1964, p. 656) noted, avoiding *I* and active-voice verbs (discussed in Section 5.31) does not guarantee objective writing. In general, use *we* only if:

○ You are writing with a coauthor.

○ *We* includes persons other than you, the author. For example, "We [people in general] say we believe *X*, but we do *Y*."

Such uses are different from beginning an article with "We [I] first review the literature. We [I] then analyze data." The latter sounds pompous, and has been justifiably termed "the regal we" (Wilson 1974, p. 2).

5.25 Sequence of Tenses. In general,

○ When writing about prior findings, theory and method, use the past tense or present perfect tense. For example: *he found, previous researchers have found,* and *I instructed the observers.*

○ Use the present tense for results that are right before the reader. For example, "Telephone surveys produce less valid data than do other survey methods."

○ Use the present tense for statements that have a continuing but general applicability, such as definitions and hypotheses.

○ Avoid the future tense.

5.26 Latin or English. In general,

○ Use Latin terms sparingly.

You may use them correctly, but your readers may not understand them. The two most commonly used terms are *i.e.* (that is) and *e.g.* (for example), and many scientists confuse even those two.

○ Use *i.e., e.g.,* and *etc.* within parentheses only. Elsewhere use, respectively: *that is, for example,* and *and so on,* as is done in this book.

Checking Clarity in Sentences

5.27 Precise Statements. Lack of precision often creates misleading sentences. For example, if you administered a questionnaire to subjects both before and after an experimental manipulation, the procedural statement should indicate this fact clearly. A sentence like "Questionnaires were administered to the subjects" is true, but incomplete.

○ Give all the necessary detail. For example: "The subjects filled out a questionnaire on attitudes before participating in the experiment. Afterward they completed another copy of the same questionnaire."

5.28 Sentence Length. The average line of typing or normal handwriting contains 10 to 12 words.

○ Try to complete at least one sentence in every two lines. If you find this task difficult, try to write sentences that a 7-year-old could understand. Then choose transitions that make the writing flow smoothly (for help, see Section 5.33).

This rule does not mean that *all* sentences should be short. Rather, long sentences should occur as infrequently as possible.

5.29 Verb-Subject Separation. In general,

○ Do not separate the subject and verb in a sentence by more than a line.

The sentence may be grammatically perfect, but the separation distracts the reader. For example, sentence [2] is more effective than [1]:

> The lack of enthusiasm for careful research on the part of the supervisors, whose plans and salaries may depend on the researchers' findings, is quite understandable.   [1]
> I can easily understand [it is easy to understand] the supervisors' lack of enthusiasm for careful research. Their plans and salaries may depend on the researchers' findings.   [2]

5.30 Double Negatives. Double negatives can be effectively used. In scientific writing, though, they are often "weaselers," used by writers who lack confidence in their findings. For example, what was the intent of the writer who said, "It is not inappropriate to say that Smith's hypothesis is incorrect"? In general,

○ Make a choice. Smith's hypothesis is either right or wrong.

When you are tempted to use a double negative anyway, first consult Perrin (1972, p. 550) or any other good grammar book.

5.31 The Passive Voice. All complete sentences have actors—someone or something that acts—and action words that tell what the actor did. Some sentences also have objects—persons or things affected by what the actor did. In the active voice, the actor is the subject of the sentence. For example,

> She evaluated the questionnaires.   [1]
> ↑   ↑   ↑
> actor   action   object

A correct passive-voice version of this sentence is:

> The questionnaires were evaluated by her.   [2]
>   ↑   ↖ ↑   ↑
>   object   action   actor

In scientific writing, sentences like [2] are often written incorrectly, as in [3], because the phrase stating the actor sounds awkward:

> The questionnaires were evaluated.   [3]
>   ↑   ↑
>   object   action   *no* actor

The failure to identify the actor often misleads readers and conceals important information. For example, suppose that following evaluation of the questionnaires,

> The decision was made to close the program.   [4]

If you have an interest in "the program," you would want to know who did the evaluation and who made the decision. Sometimes scientists use the passive voice without stating the actor to mask uncertainty with findings or to evade responsibility for an action. Sometimes they are simply imitating the frequent, incorrect use of the passive voice in scientific articles. It is ironic that the passive voice—long thought to foster un-biased reporting (see Section 5.24)—instead often permits both bias and imprecision. Use passive-voice constructions only if:

○ The actor is obvious, unknown, or unimportant.
○ You want to stress the object, use a weak substitute for the imperative, present a thought deliberately, or give variety in a passage otherwise composed completely of active-voice verbs. In all other cases, use active-voice verbs.

5.32 Doing the following exercise (suggested by Menzel, Jones, and Boyd 1961, p. 83) will produce a remarkable change in your writing:

○ Write three pages entirely in the active voice.
○ Use no form of the verb "to be."

You will find yourself promoting nouns and adjectives to verbs, and your prose will acquire new life and vitality. If you try this exercise when you are revising a manuscript, you will probably also find that the end product is approximately 10 percent shorter than the previous draft was. (Compare the lengths of sentences [1] and [2] above, and of sentences [6] and [7], in contrast to [8], in Section 5.38 below.)

Checking Clarity in Connections

5.33 Proper connections between ideas prevents misinterpre-tations. When connecting sentences, paragraphs, and sections,

○ Choose conjunctions and transitions that correctly signal the relationship of the elements being joined. Table 5.2 lists types of connections and examples.

5.34 For more detailed discussions of clarity in writing sen-tences, see Tichy (1966, Chapters 9 and 12). For assistance in

Table 5.2   Connections Between Elements of Sentences and Paragraphs

Type of Connection	Examples
Comparison and contrast	but, however, in comparison, in contrast, on the contrary, likewise, similarly, still, whereas
Conclusion to an argument	accordingly, consequently, hence, therefore, thus
Different physical locations	adjacent to, beyond, here, near, opposite to, there
Different times	afterward, after an hour (day, week, month, year, semester, etc.), before, immediately, meantime, meanwhile, then
Equal importance	first (second, third, etc.), also, and, equally important, furthermore, moreover, or, in addition
Example	for example, for instance
Subordination	although, as, as if, as though, because, if, since, so that, that, though, unless, until, when, whenever, where, wherever, whether, while
Summary or intensification of prior statement	in any event, in brief, indeed, in fact, in particular, in short, in summary, of course, to sum up

paragraph construction, see Tichy (Chapter 14). For a general discussion of clarity, see Ewing (1974, Chapter 10). When you have finished revising for clarity,

○ Prepare a clean draft. See Section 5.17 for instructions.
○ Seek collegial criticism (described in Section 6.5).

GRAMMATICAL CORRECTNESS

5.35 Eliminate grammatical errors:

○ To prevent technically inaccurate or ambiguous sentences.
○ To prevent criticism from people who can find no other way to express their distrust of what you have written.
○ To avoid insulting people who may think that you did not "care enough to send the very best."

Dangling Introductory Modifiers

5.36 Dangling modifiers are phrases and clauses that do not refer unmistakably to the words they logically modify. Dangling introductory phrases are particularly common in scientific writing. Changing the subject of the sentence often corrects the problem. For example:

> Tested on a monthly basis, the researcher soon noticed a change in the respondents.   [1]

> Tested on a monthly basis, the data soon showed changes in the respondents.   [2]

> After seeing the film, the doctor tested the respondents.
> [3]

The structure says that the researcher [1] and the data [2] are being tested; in [3], that the doctor saw the film. Logic tells us that in [1] and [2], the respondents were tested; in [3], that the respondents saw the film. Thus better sentences are:

> Tested monthly, the respondents soon showed changes.
> [4]

> After seeing the film, the respondents were tested by the doctor.   [5]

A construction similar to that in [1], [2], and [3], often used as a transition, is:

> Having found X, the data were analyzed for Y.   [6]

The structure says that the data found X. What the author meant was a sentence like [7] or [8]:

>   Having found X, I analyzed the data for Y.   [7]
>   After I found X, I analyzed the data for Y.   [8]

5.37 The following construction is particularly common in writing that includes mathematical equations.

>   Assuming that X equals Y, the equation becomes . . . .
>   [1]

Equations cannot assume. "Assuming" does not mean "if." A better sentence is:

>   If X equals Y, then the equation becomes . . . .   [2]

Misplaced Modifiers

5.38 Consider the following sentences:

>   The manipulation was applied by the researcher to 20 groups starting on Monday.   [1]
>   The two groups should be as similar as possible on all relevant variables at the beginning of the research.   [2]
>   Ten percent of the variance in voting behavior was explained for women by SES of parents.   [3]

Sentence [1] says that the researcher manipulated 20 groups that started on Monday (and on no other day). However, the author was not interested in when the groups were formed. Rather, he meant that the manipulations began on Monday. In sentence [2] the author wanted *at the initiation of the research* to tell when the variables should be similar. However, by placing that phrase where he did, he described the variables—those at the beginning and not at the end of the research. In sentence [3] the group for whom the finding holds is unclear until almost the end of the sentence. The sentence would be clearer if the group were stated earlier. These three sentences can be correctly stated as in [4], [5], and [6] to [8] respectively:

Beginning on Monday, I [the researcher] applied the manipulation to 20 groups. [4]

At the beginning of the research, the two groups should be as similar as possible on all relevant variables. [5]

For women, 10 percent of the variance in voting behavior was explained by their parents' SES. [6]

Ten percent of the women's variance in voting behavior was explained by their parents' SES. [7]

For women, parents' SES explained 10 percent of the variance in voting behavior. [8]

5.39 Errors like that in [3] are particularly common in the results and discussion sections of research reports. They occur because the author first states a finding and then qualifies it by adding either the conditions (e.g., $3 vs. $2; pressure vs. no pressure) or the groups (here, women) to which it applies. The result is almost always one or more misplaced modifiers. To avoid these errors,

○ State the qualification in an introductory phrase or clause, usually followed by a comma. Then state the finding.

If you state the finding in the passive voice as in [6] and [7], then the actor, in this case parents' SES, should immediately follow the verb. If you use the active voice, as in [8], the actor is the subject.

Incomplete Comparisons

5.40 Consider sentence [1]:

Men are four times more likely to kill themselves than women. [1]

Was the author trying to say [2] or [3]?

Men are four times more likely to kill themselves than to kill women. [2]

> Men are four times more likely than women to kill them-
> selves. [3]

Proper placement of the elements being compared clarifies the sentence. In general, when making comparisons,

○ State exactly what elements are being compared, and in what way.

EXCEPTION. Once you have established the elements in a comparison, subsequent statements of comparison may often be left grammatically incomplete. For example:

> I compared men and women. On the average, men were taller and weighed more, but women ran faster and per-
> formed intricate tasks more quickly. [4]

Completing the comparisons in the second sentence adds words and makes the sentence awkward. For example:

> I compared men and women. On the average, men were taller than women and weighed more than women, but women ran faster than men and performed intricate tasks more quickly than men. [5]

If the entire manuscript compared men and women, then most of the comparisons could be left grammatically incomplete. Indeed, the unnecessary completion of comparisons in such manuscripts is one of the more prolific sources of wordiness in scientific writing.

5.41 Give standards of comparison. For example, sentence [6] does not make a comparison even though comparison is implied by the use of *more*. Sentences [7], [8], and [9] are correct:

> This method is more precise. [6]
> This method is more precise than are other methods. [7]
> This method is more precise than Smith's method. [8]
> This method is more precise than I had expected. [9]

For [9] you may also need to give both the expected and the achieved levels.

Restrictive and Descriptive Modifiers

5.42   Restrictive modifiers are necessary to meaning. Descriptive modifiers are not. For example:

> The chief's wife, Mary, is here.   [1]
>
> The chief's wife Mary is here.   [2]

In [1] the commas show that *Mary* is descriptive; the chief is monogamous. In [2] the absence of commas shows that *Mary* is restrictive. The chief must be polygamous, because the name is needed to tell which wife is present.

5.43   Clauses introduced by *that* and *which* are special cases. Use *that* to introduce restrictive clauses and *which* to introduce descriptive ones. Commas usually precede and follow descriptive clauses. For example:

> The data, which were gathered by Jones, are accurate. [3]
>
> The data that were gathered by Jones are accurate.   [4]

If you want to say that all the data are accurate (and, incidentally, Jones gathered them), use [3]. If many people gathered data and only Jones's were accurate, use [4]. Without *that were gathered by Jones*, the statement would be untrue.

Affect or Effect

5.44   Explanations often use the words *affect* and *effect*. Sometimes writers confuse the two words. As *verbs*,

☐ *Affect* means "to influence or to have an effect, impact, or bearing on."
☐ *Effect* means "to bring about, to accomplish, to execute, or to cause."

As *nouns*,

☐ *Effect* means "result or consequence."
☐ *Affect* has a technical meaning in psychology and social psychology that is unrelated to causality.

The following sentences show correct use.

> *X affected* [*influenced, had an impact on*] Y in two ways. [1]
> *X effected* [*brought about, caused*] a change in Y.   [2]
> *X* had two *effects* on [*consequences* for] Y.   [3]
> *X* had two *effects* [*results*].   [4]

In your own sentences,

○ Substitute the bracketed meanings to help you decide which word is correct.

Quotation Marks

5.45   In scientific writing use quotation marks only for:

○ Direct quotations incorporated within a paragraph.
○ Technical terms that are not commonly known to your readers. In such cases, also give a source for the term. See Section 5.21.
○ Words you are using ironically, to mean their opposites. For example: Smith's analysis "proved" his point, but only because he omitted certain important cases.
○ Terms that you are defining. For example: "Structure" means . . . .
○ Avoid using colloquial terms, even with quotation marks. Instead, find an equivalent word in formal English.

Sexist Language

5.46   To avoid sexist language,

○ Treat members of both sexes in the same way. If you refer to men by their last names, refer to women in the same way. If you use *Dr.* for men who hold Ph.D. degrees, then use *Dr.* also for women with the same degree.
○ Treat men and women primarily as people, and not primarily as members of opposite sexes.

○ Whenever possible, replace occupational terms ending in *man* with terms that include persons of either sex. For example: *police officer* (not *policeman*); *supervisor* (not *foreman*).

○ Do not describe a woman in a way that would not be appropriate for a man. For example, do not describe a female subject as *the sprightly grandmother of three* unless you would also describe a male subject as, perhaps, *the balding grandfather of three*.

○ Do not use the term *girl* when referring to a woman.

Masculine words that denote humanity at large, such as *men* and *mankind*, are still acceptable. However, make substitutions if you can—for example, *humanity* or *human race* for *mankind*; *people* for *men*.

5.47 Masculine pronouns used to be acceptable referents for nouns that were either male or of unknown gender. For example, *the author* was nearly always *he*. Only female nouns, such as *a graduate of Mount Holyoke College*, took a female pronoun. Masculine pronouns are still grammatically correct, but when they are unacceptable to you or to a publisher, try the following suggestions:

○ Rewrite sentences to avoid using singular pronouns. For example, use [2] instead of [1]:

A *student* should have *his* papers professionally typed. [1]
Students should have *their* papers professionally typed. [2]

○ Drop the pronoun, or replace it with *a, an,* or *the*. For example, use [4] instead of [3]:

A student should not cheat on *his* assignment. [3]
A student should not cheat on *an* assignment. [4]

○ If you use cases or examples, alternate female and male examples. Subsequent use of *he* and *she* in each example can thus be of the proper gender. See Chapters 2 and 4 for examples.

5.48   If a series of sentences refers repeatedly to both males and females, and you cannot avoid using some singular pronouns,

○ Use *he* or *she* (*his* or *her*) for the first occurrence, and *he* for the rest. This approach avoids repetition and wordiness.

○ Repeat *he* or *she* periodically, as is done in this book, especially when beginning a new line of thought or a new major section of a manuscript.

This technique, suggested by Ewing (1974) and by the McGraw-Hill Book Company (n.d.), is not a grammatical standard. It is only a systematic response to a social concern, to be used only when socially necessary and only when rewriting is impossible or excessively awkward.

References to Race

5.49   Do not capitalize *black*, or even *black* and *white*, to show respect. Currently accepted practice is:

○ Treat both groups the same way. Use lowercase initial letters on both *black* and *white*, and uppercase letters on *Negro* and *Caucasian*.

Misuses of Nouns

5.50   When possible, avoid using nouns to modify other nouns. The resulting combinations of words are often unclear. For example, if a man has *guilt* feelings, does he have *guilty* feelings or feelings *of guilt*? Is a *comparative research design* a *design for comparative research*, a *comparative design for research*, or a *research design that permits comparisons*? Is a *Japan expert* an *expert on Japan* or a *Japanese expert* (on some topic)? Is *neighborhood police protection: police protection of neighborhoods* or *protection by police officers who live in the neighborhood*? Is a *multiparty cleavage system* a (political) *system split among many parties*, or a *way to split a* (political) *system composed of many parties*? Is *legislator influence* the *influence of legislators* (or *legislators' influence*) on someone or something, or someone's *influence on legis-*

lators? Is *empathy research: research to study empathy*, or *research done with empathy*? Such uses of nouns, which were born in the headlines of newspapers, are especially common in abstracts of scientific articles—an unfortunate fact, because readers should not have to read several pages before they learn just what a *Japan expert* is. To avoid confusing readers,

○ Use adjectival forms of the nouns (such as *Japanese*), combinations of nouns and prepositions (such as *on Japan*), and clauses (such as *that permits comparisons*) that express your meaning precisely.

Eliminating misused nouns can enhance the clarity of writing almost as much as a change from passive- to active-voice verbs.

5.51 Do not create grammatically meaningless nouns out of shortened names for concepts or variables. For example, an author who names two variables *hold the same job five years* and *married twice* sometimes also writes a sentence like [1] that is more clearly written as in [2]:

> The association of hold the same job five years and married twice is .5.   [1]
> The association between holding the same job five years and being married twice is .5.   [2]

The tendency to treat entire descriptive phrases as nouns can also cause subject-verb disagreement. For example, in sentence [3] the subject and verb disagree because the author treated *wishes for high social status* as a singular noun. Sentence [4] is correct.

> Wishes for high social status is common.   [3]
> Wishes for high social status are common.   [4]

Spelling; Confused and Misused Terms

5.52 In general, use *Webster's Third New International Dictionary*, but see also Sections 5.72 and 8.12. Many common words and phrases are often either confused with other terms, or are

Table 5.3 Words Commonly Misused or Misspelled

Incorrect	Correct
acknowledgement	acknowledgment
afterwards	afterward
ageing	aging
alright	all right
an hypothesis	a hypothesis
behavior	In the abstract, is singular
can not	cannot
clearcut, clear cut	clear-cut
co-author	coauthor
co-education	coeducation
comparitive	comparative
controled, controling	controlled, controlling
co-ordination	coordination
demolish (or destroy) completely (or totally)	demolish, destroy (adding *completely* or *totally* is redundant)
descernable	discernible
dichotomy	Does not mean *gap*
grey	gray
head up	head
hopefully	Does not mean "If all goes well, . . ." Describes *how* a person feels; therefore, "Hopefully I will give a paper" means that "I will be in a hopeful state of mind when I give the paper"
interaction	In the abstract, is singular
labelled, labelling	labeled, labeling
only	In general, place *only* just before the word you want it to modify
originil	original
recieve	receive
represent	Does not mean "is"
results of	Follow with a noun such as *calculation, research, observation,* but not with a name. *Results of Jones* is wrong. *Results of Jones's research* is correct
re-unite	reunite
sizeable	sizable

Table 5.3 *(Continued)*

Incorrect	Correct
suggest	Does not mean "show"
towards	toward
unique	Means "one of a kind"; use no modifiers (e.g., more, most)
use *'s* to form the possessive singular of all nouns	Examples: Smith's, Parsons's (not Parsons'), Cummings's (not Cummings')
while	Does not mean *when*
yeild	yield

simply misused or misspelled. These are shown in Tables 5.3 and 5.4. Table 5.5 lists words that scientists commonly misspell.

Numbers or Words

5.53   In scientific writing, express as words:

○ The cardinal numbers zero through nine, except as noted below, and their associated ordinal numbers (first, second, etc.).
○ Any number that begins a sentence.

Express in figures:

○ Cardinal and ordinal numbers 10 (10th) or greater.[3]
○ *Any* numbers that are units of measurement or time, ages, times, dates, percentages, fractional or decimal quantities, ratios, arithmetical manipulations, exact sums of money, scores and points on scales, numbers referred to as numerals, page numbers, series of four or more.
○ Also, numbers that refer to the same unit and are grouped within a sentence or several sentences in a sequence *if any* of the numbers is 10 or more.
○ All percentiles and quartiles.

Table 5.4 Words Commonly Confused with Each Other

Words	Meaning (Brief) or Proper Use
allude, elude	*allude:* mention; *elude:* escape
adverse, averse	*adverse:* bad; *averse:* opposed
alternate, alternative	Do not have the same meaning. Most commonly, *alternate* is an adjective; *alternative,* a noun. Check dictionary before using
basis, bases	*basis* is singular; *bases,* plural
bloc, block	*bloc:* a coalition of persons with the same goal; *block:* a mass of matter with an extended surface, plus many other meanings. See dictionary
compare to, compare with	*compare to* assumes basic similarity; *compare with,* basic dissimilarity
compose, comprise	*compose:* make up; *comprise:* encompass. Example: Once parts have been *composed,* the whole *comprises* the parts
criterion, criteria	*criterion* is singular; *criteria,* plural
datum, data	*datum* is singular; *data,* plural. *Datum* is rare. In its place use *observation, fact,* or *figure*
different from, different than (for things and people)	*different from* is correct (see Bernstein 1972, pp. 139–141)
disinterested, uninterested	*disinterested:* impartial; *uninterested:* not interested
ecology, environment	*Ecology* is the study of the relationship between organisms and their *environment*
either, each	*either:* means one or the other; *each:* means both
formula, formulas	*formula* is singular; *formulas,* plural
hypothesis, hypotheses	*hypothesis* is singular; *hypotheses,* plural
imply, infer	speakers *imply;* hearers (readers) *infer*
incredible, incredulous	*incredible:* not to be believed; *incredulous:* skeptical

Table 5.4 *(Continued)*

Words	Meaning (Brief) or Proper Use
index, indexes	*index* is singular; *indexes,* plural (*indices* is rarely used)
its, it's (also whose, who's)	*its (whose)*: possessive of it (who); *it's (who's)*: contraction of it is (who is)
less, fewer	Use *less* for quantities whose parts cannot normally be separated (e.g., structural solidarity); use *fewer* for items that can be counted (e.g., interviewers, experimenters)
like, as, as if	*Like* does not mean *as* or *as if.* In general, use *like* to compare nouns and pronouns. Use *as* to compare phrases and clauses containing a verb (e.g., Winston tastes good *as* a cigarette should)
medium, media	*medium* is singular; *media,* plural
oral, verbal	*oral:* emphasizes human utterance; *verbal:* applies to spoken or written words (connotes reducing ideas to writing)
optimal, optimum, optima	*optimal* is an adjective. *Optimum* is a singular noun; *optima,* a plural noun
over, more than	*over:* refers to spatial relationships; *more than:* used with figures Example: *more than* (not *over*) 200 questionnaires were returned
per cent, percent, percentage	*per cent,* in U.S. usage, is an incorrect spelling of *percent*[a]; *percent* should be preceded by a number. *Percentage:* a given proportion in every hundred; stated as __ percent

Table 5.4 *(Continued)*

Words	Meaning (Brief) or Proper Use
phenomenon, phenomena	*phenomenon* is singular; *phenomena*, plural
principal, principle	*principal:* first, dominant, leading; *principle:* a guiding rule or basic truth
refute, response	*refute:* argue successfully *response:* answer (no implication of success in argument)

[a] According to O'Connor and Woodford (1975, p. 88), *per cent* is the preferred spelling in British usage; in the United States, *percent* is preferred.

Table 5.5   Words Commonly Misspelled in Scientific Manuscripts

Incorrect	Correct
analyse	analyze
bi-polar	bipolar
mid-point	midpoint
non-directive	nondirective
non-schizophrenic	nonschizophrenic
over-aggressive	overaggressive
post-test	posttest
pre-test	pretest
programing	programming
re-examine	reexamine
self-	Always hyphenate when using *self* as a prefix.
wave length	wavelength

Source. Linton (1972, pp. 173–174).

Capitalization of Titles

5.54 For titles of books, articles, tables, appendixes, and so forth, in general,

○ Capitalize the first word and last word; the first word after a colon; all nouns, pronouns, verbs, adjectives, and adverbs; and all prepositions that contain more than four letters.

Underlining

5.55 Overuse of underlining rapidly diminishes its impact. Carefully chosen modifiers provide much better emphasis. Also, underlining asks a compositor (a person who sets type for printing) to use italic type. The switch in type increases the likelihood of typesetting errors. Therefore,

○ Avoid underlining for emphasis.
○ Underline foreign words only if they will be unfamiliar to readers.

BREVITY

Narrowing the Scope

5.56 If a draft is more than 20 percent longer than the final manuscript should be,

○ Consider narrowing the scope of the manuscript.

For example, an anthropologist writing about a tribe's kinship and economic structures might consider discussing only kinship. See Sections 5.7 to 5.11 for further discussion.

Deleting Unneeded Summaries and Quotes

5.57 For manuscripts shorter than 35 pages in length, *avoid summaries* except for a brief paragraph at the end. For longer manuscripts, use summaries with caution. For class papers and dissertations, see guidelines in Section B.2. To make topics easy to find,

○ Use a well-written abstract (described in Section 8.25).

○ Use brief topical headings and subheadings. See Section 5.6.

○ Use a summary sentence when you complete a lengthy argument. For example: Since x, y, and z are true, a must be true. In manuscripts of any size, *avoid quotations* when possible. Especially in research reports, a brief paraphrase of a quotation's major argument, and sometimes even a citation alone, will make the necessary point.

Editing Tables

5.58 In general,

○ Delete tables with eight or fewer entries. Instead, present the entries in the text.

○ Look for textual material that can be more efficiently presented in a table.

○ Be sure that the tables supplement rather than duplicate text.

○ Look for similarities among tables that would permit combining them.

○ See Sections 3.4 through 3.7 and 3.18 for further help.

Removing Unneeded Words

5.59 In general,

○ Remove unnecessary comparisons, as recommended in Section 5.40.

○ Do not repeat detailed descriptions. For example, if you used a sample of "teenage males from Xenia whose mothers became pregnant in August 1960," you need not repeat all of these qualifications with every use of the word *sample*. *The sample* is sufficient.

○ Rewrite passive-voice sentences into the active voice. For help and examples, see Sections 5.31 and 5.32.

5.60 In text,

○ Do not repeat the verbal representations of terms used in mathematical equations. For example, if R_d stands for rate of divorces, use only R_d after you have introduced the term and its meaning.

EXCEPTION. After a gap in use of several pages or chapters, repeat the term and its meaning once as a reminder to readers.

5.61 Use adjectives and adverbs sparingly. Some, such as *very* and *quite*, both weaken and lengthen sentences. For example, sentence [2] is both stronger and shorter than sentence [1]:

The data were very wrong. [1]

The data were wrong. [2]

5.62 More generally, the author who has written *a majority of* may not think automatically of *most* as a briefer way to say the same thing. Or, if *X is accounted for by the fact that* . . . , he or she may not think about substituting *X is caused by* or *Y causes X*.

○ Use Table 5.6 to help you remove unnecessary words.

5.63 Editing for brevity can reduce a manuscript's length by as much as 20 percent without removing the essence of either the argument or the data. Following revision for brevity,

○ Prepare a clean draft. See Section 5.17 for help.
○ Seek collegial criticism. See Section 6.6 for help.

Table 5.6   Common Wordy Phrases and Suggested Changes

Wordy Phrase	Suggested Change
accordingly	so
accounted for by	due to, caused by
add the point that	add that
aggregate	total
a great deal of	much
along the line of	like
a majority of	most
analyzation	analysis
an example of this is the fact that	for example
another aspect of the situation to be considered	as for
a number of	several, many, some
approximately	about
are of the opinion that	think that
as per	Delete
as regards	about
as related to	for, about
assist, assistance	help
as to	about (Or omit)
at the present writing	now
based on the fact that	because, since
collect together	collect
commence	begin
communicate	write, telephone (i.e., a specific verb)
concerning, concerning the nature of	about
consequently	so
construct	build
demonstrate	show, prove
due to the fact that	because, since
during the time that	while
employ	use
endeavor	try
except in a small number of cases	usually
exhibit a tendency to	tend to
few [many] in number	few [many]
firstly [secondly, etc.]	first [second, etc.]
for the purpose of	for, to
for the reason that	because, since

Table 5.6 (*Continued*)

Wordy Phrase	Suggested Change
from the point of view of	for
if at all possible	if possible
inasmuch as	since
in case, in case of	if
in close proximity	near
in favor of	for, to
initial	first
initiate	begin
in light of the fact that	because
in order to	to
(have an) input into	contribute to
inquire	ask
in rare cases	rarely
in reference [with reference] to, in regard to	about
in relation with	with
in terms of	in, for (Or omit)
in the case of	Can usually be dropped
in the case that	if, when
in the course of	during
in the event that	if
in the first place	first
in the majority of instances	usually
in the matter of	about
in the nature of	like
in the neighborhood of	about
in the normal course of our procedure	normally
in the not-too-distant future	soon
in the opinion of this writer	in my opinion, I believe
in the vicinity of	near
in view of the above, in view of the foregoing circumstances, in view of the fact that	therefore
involve the necessity of	require
is defined as	is (Will frequently suffice)
it is clear [obvious] that	therefore, clearly [obviously]
it is observed that	Delete
it is often the case that	often

Table 5.6 (*Continued*)

Wordy Phrase	Suggested Change
it is our conclusion in light of investigation that	we conclude that, our findings indicate that
it should be noted that the X . . .	the X . . .
it stands to reason	Omit
it was noted that if	if
it would not be unreasonable to assume	I [we] assume
leaving out of consideration	disregarding
linkage	link
make an examination of	examine
modification	change
necessitate	require, need
not of a high order of accuracy	inaccurate
notwithstanding the fact that	although
objective	aim, goal
of considerable magnitude	big, large, great
of very minor importance [import]	unimportant
on account of the conditions described	because of the conditions
on account of the fact that	because
on a few occasions	occasionally
on the grounds that	because
outside of	outside
partially	partly
perform an analysis of	analyze
presently	now
prior to, in advance of	before
proceed to investigate, study, analyze (the data-gathering, etc.) process	Omit *proceed to* *Process* can usually be dropped
relative to this	about this

Table 5.6 (*Continued*)

Wordy Phrase	Suggested Change
resultant effect	effect
subsequent to	after
sufficient	enough
synthesize	unite
taking this factor into consideration, it is apparent that	therefore, therefore it seems
terminate, termination	end
that is, i.e.	Usually can be deleted if phrase or clause to which it refers has been written clearly
the data show that X . . .	X . . .
the existence of	Usually can be deleted
the foregoing	the, this, that, these, those
the fullest possible extent	Omit, or use *most, completely,* or *fully*
the only difference being that	except
the question as to whether or not	whether
there are not very many	few
to be sure	of course
to summarize the above	in sum, in summary
transmit	send
under way	begun, started
usage	use
within the realm of possibility	possible, possibly
with reference [regard, respect] to	Omit (or use *about*)
with the exception of	except
with the result that	so that
with this in mind, with this in mind it is clear that	therefore

WRITING STYLE

5.64 Some writers like to revise to improve writing style. To achieve good style in reports of research,

- Write simply.
- Choose plain words.
- Correct grammatical errors.
- Avoid long sentences.
- Use the active voice.

If you have written a book, a book review, or a review article, you may want to do more revising—changing emphases, changing one word for another, adding humor, and so forth. A person's writing style can be as distinctive as a signature (see Section 1.10).

CAUTION.   Attempting to achieve a unique writing style is never a license to retain ambiguous sentences, ungrammatical constructions, or unneeded words.

READABILITY

Definition and Purpose

5.65 From a narrow perspective, readability tests show how much education a reader would need to understand a manuscript completely.

> For example, college freshmen have completed only 12 grades. Therefore, a textbook for college freshmen should not have a readability level over 12, and 10 or 11 is usually more appropriate.

Among the more important factors affecting readability are difficulty of vocabulary, grammatical complexity (length of sentences), complexity of concepts, degree to which topic is specialized, page format (type size, margins), illustrations, writing style and organization, and various mechanical aids (Gilbart n.d., p. 1). Readability tests can measure objective factors such as vocabulary difficulty and grammatical complexity. Only an expert on readability can measure the other factors.

5.66 More broadly, achieving readability means making a manuscript easy to read and understand. Textbook writers and publishers have long been concerned about readability, because a textbook will sell well only if written in language its intended audience can easily understand. However, writers of monographs, trade books, research articles, and articles for the general public should be equally concerned. The more complex an argument, the greater the need for everyday English, with a minimum of technical language and the simplest sentences that will still convey the argument. Gunning has remarked that "the best technical writing is being done by persons at the top of their professions who have done important work, understand its meaning, and write about it with confidence. They are bold enough to write simple, direct English. . . . Others, who haven't done much or who understand less clearly what they have done, write with an uneasiness that leads to fog" (Gunning 1968, p. 257). To illustrate, Gunning quoted several examples. One, from Darwin's *Descent of Man*, has a readability level appropriate for tenth graders.

Formulas to Test Readability

5.67 Doing all five steps in revision carefully can help you achieve readability. After you complete them,

○ Use the Smog Index or the Gunning system to help you determine how successful you have been.
○ Because the simplicity of the formulas limits their reliability, consider the results they give as suggestive, not absolute.

5.68 Two Common Formulas. The Smog Index is probably the simplest formula:

○ Take 10 consecutive sentences from the front, 10 from the middle, and 10 from the end of a manuscript.
○ Count the number of words in all 30 sentences with 3 or more syllables in them.
○ Take the square root, and add 3.

The result is the approximate grade level for which the writing is most appropriate (McLaughlin 1969). The author of a pamphlet on family planning for persons who average 10 years of schooling should not have an index of 14 or 15 (mid-college). For scholarly writing 16 is appropriate, although lower levels are usually more acceptable to readers. For the Gunning system:

○ Calculate the average sentence length per 100 words.
○ Count the number of words of 3 syllables or more per 100 words.
○ Add the results of the first two steps and multiply by 0.4.

The result is the approximate grade level (Gunning 1968, pp. 38–39). For writers who dislike numbers, Gunning (1968, pp. 42–43) gives three other rules that help writers to improve readability:

○ Consider who the reader will be.
○ Avoid long sentences.
○ Use long words as little as possible.

If you use either system regularly, the search for simpler words and less complex sentences soon becomes automatic.

5.69 Other Readability Tests. The Dale-Chall test (Dale and Chall 1948), the Flesch test (Flesch 1951; see also 1974, Chapter 13), the Fry test (Fry 1968) and others, while probably more accurate, are more complex. If you need to use them,

○ Seek help from a specialist on readability.

APPROPRIATE LENGTHS FOR MANUSCRIPTS

5.70 Teachers often define the lengths of class papers and dissertations. Scientists writing journal articles must usually restrict their articles to the lengths set by the journals they have chosen.

○ When writing a journal article, consult the limits on length given in Table 7.1.

The general rule for the manuscript of a book is:

○ Write no more than is necessary to discuss the topic thoroughly but efficiently.

Resnikoff and Dolby (1972, p. 10) proposed an empirical definition of length. After a detailed study of libraries' information-storage and retrieval systems, they came to the following conclusions: "An abstract is approximately 1/30th the size (in number of characters) of the technical paper it abstracts"; an index, one-thirtieth the size of the book it indexes; the table of contents, one-thirtieth the size of the index; a book title, one-thirtieth the size of the book's table of contents.

TYPING AND PROOFREADING

5.71 When you have finished writing and revising,

○ Type the final manuscript. For instructions, see Section 5.17. For instructions specific to journal articles, see Chapter 8. For instructions specific to books, see Chapter 12. For guidelines on typing class papers and dissertations, see Section B.3.
○ Proofread carefully. For instructions, see Sections 8.84 and 11.32.

RESOURCES FOR WRITERS

General Aids

5.72   Dictionaries.   As a guide to spelling for American publications,

○ Use *Webster's Third New International Dictionary of the English Language* (3d ed., unabridged, 1961) or *Webster's New Collegiate Dictionary* (1975; based on *Webster's Third*).

For British publications,

○ Use *The Oxford English Dictionary* (1933). Supplement it with *A Dictionary of Modern English Usage* (Fowler 1965), which is based on *The Oxford English Dictionary*.

For information on people and places,

○ Use *Webster's Biographical Dictionary* (1972) and *Webster's New Geographical Dictionary (1972)*.

5.73   Thesauruses.   *Roget's International Thesaurus* 3d ed., 1962) provides more lists of words with similar meanings than does a dictionary. Flesch (1974, p. 156) recommends the *Thorndike-Barnhart Dictionary* as the best source of simple synonyms. See also *Webster's New Dictionary of Synonyms* (1973).

5.74   Quotations.   Bartlett's *Familiar Quotations* (1968 ed.) gives familiar quotations and their sources.

5.75   Grammar and Writing.   *Effective Writing* (Tichy 1966) was designed in part for writers in the natural and physical sciences. Therefore, while her topic is writing in general, her advice is often more than ordinarily helpful to social and behavioral scientists. She spends considerably more time than I do on organizing, outlining, writing, revising, beginning paragraphs, correcting grammar, and improving writing style.

Writing for Results (Ewing 1974) is a helpful guide for writers in business. *Little English Handbook* (Corbett 1973) is a clear, brief grammar book. *Elements of Style* (Strunk and White 1959) is a brief, classic grammar book. *Writer's Guide and Index to English* (Perrin 1972) is an excellent college textbook on expository writing, with a useful index to English. *A Manual for Writers of Term Papers, Theses, and Dissertations* (Turabian 1973) is much used by students. *The Careful Writer* (Bernstein 1965) is an entertaining dictionary of terms that are often misused or confused with each other.

5.76 Readability. *Reading Expectancy and Readability* (Pescosolido and Gervase 1971) lists documents on, and gives explanations of, readability.

Resources for Scientific Writing and Publishing

5.77 *Writing Research Papers* (Lester 1971) describes every step in the research and writing process. Lester's instructions conform to those of the Modern Language Association (MLA), but he also describes documentation in other editorial styles (Chapter 8). *Writing Scientific Papers in English* (O'Connor and Woodford 1975) is also useful. *The Student Sociologist's Handbook* (Bart and Frankel 1971) is helpful to undergraduates in sociology and social psychology. Graduate students might want to read *Scientific Writing for Graduate Students* (Woodford 1968). *Writing a Technical Paper* (Menzel, Jones, and Boyd 1961) takes its examples from natural and physical sciences, but is still very useful to social and behavioral scientiests who are writing for publication. The book is small and well written. Do not let its age deceive you into thinking it is obsolete.

5.78 *The Technique of Clear Writing* (Gunning 1968, pp. 254–274) offers a more general discussion of technical writing. The APA's *Publication Manual* (1974) and Linton's *Simplified Style Manual* (1972) consider scientific report writing for psychologists. APA (1974, pp. 35–37) also discusses the metric system and gives abbreviations. "Tabular Presentation" (Davis and Jacobs 1968), *Say It with Figures* (Zeisel 1968), *A Manual of*

Style (University of Chicago Press 1969, Chapters 11 and 12), APA (1974), and Linton (1972, Chapter 6) explain how to prepare tables and figures. Zeisel also discusses other aspects of using numbers.

5.79 Some books and articles are designed especially for publishing authors.

○ Acquire the most commonly used editorial style guides in your discipline.

Chapter 8 lists and describes the editorial styles most widely used by social- and behavioral-science journals. Some—for example the APA's manual (1974) and the Modern Language Association's *Style Sheet* (1970)—include sections on grammar and writing. The University of Chicago Press's *A Manual of Style* (1969), the most widely used style manual in book publishing, is also used by many journals. This book gives detailed instructions for using two fundamentally different editorial styles. Chapter 8 describes (Section 8.4) and gives examples of both. More than just a style manual, this book systematically discusses both English grammar and manuscript preparation, and explains requirements from the publisher's perspective. Often, knowing the reason for a rule helps a writer to follow it better and make accurate decisions in situations not covered by rules. Also helpful are some of the other style guides prepared by various publishing houses, for example *Author's Manual* (Harper & Row 1966), and given to authors at the time they sign contracts. McGraw-Hill's (n.d.) "Guidelines for Equal Treatment of the Sexes" gives many examples of ways to avoid sexist language (available from McGraw-Hill's Public Information and Publicity Department).

5.80 "Thesis to Book" (Holmes 1974, Parts 1, 2, and 3) is helpful to scholars trying to write books based on their doctoral dissertations. See Sections 13.6 and 13.7 for details.

SUMMARY

5.81   In this chapter I first discuss revising overall organization and content (Sections 5.2 to 5.17). I next examine revising for clarity (5.18 to 5.34), grammatical correctness (5.35 to 5.55), brevity (5.56 to 5.63), and style (5.64). I also discuss readability (5.65 to 5.69), lengths of manuscripts (5.70), and typing and proofreading (5.71). The last sections (5.72 to 5.80) list resources to help authors improve their writing.

NOTES TO CHAPTER 5

1.   Occasionally authors combine the standard title with a specific descriptive title. For example, White, Boorman, and Breiger (1976) used *Methods: Phenomenology and Algorithms* to title a method section that described a mathematical technique for analyzing social structure.

2.   Gunning (1968, pp. 259–260) has suggested that both the abuse of technical language and the creation of new terms often result from scientists' professional insecurity and the desire "to persuade others (and perhaps convince themselves) that they know a great deal." Tichy (1966, p. 213) has spread the blame more broadly: "Until the learned societies assume their aesthetic, and possibly their ethical, responsibility for improving language, the best that a writer can do is use the technical terms of his own specialization sparingly and avoid the needless use of technical language from other specializations."

3.   For books in disciplines other than psychology, some publishers prefer that authors use words for cardinal and ordinal numbers up to 100 (100th). The editorial styles of some journals, particularly those whose articles are largely nonquantitative, also require that authors use words for numbers up to 100 (100th).

CHAPTER SIX

Critics, Criticism,
and Coauthors

INTRODUCTION

6.1 No piece of published writing is ever the author's alone.
Even scientists who do not consult with others as they write
usually alter their manuscripts in response to the suggestions of
journal and book editors and referees. Indeed, the author who
does not seek and respond to criticism usually publishes very
little. The unwritten rules that govern scientists' relations with

112

each other, with journal editors, and with book publishers are usually known by experienced scientists, but newcomers must learn by watching, listening, and asking questions. In this chapter I discuss working with collegial critics, editorial consultants, and coauthors. Relations with journal editors and with book publishers are discussed in Parts II and IV. Read this chapter both as an author and as a critic.

SEEKING AND USING CRITICISM

The Value of Criticism

6.2   Some scientists fear letting others see their work until it is nearly finished—at least from their perspective. Some fear criticism per se because it can be unpleasant (see Section 6.8). Some fear being caught in errors and omissions, although eliminating errors may be the best reason for seeking help. Others do not realize that collegial assistance is a common, reciprocal occurrence. This failure may result from the normal requirement, during undergraduate and graduate days, that papers be the work of only one person, who subsequently receives a grade on that work. Still others equate asking a colleague to read a manuscript with submitting a thesis chapter to an adviser. However, the thesis relationship is usually a subordinate-to-supervisor relationship, while the collegial relationship is usually one of equals. Certainly many colleagues respond in blunt terms that seem rather superior and unfriendly, but this bluntness is often unintentional. Because the critic is trying to return an evaluation quickly, he or she has not taken the time to be tactful. Finally, some scientists fear having their ideas stolen. (Some scientists prevent stealing by circulating their unpublished manuscripts so widely that a stolen idea would promptly be recognized as such.)

6.3   Nevertheless, the benefits of criticism argue strongly for setting aside such fears. By contributing a viewpoint different from yours, good collegial critics can stimulate your thinking and improve your writing. Increasingly, journals' *Instructions to*

Contributors are recommending that authors seek such criticism before submitting their articles for possible publication. On each manuscript,

○ Choose collegial critics for their substantive, theoretical, or methodological competence on the topic; frankness; and reputation for prompt, thoughtful responses.
○ Optional: to test the breadth of communication, you may also want a critic with a substantive orientation different from yours.

By analyzing your writing and editing your manuscripts, editorial consultants can also help you clarify your thinking and improve your writing. *The Literary Marketplace* (*LMP*; described in Section 14.7) lists free-lance editors in many geographical areas.

What Help to Request, and When

6.4   Postdissertation Advice.   If you want to publish a manuscript based on your doctoral dissertation, but do not know whether a book or articles are more appropriate,

○ Request advice, perhaps from your dissertation adviser.

6.5   Criticism of Organization and Content.   After completing a first draft and revising to improve organization and content (see Sections 5.2 to 5.16) and clarity (5.18 to 5.34),

○ Ask an editorial consultant to evaluate the organization and clarity.[1] Some sections may be unneeded, unclear, redundant, or more effective if placed elsewhere in the manuscript.
○ Ask at least one colleague to evaluate the organization and to look for errors and omissions in content.

If you ask for such comments before investing months in revising for grammatical correctness, brevity and writing style, you will more readily accept sweeping suggestions for change, or even throw away the manuscript if necessary. For example, if the manuscript's central argument has been made before, but in literature that you have not read, an experienced colleague may catch that fact and save you both time wasted on further revising and the public embarrassment of having an outsider make the discovery. Or a colleague may discover that you did an analysis improperly (not uncommon, given today's sophisticated statistics and methods). When done properly, the results prove both insignificant and uninteresting. In such cases the colleague has done you a favor, but you may find it hard to feel grateful if you have already invested months in rewriting and polishing.

6.6   Criticism of Grammatical Correctness, Brevity, and Writing Style.   After revising for grammatical correctness (Sections 5.36 to 5.54), brevity (5.56 to 5.62), and style (5.64),

○ Ask an editorial consultant to do mechanical editing: correct spelling, punctuation, and misplaced prepositional phrases; remove unnecessary words; rephrase awkward sentences; check the reference list with references in the text.

○ Ask a colleague to read the manuscript as if he or she were a referee. He may find minor errors, inconsistencies, obscurities, sentences that can be deleted, and so forth. If possible, choose a colleague who did not see a previous draft.

○ If you do not know what publisher is most appropriate for the manuscript, ask for suggestions.

How to Ask for Help

6.7   When asking for help,

○ Make a personal request. Write a letter if you want help from someone not employed at your institution.

○ Never ask for any kind of help without first having tried to correct problems yourself.

○ Always give critics a clean, typed draft.

○ Tell the critic, in writing, precisely what kind of criticism you want (see Sections 6.4 to 6.6).

○ Offer help in return.

How to Use Criticism

6.8 Even well-published authors often find it hard to accept criticism gracefully. However good the criticism is, accepting it often requires the author to feel, even if only temporarily, that he or she has failed. Tactlessness on the critic's part may make acceptance even more difficult. Also, almost invariably some criticisms are "wrong." For example, consider outline [1]:

  I. Problem statement   [1]
  II. Theory
 III. Sexuality
 IV. Dating behavior
  V. Summary

The author using this outline had five first-order headings (defined in Section 8.31) in his manuscript. The text for the third, *Sexuality*, was three pages long. A journal's referee, misled by the fact of the separate heading, remarked that sexuality was important enough to the author's theory to merit more than three pages of discussion. The author was frustrated by the criticism because he had gone on to examine the effects of sexuality on dating behavior. However, he sought help from another critic, who suggested that the problem might be resolved simply by reorganizing the outline as [2]:

  I. Problem statement   [2]
  II. Theory
 III. Sexuality
    A. Definition and description
    B. Effects on dating behavior
 IV. Summary

In the manuscript, what had originally been the third and fourth first-order headings became, instead, one first-order heading, *Sexuality,* and two second-order headings: *Definition and Description* and *Effect on Dating Behavior.* The revised manuscript was subsequently accepted for publication.

6.9 Some might object that the critic should have read more carefully, but that objection misses an important point:

☐ Critics should not have to read with unusual care.

If an author is not switching topics, the heading should not imply that he is. Situations like this one happen frequently, particularly with referees, because the author cannot talk directly with the critic and get to the heart of the difficulty. Authors become very frustrated if they fail to realize that a genuine problem exists even if the critic has "misdiagnosed" it and, thus, described it inaccurately.

6.10 Clearly, criticism cannot always be accepted at face value. In the case just described, if the author had accepted the criticism without question, his revision might well have damaged the manuscript. However, had he simply rejected the observation, he would not have improved the article. When baffled by a critic's comments,

○ Assume that something is wrong somewhere.
○ Consult again with the critic, if possible. If not, seek help from a third party.
○ Ask questions politely. Never quibble or protest. Such action may cost you the critic's future help.

6.11 Similarly, an editorial consultant may misinterpret your meaning and thus edit a sentence or paragraph so that it does not say what you intended. In such cases, the original text is usually unclear. When correcting such editing,

○ Do not restore the original.
○ Try different phrasing.
○ Discuss such problems with the consultant. Doing so will often improve the editing on subsequent manuscripts.

6.12   When you have completed a manuscript,

○ Reread the consultant's editing and general comments.
○ List the types of errors that recur. If asked, some consultants will make the list for you.
○ Note how the consultant corrected the errors. Also read Chapters 2, 3, and 5 for other suggestions.

In your next manuscript, concentrate on correcting the most frequent errors. When you complete that manuscript, make a new list of errors and treat it like the previous one. If you repeat this procedure with each manuscript, your writing will soon show noticeable improvement. If, when you make your first list, you find many different types of error,

○ Concentrate first on correcting errors that affect organization and content (see Sections 5.2 to 5.16). Next, work on improving clarity and grammatical correctness (5.18 to 5.54). Concentrate next on brevity (5.56 to 5.62) and last on writing style (5.64).

Relationships Between Critics and Authors

6.13   Collegial assistance should not be taken for granted. It may be withheld, or withdrawn at any time. Nevertheless, authors who request criticism on a manuscript usually want detailed comments, and as soon as possible. Critics usually assist most graciously when the author inquires about, and respects constraints on, their time. Authors usually accept criticism most easily when the critic has tried to be tactful as well as incisive.

> For example, "The connection between the first two sections needs to be stated more clearly" is a more tactful comment than "There's no connection between the first two sections."

6.14   If you work with a consultant, you may find that certain circumstances make it easier for you to accept criticism. You may prefer that editing be done in pen rather than pencil, a fine-point pen instead of a medium, or green ink instead of blue. You may prefer general comments on writing to be delivered verbally as well as in writing. You may prefer to converse in your office rather than in the consultant's. Any number of small variables may enhance the author-editor relationship.

○ If you have preferences, state them.

6.15 When you have completed a manuscript,

○ Acknowledge the help you received. See Sections 8.56 to 8.59 and 12.28 for instructions and examples.
○ Give each critic a copy of the completed manuscript.
○ Return the favor directly to those who helped you, or help others as carefully as you were helped.

6.16 Occasionally, when critics have commented extensively, authors invite them to become coauthors. Occasionally, also, a colleague makes extensive comments or changes and then demands inclusion as a coauthor. Such situations can be unpleasant, particularly if the assisting party has higher professional status than the author holds. The best way to resolve such situations is for critics to prevent them. If, in reading a draft, you feel that substantial revision is needed and that you should receive coauthorship status if you do revise,

○ Say so *before* making any other suggestions.

WORKING WITH COAUTHORS

The Difficulty of Determining Authorship

6.17 Coauthorship is a special case of collegial assistance. At its best, coauthorship results when two or more scientists combine their strong points to do, and then to publish, scientific research. At its worst, coauthorship causes stress and resentment. One major question is: What is an author? Price (1964, p. 656) argued that only persons who have contributed to the writing of a manuscript are entitled to either authorship or coauthorship. Today that prescription is far too limiting. In contemporary social and behavioral science, computation and analysis have become increasingly complex. Scientists who have not learned the latest statistical and methodological techniques depend heavily on the methodological and computional skills of colleagues and graduate students. In such cases the assistants contribute quite as much to a manuscript as does the principal investigator, even though they may not write a word. In short, the right to authorship is hard to determine. Also, different disciplines use different criteria to determine what an author is, and current criteria are changing (Zuckerman 1968, p. 291). The merits of various practices aside, scientists need to know the practices and their implications.

Patterns of Ordering Names

6.18 Zuckerman (1968) identified three patterns of ordering names on multiauthored papers. The "equality pattern," designed to show that all authors made an equal contribution, consists of alphabetized and reverse-alphabetized last-name sequences. For example:

> Abrams, Adams, and Allen
> Allen, Adams, and Abrams

The second pattern emphasizes *one name* by placing it *out of order*, as the first or last name, in an otherwise sequential series. For example:

> York, Adams, Berk, and Cone
> Cone, Berk, Adams, and York

The third, an alphabetically random pattern, gives prime visibility to the first author and less to each of the rest in turn (see Zuckerman 1968, p. 278–289; also Mitchell 1968, p. 96).

6.19 The confusing aspect of these patterns is that for any given set of coauthors, the name order may not mean what it seems to mean. For example, if three coauthors are making equal contributions to three or more articles, they may have agreed that the order will be alphabetical on the first and reverse-alphabetical on the second. On the third, though, the middle person will be named first. Readers who see the third paper in isolation from the rest may misunderstand the first author's role. Take another example. Random name order is often interpreted as showing that each succeeding author did less work than each prior author. However, the first author may be the principal investigator of a research team, while the other authors are research assistants. The principal investigator may have done little other than to obtain funding and supervise the research, but he or she controls the research and if he wants his name first, there is little the assistants can do (see Mitchell 1968, pp. 95–96).[2]

A Prescription for Preventing Difficulties

6.20 Whatever the differences in status and quality of personal relationship, scientists who are working together should:

○ Make written agreements, before manuscript preparation, about what contribution will earn an acknowledgment of thanks and what will earn coauthorship.
○ If coauthorship is a possibility, specify name order for each manuscript.

Titles are not necessary to such agreements. Designate manuscripts, for example, as "the first article" and "the second article."

SUMMARY

6.21 In this chapter I discuss the value of criticism (Sections 6.2 and 6.3), what help to request and when (6.4 to 6.6), how to ask for help (6.7), how to use criticism (6.8 to 6.12), and relationships between critics and authors (6.13 to 6.16). I then discuss the difficulty of determining authorship (6.17), patterns of ordering coauthors' names (6.18 and 6.19), and ways to avoid disagreements over name order (6.20).

NOTES TO CHAPTER 6

1.   In general, do not request mechanical editing (see Section 6.6) at the same time. Because reorganization often changes whatever mechanical editing has been done, trying to have both steps done simultaneously usually wastes money and time.

2.   Zuckerman (1968, pp. 283–285) noted an interesting contrast between the behavior of Nobel Laureates and that of other scientists. Many of the former intentionally placed their names last in the hope of benefiting their co-workers; the non-Nobel Laureates more often placed themselves first.

Part Two

AUTHORS, ARTICLES, AND SCHOLARLY JOURNALS

CHAPTER SEVEN

Journals: What Kind, How Many, Which, and Why

INTRODUCTION

Difficulty of Getting Articles Accepted for Publication

7.1   Many authors have trouble finding journals willing to publish their articles. Sometimes the content of the articles is not publishable anywhere. Often, though, the authors have handicapped themselves unnecessarily. They know only the

125

two or three most prestigious journals in their disciplines and a few that publish articles on topics of special interest to them. As a result many sociologists, for example, send their articles first to the *American Sociological Review (ASR)* or the *American Journal of Sociology (AJS)*. Rejection of an article by either journal is usually followed by submission to the other. Only after two or three rejections—sometimes accompanied by confusingly different critiques (see McCartney 1973b, p. 444)—will the author seek a journal especially suited to the article's degree of importance and level of specialization. That search is often complicated because many journals' titles do not indicate preferred subject matter. Table 7.1 below gives many examples.

Advantages and Disadvantages of Prestigious Journals

7.2   Articles published in prestigious journals are widely read, and they often confer greater status on their authors than do articles published in other journals. However, the cost of rejection—a likely possibility, since many of the most prestigious journals reject more than 85 percent of the articles submitted to them—can be high.

☐ Refereeing can take between 2 and 12 months.
☐ Findings can become obsolete.
☐ In heavily researched areas, an author's findings may be discovered and published by other researchers. See Merton (1961) on simultaneous discoveries.

Value of Seeking the Most Appropriate Journal

7.3   Most authors spend months preparing each article. That investment should justify spending one or two hours more to find the most appropriate journal. Some scholars object to any such attempts at "marketing," arguing that any worthy article will get published without such efforts. However, articles unacceptable to the most prestigious journals are not necessarily worthless. If carefully done, such articles are important to the cumulation of research and theory on their topics and should, therefore, be part of the archival literature. Certainly poor articles—poorly analyzed or poorly written—get published, often because of their authors' skill at finding appropriate journals. However, skillful marketing can also be used on good articles with limited importance, to the benefit of their authors and of science.

7.4 When choosing a journal,

○ Evaluate the degree of importance and level of specialization of your article's topic.
○ Consider the topical preferences and the readerships of various journals.

HOW TO EVALUATE AN ARTICLE

Important Criteria

7.5 Data, methods, analysis, implications, conclusions, and writing determine an article's relative importance. Some data are national or cross-national; others are local. Some are complete and clean. Others are skimpy or full of coding and other errors that you cannot correct. Some data permit sophisticated analytic techniques. Other data defy analysis more complex than marginal counts and cross-tabulations. Methodologically, some articles break new ground, as did the first sociological articles using path analysis. Others use conventional techniques. Implications and conclusions are also important.

Examples

7.6 For example, cross-cultural research has long been difficult because most data-gathering instruments cannot be made equally appropriate *and* equivalent for two or more cultural settings. An article presenting a solution to this problem that works with one or more instruments would probably be important to researchers in several disciplines. An article disproving a central argument of a major theorist would probably also be important. However, an article disproving a minor or little-used argument of a major theorist would probably be less important than the other two, no matter how good the analysis and writing were. Although it sometimes seems hard to believe, even the best scientists write relatively few important articles—a fact that other scientists may find comforting. Many research projects yield both important and less important articles. Both use the same data and quality of analysis. Only relative importance and level of specialization differ, but that fact still limits the publishing possibilities for the less important articles.

> For example, the *Journal of Marriage and the Family* might be the most appropriate journal for a sociological article on family structure. Submit such an article to the *ASR* only if (1) it makes a substantial contribution to general theory or methodology or (2) the data are of high quality and either strongly support or strongly reject previous, controversial findings.

Importance of Collegial Help

7.7 When evaluating an article's importance and level of specialization,

○ Seek collegial help. Colleagues' greater objectivity will more closely resemble that of referees. See Sections 6.2 to 6.6 for help.

HOW TO CHOOSE AND EVALUATE JOURNALS

How to Choose a List of Possible Journals

7.8 Table 7.1. To obtain a list of possible journals for a specific article,

○ Examine the first two columns and the index of Table 7.1, which is printed at the end of this chapter.

○ List journals that appear to publish articles on your topic or
  on closely related topics.

Table 7.1 shows characteristics and topical preferences of more
than 500 journals in the social and behavioral sciences. As far as
I could determine, all use referees or editors to evaluate articles
and all accept unsolicited articles. These journals are in social
and cultural anthropology, business research, communication
studies, economics, education, information science, linguistics,
political science, psychiatry, psychology, psycho- and socio-
linguistics, sociology, general social science, and applied
mathematics and statistics. I could not organize by discipline
because of the extensive overlap in subject matter. Appendix A
explains the procedure for choosing journals. Notes to the table
give abbreviations and details. An index by subject matter
follows the notes. Order of entries is alphabetical by word,
disregarding initial *a, an,* and *the*.

7.9   Other Sources.   For lists of other journals,

○ See Table A.1 in Appendix A of this book.
○ See Rhoades (1974) for a list of journals in sociology.
○ See Silverman and Collins (1975, Appendix F) for a list of
  journals in education.
○ Examine the lists of journals covered by various indexes and
  abstracting services. See Section A.5 for help.
○ Use your library's copy of *Journal Citation Reports* (part of
  SCI; prepared by the Institute for Scientific Information) to
  identify journals whose orientation is similar to that of your
  article.
○ List the journals that have published the articles you cite.
  One of them might want to publish your article to follow up
  an earlier one.
○ List journals named in the reference lists of recent articles and
  books that you cite.
○ If your article is on radical or critical social science, consult
  "Short Journal Reviews," a regular feature in *Telos* (see, e.g.,
  the spring and summer issues in 1975).

○ Examine journals in disciplines other than your own.
○ Ask colleagues for suggestions.

7.10 Suggestions for Cross-Cultural and Geographic-Area Researchers.   If you are writing about cross-cultural research or if your article is on a specific geographical area,

○ Consult journals that specialize in articles on that area.
○ Locate the journals by looking through your library's catalog or through indexes for journals whose names include the name of the area. See Section A.2 for help.

7.11 Sources of Editors' Names and Addresses.   If your library does not have a given journal,

○ Obtain its address and editor's name from *Ulrich's International Periodicals Directory* or *The Directory of Publishing Opportunities*.
○ Write to the editor, describe your article, and ask if you should submit it. Also request a description of preferred topics and instructions on style.

How to Evaluate Journals

7.12 Eliminating Journals Because of Inappropriate Topical Preferences of Readers.   From these sources you can compile a list of many journals that might be appropriate for your article. Make a copy of the list to use with future articles. Next, to obtain detailed information on journals' topical preferences and readership,

○ Read each journal's statement of purpose. This information is usually near the front of each issue or with the instructions to contributors.
○ Skim several articles in more than one issue of each journal.
○ Look for announcements of future issues on specific topics. These often include invitations to submit articles for consideration.

This information will probably show you that at least half of the journals on your list are inappropriate.

7.13 Eliminating Journals. For the remaining journals, evaluate quality and stability. Both elements can change over time, and from one editor to the next. Use the following information to help you evaluate:

☐ Your own judgment of articles in a journal.

☐ Your colleagues' opinions of articles.

☐ The journal's age. Older journals are usually more stable financially and have had a longer time in which to establish a reputation. Financial instability can cause a journal to cease publication abruptly. Authors usually find little comfort in a meaningless letter of acceptance.

☐ Size of circulation. In general, the larger the readership, the higher the journal's quality.

☐ Ownership. Journals owned by nonprofit associations, such as the American Psychological Association, need to break even, but they are not publishing journals primarily to earn a profit. Firms such as Academic Press often publish high-quality journals, but they also want to earn a profit.

Most journals publish data on age, circulation, and ownership at least once a year, often at the end of the last issue in each volume. Rhoades (1974) gives this information for many of the journals in his collection. See also the latest edition of *The Directory of Publishing Opportunities*.

7.14 You may also want to read articles on quality of journals. For example, Jakobovits and Osgood (1967) discussed the connotations of 20 psychological journals to professional readers. Oromaner (1970, p. 246) listed rankings of several journals in sociology. Sociologists might want to read Lin's (1974) description of stratification within the formal communication system in American sociology. The most likely place to find such articles is in your discipline's journal on the profession.[1] With this information, you can probably eliminate several more journals and rank the rest in order of preference.

7.15 Next, evaluate the remaining journals on the following criteria, listed in order of relative importance to most authors.

○ Preferred length of article is either well over or well under the length of yours. See column 4 in Table 7.1 for help. In general, article length varies by discipline. For example, psychological journals generally publish shorter articles than do sociological journals, which generally publish shorter articles than do journals in political science.[2]

○ Format does not fit your subject. See column 5.

○ Use of tables or illustrations is restricted or prohibited.

○ Acceptance rates are too low. See column 7.

○ Lag between submission and publication is too long. See column 6.

○ Submission fee is required. See column 7.

○ Editorial style is one you do not like to use. See column 5.

7.16 Making a Final Choice.   After you choose a journal,

○ Obtain the editor's name and address. Note 5 of Table 7.1 shows the common locations for that information. If you already have this information, check it. The turnover rate for editors is high.

○ Check editorial style closely. Column 5 gives general style, but most journals make small deviations. Chapter 8 gives details on what to check.

I show editorial style because when you draft an article, you must choose a style for documentation and headings. If you draft in a style close to that of the journal you have chosen, preparing the final draft in proper style will be easy.

7.17 Finding Journals for Subsequent Articles.   Do not throw away the list on which you made notes. File it with the duplicate copy of the original list (Section 7.12). Having that information will help you find an appropriate journal more quickly the next time you write an article on a similar topic.

SUMMARY

7.18 In this chapter I first discuss the difficulty of getting articles published (Sections 7.1 to 7.4). I then show how to evaluate articles (7.5 to 7.7) and how to choose and evaluate journals (7.8 to 7.17). To help in these tasks, I list more than 500 journals in the social and behavioral sciences (Table 7.1). The table shows preferred subject matter, length of articles, editorial style, format, publication lags, and acceptance rates. Following the guidelines can help you get your articles published as rapidly as possible in the best journal possible.

NOTES TO CHAPTER 7

1. Some scientists want journals to publish "journal reviews." Each review would report a journal's history, sponsorship, size, circulation, and cost as well as qualitative assessment of the journal's function, readership, and relative standing with respect to other journals (e.g., see Bunnett 1975).

2. Variations in different disciplines aside, for most authors and most journals, no article will be published in a form that is longer than is absolutely necessary. Almost inevitably this means that articles are shorter than authors would like, but not as short as editors would like.

Table 7.1 Characteristics of Journals in the Social and Behavioral Sciences

(1) Name of Journal[1]	(2) Topics[2]	(3) Number of Copies, Abstract[3]	(4) Article Length[4] (typed pages)	(5) Style[5]	(6) Lag[6] (months)	(7) Miscellaneous[7]
1 Academic Therapy	I:exceptional child; normal I.Q. or better	2;—	12–34	MSH	—	—
2 Acta Psychologica	I:psychonomics	2;150	20m	sMSN*	—	—
3 Acta Sociologica	Sociol.:European area	2;4	12–36	sMSN	—	—
4 Administration and Society	I:comp. public adm.	3;—	40m	Sage	—	—
5 Administrative Science Q.	I:res., theory, organizational behav.	3;99m	18–60;35	ASA*;9/75	3½;5r	A 6.2%r
6 Adolescence	I:title	2;—	7–27,10	sAPA	1;18r	A 49%r; write first
7 Adult Education	I:res., theory, title	3;125m	17–40;25	sMSH	—	Use triple-spacing
8 Alberta J. of Educational Research	I:res. on ed.	2;100	12–39;17	APA*	—	—
9 Am. Anthropologist	Anthrop.:res. and theory	3;75m	24–38	sMSN;9/74	6–15	sf $25n
10 Am. Behavioral Scientist	I:res., rev., title	ni;—	4–70	Sage	—	—
11 Am. Economic Rev.	Gen. ecs.	2;—	50m	sAPA	—	sf $15, $30
12 Am. Economist	Gen. ecs.	1;—	5–20	sJASA	—	—
13 Am. Educational Research J.	I:theory, res. on ed.	3;120	12–35	APA*	4;4r	A 10%r
14 Am. Ethnologist	Anthrop.:ethnol.	3;75	16–48	sMSN;8/75	6–15	sf $25n
15 Am. J. of Agricultural Economics	Res., theory:title	3;100	15–33	sMSN	2;6	—
16 Am. J. of Community Psychology	Psych.:soc. psych.	3;150	8–45;17	APA	2;12r	A 20%r
17 Am. J. of Economics and Sociology	I:title	ni;130	10–50	sMSH	—	—
18 Am. J. of Mental Deficiency	I:title	3;130	10–20;14	APA*	1;12r	A 11.6%r
19 Am. J. of Political Science	Gen. pol. science	3;100	22–40	sMSN	—	—
20 Am. J. of Orthopsychiatry	I:human behav.	2;75	20–30	sJASA	6;9r	A 24%r
21 Am. J. of Psychology	Exp. psych.	2;100	10–40;20	sAPA*	4;11r	A 12%[8]
22 Am. J. of Sociology	Gen. sociol.	3;100m	20–40;30	sMSN	—	—
23 Am. Political Science Rev.	Gen. pol. science	ni;150m	25–61	sMSH	—	—
24 Am. Politics Q.	I:title	3;—	25m	Sage	—	—
25 Am. Psychologist	Psych.	3;120m	17–48	APA	2;4r	R 53%[9]
26 Am. Sociological Rev.	Gen. sociol.	4;150m	30m	ASA	2;6r	A 8.7%[10]
27 Am. Sociologist	Professional concerns of sociologists	5;150m	11–20;13	ASA	3;3	A 17%[11]

28 Animal Learning and Behavior	Exp. psych. (animals)	3;150m	9–21;15	APA*	3–12	—
29 Anthropologica	Anthrop.::cult., soc.	ni;80	30–50	sMSN	—	Write abstract in French
30 Anthropological Q.	Gen. anthrop.	2;150m	10–28	sMSN	—	—
31 Antitrust Law and Economics Rev.	I:theory of ind. organization	ni;—	18–40	sMSH	—	—
32 Archives Européennes de Sociologie; see European J. of Sociology						
33 Archives of Sexual Behavior	I:title	4;250m	16–26	sSA*	—	—
34 Arctic Anthropology	Anthrop.::title	ni;125	21–80	sMSN	—	—
35 ASIS	I:inf. science	2;200m	15–50	sJASA*	—	—
36 Aust. and New Zealand J. of Sociology	Gen. sociol.	3;—	10–20	sASA	3;6^r	A 30.7%^{r}
37 Aust. Economic History Rev.	I:ec. and bus. hist.	ni;—	32m	sMSH	—	—
38 Aust. Economic Papers	Gen. ecs.	ni;—	18–44;26	sMSH	—	—
39 Aust. J. of Politics and History	I:title	ni;—	12–40	sMSH	—	—
40 Aust. J. of Psychology	Gen. psych.	3;100	18m	APA*	—	—
41 AV Communication Rev.	I:theory, res. on audiovisual tech. in ed.	3;—	16m^r	APA	4;5^r	A 14%^{r}
42 Behavior Research Methods and Instrumentation	I:title	3;125	6–25	sAPA[12]	—	A 59%^{r}
43 Behavior Science Research	Meth., theory in cross-cult. res.; ethnogr. data	ni;75	36m^r	sASA	3;9^r	A 40%^{r}
44 Behavior Therapy	I:theory, res. in behav. modification	2;200	6–20;15	APA*	—	—
45 Behavioral Science	I:living and nonliving systems	3;250m	15–50;26	sAPA*	6–12	—
46 Behaviour Research and Therapy	Psych.::title	2;200m	7–24;20	sMSN*	7–9[13]	—
47 Biological Psychology	Res.::title	3;150m	15–30;22	sSA*	—	—
48 Brain and Language	I:title	3;100m	16–42	sMSN	—	—
49 Br. J. of Addiction	I:title	2;100m	12–24	sAPA*	—	—
50 Br. J. of Criminology	I:crim., delinquency, deviance	ni;—	4–36;20	sSA	—	—
51 Br. J. of Educational Psychology	I:title	ni;125	14–34;24	SA*;11/74	8–12	A 28%[14]
52 Br. J. of Medical Psychology	I:title	2;—	8–41;24	SA	—	—
53 Br. J. of Political Science	I:pol. science	2;—	8–48	sMSH	—	—
54 Br. J. of Psychology	Gen. psych.	2;175	28m	SA*	10–18	—
55 Br. J. of Social and Clinical Psychology	Theory, res., rev.:title	ni;400m	20m	SA*	18–27	—
56 Br. J. of Sociology	Gen. sociol.	ni;—	24–40;30	sMSH	—	—
57 Bull. of the Midwest MLA	I:lang., lit.	ni;—	32m	MLA	—	—

Table 7.1 (Continued)

(1) Name of Journal[1]	(2) Topics[2]	(3) Number of Copies, Abstract[3]	(4) Article Length[4] (typed pages)	(5) Style[5]	(6) Lag[6] (months)	(7) Miscellaneous[7]
58 Bull. of the Psychonomic Society	Psychonomics	1;125	8m	APA*	3–4	Accepts articles written or sponsored by Society members A 31%r
59 California J. of Educational Research	Gen. ed.:res., rev., projects	2;150m	12m	APA	1,6r	—
60 Can. and International Education	I:ed. and society	2;100	26–46	sMSH	—	—
61 Can. J. of African Studies	I:title	1;150m	12–24	MSH	—	—
62 Can. J. of Behavioural Science	Res., theory and applied psych.	2;120m	11–48;20	APA*	5–28	Pub. ch.
63 Can. J. of Economics	Gen. ecs.	3;150	9–36;27	sMSN	—	sf $14n
64 Can. J. of Political Science	I:pol. science	3;250	30–90	sMSH	—	—
65 Can. J. of Psychology	Theory and exp. psych.	3;100m	17m	APA*	6–18	Pub. ch.
66 Can. J. of Sociology	Sociol. of interest to Canadians	2;125	30–45	sASA	—	—
67 Can. Psychological Rev.	Gen. psych.	3;100	10–26	APA*	—	—
68 Can. Public Policy	I:title	3;100	10–37	sMSN	—	—
69 Can. Rev. of Sociology and Anthropology	Gen. sociol., anthrop.	2;100m	13–30	ASA	3r;14	A 14.6%r
70 Child Care Q.	I:title	3;50m	4–24	APA	3;8r	A 50%r
71 Child Development	Res., theory, rev.:title	2;100	20m	APA*	—	Author may suggest referees
72 Child Psychiatry and Human Development	I:title	2;100	16m	sJASA	2;12r	A 50%r
73 Child Welfare	I:title	2;40	12–16	sJASA	1,9r	A 40%r
74 Co-Existence	Sociol., ecs.:comp.	ni;—	10–54	sMSH	—	—
75 Cognition	I:functioning of the mind	3;100	13–52	sSA	3;3r	—
76 Cognitive Psychology	I:cognitive psych.	3;125	18–56	APA*	5–6;13	—
77 College Student J.	Res., theory:title	2;120	No limit	APA*	—	Pub. ch.
78 Communication Research	I:title	3;200m	18–45	Sage	—	—
79 Community Mental Health J.	I:title	2;100	16m	APA;F74	3;18r	A 10%r

80 Comparative Education	I:title, plus area ed.	2:200m	10–21	sJASA	3–5[13]	—
81 Comparative Education Rev.	I:title, plus area ed.	3;150m	15–33	MSH	—	—
82 Comparative Political Studies	Cross-nat.:title	3;—	25m	Sage	2;5[r]	—
83 Comparative Politics	I:title	3;—	30–58;46	sMSH	—	—
84 Comparative Studies in Society and History	I:title	2;—	10–90	sMSH	—	—
85 Counselor Education and Supervision	I:title	3;175m	12–24	sAPA	3[15]	—
86 Crime and Social Justice	I:radical crim.	3;—	16–52	sASA	—	—
87 Criminology	I:res., meth., title	3;150	15–41;30	Sage	2;5[r]	—
88 Current Anthropology	Gen. anthrop.	ni;300m	8–24	sMSN;6/65	—	—
89 Curriculum Theory Network	I:title	ni;—	5–30;15	sMSN	—	—
90 Demography	Population res.	2;100m	15–20[r]	sMSN;2/72	4;5[r]	A 18%[r]
91 Development and Change	I:title	ni;—	28m	sMSH	—	—
92 Developmental Psychology	Title	3;100	11–44;20	APA*	8–12	R 80%[9]
93 Dissent (New York)	J:radical ideas; views on socialism and democracy	ni;—	12–35	sMSH	—	—
94 Econometrica	Ec. theory in relation to stat., math.	3;75	20–65;30	sJASA	15–29	—
95 Economic Development and Cultural Change	I:title	ni;—	8–48;24	sMSH	—	—
96 Economic Inquiry	Gen. ecs.	3;100	13–28;22	sMSN	—	sf $15, $30
97 The Economic J.	Gen. ecs.✓	3;100m	36–94	sMSN	6[13]	sf $25n
98 The Economic Record	Gen. ecs.	ni;100m	26m	sJASA	2–6[13]	—
99 Economic and Social Rev.	I:soc. science	ni;—	36–56	sJASA	3;3[r]	A 50%[r]
100 Economica	Ec., stat. ec. hist.	2;—	20–40;24	sSA	—	—
101 Economy and Society	I:title	ni;300m	33–78;51	sMSH	—	—
102 Education	Gen. teacher ed.	2;120m	12m	APA	—	—
103 Education in Eastern Africa	Ed.:title	ni;—	8–20	sMSH	—	—
104 Educational Administration Q.	I:title	3;—	14–42	sMSH	—	—
105 Educational Forum	Gen. ed.	ni;—	16m	MSH	1;6[f]	—
106 Educational and Psychological Measurement	I:title	2;100	varies; see (7)	APA*	varies; see (7)	(4) and (6) vary with type of article
107 Educational Record	Contemporary higher ed.	ni;75	10–28	sMSH	—	—
108 Educational Research	Gen. ed.	2;125	12m	sSA	—	—
109 Educational Technology	I:title	ni;—	5–35	sAPA	—	—

Table 7.1 (*Continued*)

(1) Name of Journal[1]	(2) Topics[2]	(3) Number of Copies, Abstract[3]	(4) Article Length[4] (typed pages)	(5) Style[5]	(6) Lag[6] (months)	(7) Miscellaneous[7]
110 Educational Theory	I:title	4;—	14–30;10	sMSH	—	—
111 Elementary School Guidance and Counseling	I:title	3;75	10–16	APA	—	—
112 Elementary School J.	Elementary ed.	ni;—	14–38	sJASA	—	—
113 Environment and Behavior	I:res., theory,title	ni;—	26–54	Sage	2;5r	—
114 Environment and Planning	I:title	3;125	15–90	sSA	2–19[13]	—
115 Et al.	Gen. soc. science	ni;—	12m	sASA	1;5r	—
116 ETC., A Rev. of General Semantics	I:title	2;—	10–24	APA	2;10r	A 24%r
117 Ethics in Science and Medicine	I:title	2;500m	16–70	sMSH	—	A 39%r
118 Ethnicity	Ethnic relations	3;—	13–45	sMSN	4;10r	—
119 Ethnology	Anthrop.:cult., soc.	ni;—	100m	sMSN	—	—
120 Ethos	Relationship between individual and soc. milieu	3;—	24–44	sMSN	—	—
121 European J. of Political Research	European comp. politics and int. relations	3;200m	20–80	sSA	—	—
122 European J. of Social Psychology	Gen. soc. psych.	3;175m	8–70;40	sSA	5;5r	A 32%r
123 European J. of Sociology	Gen. sociol.	ni;—	39–99	sMSH	—	A 42%r
124 Evaluation	I:human service decision making	ni;—	15m	sMSH;Sp/74	3;8r	A 30%r
125 Exceptional Children	I:title	ni;—	6–10r	APA	4;6r	A 17.5%r
126 Explorations in Economic History	I:title	2;—	18–35	sMSN	—	—
127 Family Coordinator	I:help for family practitioner	3;100m	12–20r	sAPA;1/75	2;6r	A 25%r
128 Family Process	I:family res.	2;150m	11–50	sJASA	3;4r	A 21%r
129 Forum	I:modern lang. studies	ni;—	17–50	sMSH	—	—
130 Foundations of Language	I:lang. and philos.	ni;—	28–92	sMSN	—	—
131 Futures	I:forecasting and planning	ni;150m	10–16	sMSH	—	—
132 Futurist	I:forecasting and planning	ni;—	12–42	ni;see (7)	6;8r	References are in text
133 Georgia Political Science Association J.	Gen. pol. science	4;125m	13–48	Tur	—	—

134 Growth and Change	I:regional dev.	ni;—	14m[r]	sMSH	3;12[r]	A 20%[r]
135 Harvard Business Rev.	Bus. philos. and practice	ni;125	15–40	sMSH	1;3[r]	A 7%[r]
136 Harvard Education Rev.	Gen. ed.	3;250m	40m[t]	MSH,MSN	2;4[t]	Uses both styles
137 Health and Society; see Milbank Memorial Fund Q.						
138 Higher Education	I:title	ni;250m	15–40	sMSN[15]	—	—
139 History of Childhood Q.	Psychohistory	ni;—	5–84	MSH	—	—
140 History of Political Economy	I:title	2;—	5–65	MSH	—	—
141 Human Context	Philos. and methodology of sciences of man	ni;—	33m	sMSH	2;9[r]	A 10%[r]
142 Human Development	Psych.:title	2;100m	20–40	sAPA	—	Pub. ch.
143 Human Factors	I:title	3;150m	17–48	sAPA*;2/75	12–18	—
144 Human Organization	Applied anthrop. and soc. science	4;200	21–48;30	MSN	—	sf $10n
145 Human Relations	I:res.,title	ni;150	5–18	sAPA	—	—
146 Improving College and University Teaching	I:title	ni;50	7m[r]	sMSH	3;12[r]	A 83%[r]
147 Industrial and Labor Relations Rev.	I:title	ni;—	25m[r]	sMSH	3;3[r]	A 15%[r]
148 Inquiry	I:med. care	3;100m	17–30	sMSH	—	—
149 Industrial Relations	I:ecs. and sociol.	ni;—	10–45	sMSH	2;8[r]	—
150 Instructional Science	I:title	ni;200	24–80	sMSN	—	—
151 Insurgent Sociologist	Radical sociol.	ni;—	5–50	sMSH	—	—
152 Intellect	I:soc. ed.	ni;—	14m[r]	sMSH	1;6[r]	A 20%[r]
153 Inter-Am. Economic Affairs	Ec:title, area and comp.	ni;—	10–42	sMSH	—	—
154 International Affairs	Pol. science:int. studies	ni;—	19–44	sMSH	—	Write first
155 International Economic Rev.	Quantitative ecs.	3;—	8–40	sJASA	—	—
156 International Interactions	I:title	3;150m	10m	sMSN	2[r,15]	A 13%[r]
157 International J.	I:int. affairs	2;—	30–66	sMSH	—	—
158 International J. of Aging and Human Development	I:title	3;100m	8–60	APA*	2–3[15]	—
159 International J. of Am. Linguistics	I:title	ni;—	30–42	sMSH	—	—
160 International J. of Comparative Sociology	I:comp. sociol., anthrop., and pol. science	2;—	28m	sASR	1,8[r]	—
161 International J. of Contemporary Sociology	Gen. sociol.	2;—	6–48	sMSH	2;12[r]	A 38%[r]

Table 7.1 *(Continued)*

140

(1) Name of Journal[1]	(2) Topics[2]	(3) Number of Copies, Abstract[3]	(4) Article Length[4] (typed pages)	(5) Style[5]	(6) Lag[6] (months)	(7) Miscellaneous[7]
162 International J. of Criminology and Penology	I:title	2;—	17–30	sMSH	—	—
163 International J. of Environmental Studies	I:title	2;200m	16–56	sMSH	5–6	—
164 International J. of Group Tensions	I:conflict and violence	ni;—	9–45;12	Sage	—	—
165 International J. of Mental Health	I:title	ni;—	18–46	sMSH	—	—
166 International J. of Psychology	Res., theory:title	ni;200m	16–32	APA	—	Prepare abstract in French
167 International J. of Social Economics	Gen. soc. ecs.	2;100m	20–40	sMSH	—	Write first
168 International J. of Social Psychiatry	Exp. clin. psych.; med. sociol.	4;100m	8–30	sAPA*	—	—
169 International J. of Sociology of the Family	I:title	ni;150	14–34	ASA	2;9r	—
170 International Migration Rev.	I:title	2;—	20m r	sASA	6;9r	A 30%r
171 International Rev. of Administrative Science	I:public adm.	ni;—	16–24r	sMSH	2;9r	—
172 International Rev. of Education	I:ed.	2;350m	20m	sMSH	—	—
173 International Rev. of Modern Sociology	I:esp. res., theory on cross-nat. and cross-cult. sociol.	2;150	13–46	sASA	2;9r	—
174 International Statistical Rev.	Gen. stat.	2;500m	11–56	sMSN	—	—
175 International Studies Q.	I:theory, title	3;300m	14–42	Sage	2;9r	—
176 Intersections	I:urban and environmental studies	ni;—	20m	MLA	—	—
177 Issues in Criminology	I:title	2;200	27–47	sASA	3;2r	A 16%r
178 Japanese Psychological Research	Gen. psych.	2;120m	26m	sMSN*	1–6	—
179 Jewish J. of Sociology	Sociol.:related to Jewish life	ni;—	13–36;32	sMSH	—	—
180 J. for the Scientific Study of Religion	I:title	3;150	20–46	sASA;3/75, p.65	5;3r	A 28%r
181 J. for Special Educators of the Mentally Retarded	Res.:title	2;100m	1–12;3	sAPA	—	—
182 J. for the Theory of Social Behaviour	I:theory, meth., title	3;—	13–58	Many	—	—

183 J. of Abnormal Child Psychology	Psychotherapy in childhood and adolescence	3;150	11–72;12	APA*	—	—
184 J. of Abnormal Psychology	Res., theory:title	3;175m	11–42;17	APA	5–15	R 70%[9]
185 J. of African Studies	I:title	ni;—	30–50	sMSH	—	—
186 J. of Alcohol and Drug Education	I:title	ni;—	8–18	Many	—	—
187 J. of Am. Folklore	I:title	ni;—	18–56	sMSH	3;5[r]	A 44%[r]
188 J. of the Am. Institute of Planners	I:res., theory on urban planning	ni;150	28–44	sSage	3;6[r]	A 13%[r]
189 J. of the Am. Statistical Association	I:theory, meth., and applied stat.	4;100	8–37;15	JASA	12–36	—
190 J. of Anthropological Research	Gen. Anthrop.	ni;150m	9–57	sMSN	—	—
191 J. of Applied Behavior Analysis	Title	5;100	7–18;11	APA*;Su74, p. 242	4;5	—
192 J. of Applied Behavioral Science	I:science and tech. of soc. change	4;150m	6–25	APA	3;18	—
193 J. of Applied Communications Research	I:title	ni;—	4–16[r]	sMSH	2;3[r]	A 44%[r]
194 J. of Applied Psychology	Psych.:title	3;120m	11–20	APA*	15	R 75%[8]
195 J. of Applied Social Psychology	Psych.:title	2;120	18–49	APA*	3;4[r]	A 10%[r]
196 J. of Asian and African Studies	I:title	2;—	28m	sASA	—	—
197 J. of Asian Studies	I:title	3;—	35m	MLA	—	—
198 J. of Baltic Studies	I:title	2;—	16–26	MLA	—	—
199 J. of Behavior Therapy and Experimental Psychiatry	I:title	3;100m	5–25	sMSN	4;15	—
200 J. of Behavioral Economics	I:title	3;500m	16–28	sJASA	—	Special instructions for footnotes
201 J. of Behavioural Science	I:title, esp. African	2;120m	10–15	sAPA	—	—
202 J. of Biosocial Science	I:title	2;5% of text m	4–61;39	sSA*	5–11[13]	—
203 J. of Black Studies	I:title	2;—	25m	Sage	2;5[r]	—
204 J. of Broadcasting	I:title	2;—	10–15[r]	sMSH;Sp74, p. 255	1;3[r]	A 17.5%[r]
205 J. of Child Language	I:title	2;120m	45m	sSA	6–13	—
206 J. of Child Psychology and Psychiatry and Allied Disciplines	I:title	2;100m	20–28;24	sSA*	9–13[13]	—
207 J. of Clinical Psychology	I:title	ni;125	6–76;9	sAPA*	—	—

Table 7.1 *(Continued)*

(1) Name of Journal[1]	(2) Topics[2]	(3) Number of Copies, Abstract[3]	(4) Article Length[4] (typed pages)	(5) Style[5]	(6) Lag[6] (months)	(7) Miscellaneous[7]
208 J. of College Student Personnel	I:res. on personnel and guidance	3;50m	14m	APA*	7–20	Avoid generic masculine pronoun
209 J. of Communication	I:title, theory, res., policy	2;—	28–40r	sJASA	1;3r	A 17%r
210 J. of Comparative Administration; see Administration and Society						
211 J. of Comparative Family Studies	I:title	ni;150	11–68;38	sASA	—	—
212 J. of Comparative and Physiological Psychology	I:title	3;120	10–46;24	APA*	11–19	R 62%[9]
213 J. of Conflict Resolution	I:res. on war and peace	3;150	28–67	Sage	3;8r	A 25%r
214 J. of Consulting and Clinical Psychology	Psych.:title	3;175m	6–19;9	APA*	6–11	R 78%[9]
215 J. of Correctional Education	I:title	2;—	10m	sAPA	—	—
216 J. of Counseling Psychology	Res., theory, meth.:title	2;175m	5–21;16	APA*	6–12	R 77%[9]
217 J. of Criminal Justice	I:title	3;125	24–32	sMSN	—	A 20%r
218 J. of Criminal Law and Criminology	I:title	2;—	15–66	sMSH[16]	4;3r	—
219 J. of Cross-Cultural Psychology	I:title	3;125	20m	Sage*	2;5r	—
220 J. of Curriculum Studies	Theory, meth., and practice of teaching	ni;—	20m	MLA	—	—
221 J. of Developing Areas	I:title	3;—	30mr	MSH	3;12r	A 5%r
222 J. of Developmental Studies	I:ec. and pol. dev.	ni;150	15–45;28	sMSN	15–21	—
223 J. of Econometrics	Theory and applied:title	3;100	34–87	sMSN	15–21	—
224 J. of Economic History	I:title	3;100	14–59;33	sMSH	—	—
225 J. of Economic Issues	Nonquantitative ecs.	3;—	13–67;27	sMSH	—	—
226 J. of Economic Studies	I:title	2;100m	14–48	sMSN	—	—
227 J. of Economic Theory	Title:emphasis on math.	3;100m	19–66	sJASA	7–21	—
228 J. of Education	I:contemporary ed.	3;120m	5–15	APA	—	—
229 J. of Education for Social Work	I:title	3;75	14m	MSH	—	—
230 J. of Educational Measurement	Title	3;150m	4–32;23	APA*	10–15	—
231 J. of Educational Psychology	Title	3;120m	8–34;17	APA*	—	R 79%[9]

						Pub. ch.[t]
232 J. of Educational Research	Title	1;120m	6–12	sJASA*	1;11[t]	A 17%[r]
233 J. of Educational Thought	I:ideas on ed.	3;75m	28m	sMSH	3;4[r]	—
234 J. of Ethnic Studies	I:title	2;—	14m[r]	MLA	2;5[r]	—
235 J. of the Experimental Analysis of Behavior	Psych.:title	2;150	12–36;30	APA*	11–18[13]	—
236 J. of Experimental Child Psychology	Title	3;120m	10–32	APA*	10–14	
237 J. of Experimental Education	I:esp. sophisticated technical problems	2;120m	12–20	sJASA	1;6[t]	Pub. ch.
238 J. of Experimental Psychology	4 parts, as follows:					
239 General	Title	3;175m	7–100	APA*	5–12	R 78%[9]
240 Human Perception and Performance	Title	3;175m	22–45	APA*	8–11	R 82%[9]
241 Animal Behavior Processes	Title	3;175m	25–45	APA*	7–16	R 84%[9]
242 Learning and Memory	Title	3;175m	12–38	APA*	9–11	R 75%[9]
243 J. of Experimental Social Psychology	Title	3;200m	14–72	APA*	7–20	—
244 J. of Family Counseling	I:title	2;"short"	10–20	APA	—	—
245 J. of General Education	I:title	ni;—	16–24	sMSH	—	—
246 J. of General Psychology	Title	2;125	10–19;17	sJASA*	1;8	Pub. ch.
247 J. of Genetic Psychology	Dev. and clin. psych.	2;150	11–27;17	sJASA*	10–20[13]	Pub. ch.
248 J. of Health and Social Behavior	I:title	3;150m	14–37	ASA	2;8[r]	A 18%[17]
249 The J. of Higher Education	I:title	2;150	14–34	MLA;Sp74	2;4[r]	A 11%[r]
250 J. of the History of the Behavioral Sciences	I:title	2;100m	10–39	sJASA	—	—
251 J. of the History of Ideas	I:title	2;—	40m	sMSH	—	—
252 The J. of Human Resources	I:res. on ed., manpower, and welfare resources	3;100m	20m	sJASA	3;9[r]	A 11%[r]
253 J. of Humanistic Psychology	Title	2;—	7–50;17	APA	—	—
254 J. of Industrial Economics	Title	2;100m	14–56	sJASA	—	—
255 J. of Interamerican Studies and World Affairs	I:title	2;—	25–35[r]	Sage	2;9[r]	—
256 J. of International Affairs	I:title	ni;—	13–38	sMSH	—	—
257 J. of International Economics	Theory:int. trade, balance of payments	3;100m	35–110	sMSN	6–18	—

Table 7.1 (Continued)

(1) Name of Journal[1]	(2) Topics[2]	(3) Number of Copies, Abstract[3]	(4) Article Length[4] (typed pages)	(5) Style[5]	(6) Lag[6] (months)	(7) Miscellaneous[7]
258 J. of International Law and Economics	I:title	ni;—	36–80	sMSH	—	—
259 J. of Law and Economics	I:title	ni;—	7–62	sMSH	—	—
260 J. of Learning Disabilities	I:title	ni;150	14–26;22	sMSH	—	—
261 J. of Leisure Research	I:res., theory on leisure	5;150	14m	sAPA*	3;7r	A 27%r
262 J. of Linguistics	I:title	ni;—	6–52	sMSN*	9–12	—
263 J. of Marketing	I:title	4;—	16–24	sMSN	2;6r	A 18%r
264 J. of Marriage and the Family	I:title	2;100m	5–52;32	sASA;5/75	2;12r	A 16%r
265 J. of Marriage and Family Counseling	I:title	3;100m	10–30	sAPA;4/75	—	—
266 J. of Mathematical Economics	I:title	3;100m	16–28	sMSN	6–17	—
267 J. of Mathematical Psychology	I:title	3;125	20–35;33	sAPA*	4–11	—
268 J. of Mathematical Sociology	I:title	3;120m	31–49	sMSN	4;4r	A 30%r
269 J. of Modern African Studies	I:title, esp. ecs. and politics	ni;—	24m	sMSH	—	—
270 J. of Monetary Economics	I:title	3;100m	20–70	sMSN	—	—
271 J. of Money, Credit, and Banking	Ec.:title	ni;—	25–49;39	sJASA	—	—
272 J. of Motor Behavior	I:human motor behav.	3;150m	18–36	APA	2,4	—
273 J. of Negro Education	I:title	2;—	15m	MSH	4;18r	—
274 J. of Parapsychology	Title	ni;250	14–30	APA*	—	—
275 J. of Peace Research	I:res., resolving conflict	3;250	7–24;12	sMSH;sMSN	—	—
276 J. of Peace Science	Theory, res.:peace and conflict	3;100	22–112	sMSN	—	sf $10a
277 J. of Personality	I:title	3;—	20m	APA*	9–14	Pub. ch.
278 J. of Personality Assessment	I:title	2;120m	5–36	APA*	4;12	A 49%r
279 J. of Personality and Social Psychology	I:title	2;175m	25m	APA*	6–20	R 87%[9]
280 J. of Physical Education	I:title	2;200m	6m	Many;7/75, p. 163	—	—

No.	Journal	Scope	Freq.				
281	J. of Physical Education and Recreation	I:title	ni;—	6–18	Many	—	—
282	J. of Police Science and Administration	I:title	2;—	5–36;18	sMSH	—	—
283	J. of Political Economy	I:title	3;100m	24–65;32	sMSN	—	sf $25a
284	J. of Political and Military Science	I:title, esp. comp.	3;150m	20–48	sASA	3;3[r]	A 8.5%[r]
285	J. of Politics	Gen. pol. science	2;—	25m	sMSH	—	—
286	J. of the Polynesian Society	I:Polynesian area res.	1;—	22–45	sMSN	—	—
287	J. of Popular Culture	I:title	ni;—	10–12	MLA	1;18[r]	A 25%[r]
288	J. of Psycholinguistics	I:title	4;150m	16–44	sMSN	11–22	—
289	J. of Psychology	Gen. psych.	2;150	10–21;14	sIASA*	2–6	Pub. ch. A 72%[r]
290	J. of Public Economics	I:title	3;100m	8–54;19	sMSN	10–21	—
291	J. of Reading Behavior	I:res., theory, title	5;120m	12–28;20	APA*	—	—
292	J. of Research and Development in Education	Ed.:title	ni;—	13–46	sAPA	—	—
293	J. of Research in Crime and Delinquency	I:res., theory, title	4;300m	30m	Many	10[,15]	A 18%[r]
294	J. of Research in Personality	I:title	2;120m	13–61	APA*	—	—
295	J. of Research in Science Teaching	I:title	3;200m	11–37;21	APA*	9–10[13]	—
296	J. of the Royal Statistical Society	Gen. stat.	ni;120	24–58	sSA	—	—
297	J. of School Psychology	I:title	3;100	15–48;20	APA	2;12[r]	A 20%[r]
298	J. of Sex Research	I:title	2;200	18–40	sAPA	2;12[r]	—
299	J. of Social History	I:title	ni;—	22–100	MSH	—	—
300	J. of Social Issues	Psych. aspects of soc. issues	ni;150	7–41;34	sAPA	—	—
301	J. of Social Policy	I:title	2;200m	20–40	sMSH	—	—
302	J. of Southeast Asian Studies	I:title	2;—	16–32	sMSH	—	—
303	J. of Southern African Studies	I:title	3;—	22–45	sMSH	—	—
304	J. of Special Education	I:res., theory, rev. on title	3;300m	15–35	APA	—	—
305	J. of Steward Anthropological Society	Anthrop.:theory, esp. by graduate students	2;—	13–26	sASA	Immediate[13]	—
306	J. of Structural Learning	Psych., ed.:title	2;—	4–16	sAPA	6	—
307	J. of Teacher Education	I:title	2;—	24m	MSH	—	—
308	J. of Urban Analysis	I:title	3;150m	36–84	sMSH	—	—

Table 7.1 (*Continued*)

(1) Name of Journal[1]	(2) Topics[2]	(3) Number of Copies, Abstract[3]	(4) Article Length[4] (typed pages)	(5) Style[5]	(6) Lag[6] (months)	(7) Miscellaneous[7]
309 J. of Verbal Learning and Verbal Behavior	I:title	4;120m	13–71;29	sAPA	6-10	—
310 J. of Vocational Behavior	I:theory, res., on title	2;200	11–30;19	APA*	11–14	—
311 Language in Society	I:title	2;150	8–50	sSA	—	—
312 Language Learning	I:applied ling.	2;200m	20–72	sMSN	—	—
313 Latin Am. Research Rev.	I:title	ni;—	24–88	Many	—	—
314 Law and Contemporary Problems	I:title	ni;—	38–210	sMSH	—	—
315 Law and Society Rev.	I:res., on law and society	ni;—	34–88	sMSN	—	A 11%[r]
316 Learning and Motivation	I:theory, res., title	4;150m	14–33	sAPA*	10:10	—
317 Life-Threatening Behavior; see Suicide						
318 Lingua	Gen. ling.	1;200m	40–75	sMSN	—	—
319 Linguistic Inquiry	Gen. ling.	3;—	7–75	sMSN	—	—
320 Linguistics	Gen. ling.	ni;—	15–40	sASA	—	—
321 McGill J. of Education	Gen. ed.	2;—	12m	sMSH	—	—
322 Man	Gen. anthrop.	ni;—	6–40	sMSN	—	—
323 Man in the Northeast	Anthrop.:title	1;75m	15–35	sMSN	—	—
324 Manchester School of Economics and Social Studies	Gen. ec.	ni;—	17–79	sMSH	4;4	—
325 Mankind	Gen. anthrop.	ni;—	8–34;18	sMSN	5–7	—
326 Mankind Q.	I:race and inheritance	3;100m	13–42	sMSH	—	—
327 Measurement and Evaluation in Guidance	I:title, emphasis on applications	3;175	9–22;13	APA*	2–3[15]	—
328 Memory and Cognition	Human exp. psych.	3;150m	11–33;20	APA*[12]	8–15	—
329 Mental Retardation	I:title	3;100m	10m	APA*	3–5[15]	—
330 Merrill-Palmer Q. of Behavior and Development	I:human dev.	2;"yes" see (7)	10–25;18	APA	—	Abstract not printed
331 Milbank Memorial Fund Q.: Health and Society	I:title	3;200	40m	sASA	2;3[r]	A 18%[r]

No.	Journal	Description					Notes
332	Middle Eastern Studies	I:title	ni;—	18–54	sMSH	—	—
333	Midwest Rev. of Public Administration	I:title	4;—	16m	sMSH	—	—
334	Minerva	I:science, learning, and policy	ni;—	28–69	sMSH	—	—
335	Modern Age	I:title	ni;—	27–39	sMSH	—	—
336	Modern Asian Studies	I:title	2;—	8–32	sMSH	—	—
337	Multivariate Behavioral Research	I:title	3;120	65m	sAPA*	3;13	Pub. ch.
338	NASPA J.	I:res., student personnel adm.	ni;—	8–21;10	MSH	—	Emphasizes applications
339	National Association for Women Deans, Administrators, and Counselors	I:res. interesting to readers	2;—	12m	APA	—	—
340	Neuropsychologia	Exp. psych.	2;100m	10–37;26	sAPA*	5–9	—
341	New Atlantis	I:urban and regional problems	ni;—	9–97;32	sMSH	—	—
342	New Left Review	I:Marxism, radical thinking	ni;—	24–90	sMSH	—	—
343	New Universities Q.: Culture, Education, and Society	I:title	ni;—	10–31	sMSH	—	—
344	New York University J. of International Law and Politics	I:title	2;200m	30–48	sMSH	—	—
345	New York University Education Q.	I:ed., health	ni;—	29–30	sMSH	—	—
346	New Zealand J. of Educational Studies	Ed.::New Zealand and Pacific area	ni;100	18–20	sSA	—	—
347	Northwest Anthropological Research Notes	Gen. anthrop.	ni;150	1–65	sMSN	—	—
348	Occupational Psychology	I:title	2;200m	20m	sMSN	—	Avoid technical language
349	Orbis	I:int. relations	ni;—	18–54	sMSH	—	—
350	Oxford Bull. of Economics and Statistics	Stat. applications to ec. and soc. problems	2;100m	17–42	sJASA	—	—
351	Oxford Economic Papers	I:ec., ec. hist., public adm.	2;100m	15–30	sMSH	—	—
352	Pacific Affairs	Pol. science: title	ni;—	28–36	sMSH	—	—
353	Pacific Sociological Rev.	Gen. sociol.	2;125	11–40	sASA	2;5^r	—
354	Papers in Linguistics	Title	2;100m	10–70	sMSN	—	—
355	Parliamentary Affairs	Pol. science: cross-cult., title	ni;—	8–48	sMSH	—	—
356	Peabody J. of Education	Gen. ed.	3;—	6–20;6	MLA	1–3^{1,13}	—
357	Peace and Change	I:title	3;—	20m	sMSH	4;5^r	—

Table 7.1 (*Continued*)

(1) Name of Journal[1]	(2) Topics[2]	(3) Number of Copies, Abstract[3]	(4) Article Length[4] (typed pages)	(5) Style[5]	(6) Lag[6] (months)	(7) Miscellaneous[7]
358 Peace and the Sciences	I:title	ni;—	12–75	sMSH	—	—
359 Perceptual and Motor Skills	I:title	2;150	32m	sAPA*	2–6[13]	—
360 Personnel and Guidance J.	Ed.:title	3;—	8–14[r]	APA	2;5[r]	A 17%[r]
361 Personnel Psychology	Title	3;—	8–40	APA*	—	Many nonscientific readers
362 Phi Delta Kappan	Gen. ed.	ni;—	6–8	MSH	4;8[1]	—
363 Philosophy and Phenomenological Research	I:title	ni;—	16–38	sMSH	—	—
364 Philosophy of the Social Sciences	I:title	ni;—	20–50;25	sMSH	4–16	—
365 Philosophy and Public Affairs	I:title	1;—	12–57	sMSH	—	—
366 Phylon	I:race and culture	3;—	10–21;18	MSH	—	—
367 Physiological Psychology	Res., theory, rev.::title	3;150m	2–11;4	APA*	9;5	—
368 Plains Anthropologist	Anthrop.:plains and adjacent areas	ni;100	10–36;16	sMSN	8–11	—
369 Planner	I:urban planning	ni;—	16m	sMSH	—	—
370 Planning and Administration	I:title, local government	2;—	12m	sMSH	—	—
371 Policy and Politics	I:title	2;—	18–46	sMSH	—	—
372 Policy Sciences	I:improvements in policymaking	ni;150	13–43	sMSH	—	—
373 Policy Studies J.	I:title	ni;—	6–16;10	sMSH	—	—
374 Political Anthropology	I:title	3;100m	20–54	sMSN	—	—
375 Political Methodology	Pol. science:meth.	2;150m	40–88;56	ASA	—	—
376 The Political Q.	I:pol. science	ni;—	12–35	sMSH	—	—
377 Political Science	Gen. pol. science	ni;—	14–32;25	sMSH	—	—
378 Political Science Q.	Gen. pol. science	2;200m	26–54;32	sMSH	5;7[r]	A 12.5%[r]
379 Political Studies	Gen. pol. science	2;—	26–44	sMSH	—	—
380 Political Theory	I:pol. philos.	2;—	25m	sMSH	—	—
381 Politics	I:Aust., Asian politics	3;—	16m	sMSH	—	Write first

382 Politics and Society	I:radical soc. science	2;—	25–91	sMSH	3^{15}	—
383 Polity	Gen. pol. science	2;—	18–92	sMSH	—	A 30%[r]
384 Population Studies	I:title	ni;200	10–86	sMSH	$1\text{–}6^{r,13}$	R 65%[9]
385 Professional Psychology	Training, practice, and teaching of psych.	3;150	8–35;17	APA	16^9	—
386 Programmed Learning and Educational Technology	I:title	2;200m	4–32	sMSN*	—	—
387 Psychiatry	I:interpersonal processes	2;150	12–43	sAPA	$3;11^r$	A 17.5%[r]
388 Psychological Bull.	Psych.::rev. and interpretations of res. and meth.	2;175m	32–66	APA	$2;12^r$	R 79%[8]
389 Psychological Medicine	I:title	2;50	11–54	MSN*	$2,2^r$	A 33%[r]; Pub. ch.
390 The Psychological Record	Gen. psych.	2;125	4–37	APA*	$1\text{–}4^{13}$	—
391 Psychological Reports	Gen. psych.	ni;125	4–32	APA*	12–18	—
392 Psychological Research	I:perception, learning, communication	ni;150	20–52	sAPA*	—	A 20%[r]
393 Psychological Rev.	Theoretical psych.	3;175m	16–69	APA	$1,7^r$	R 86%[9]
394 Psychological Studies	Gen. psych.	2;150	4–27	APA*	—	—
395 Psychology	Gen. psych.	ni;120m	4–49	APA*	$1,3^r$	A 67%[r]; Pub. ch.
396 Psychology in the Schools	I:title	3;150	4–21	APA	—	—
397 Psychometrika	Quantitative psych.	3;100m	16–60	APA;3/67	$3,9^r$	A 20%[r]
398 Psychophysiology	I:title	4;175m	2–70	APA*	—	—
399 Psychotherapy: Theory, Research, and Practice	I:title	ni;—	7–23;15	APA	—	—
400 Public Administration (England)	I:title	ni;—	50–60	MSH	—	—
401 Public Administration Rev.	I:public adm.	4;150m	16^r	MSH	$3;10^r$	A 13%[r]
402 Public Finance	I:title	ni;—	16–52	sJASA	—	—
403 Public Finance Q.	I:title	$3;175m_{1j}$	18–41	Sage	—	—
404 Public Opinion Q.	I:title	2;—	4–35	sMSH	—	In general, no studies based on student samples
405 Public Policy	I:title	2;—	22–47	sMSH	—	—
406 Public Welfare	I:welfare	ni;—	15–20	MSH	$1,2^r$	A 43%[r]
407 Publius	I:federalism	2;—	16–56	sMSH	—	—
408 Quality and Quantity	Math., stat., meth. used in soc. science	ni;150	18–37	sMSN	—	—

Table 7.1 (*Continued*)

(1) Name of Journal[1]	(2) Topics[2]	(3) Number of Copies, Abstract[3]	(4) Article Length[4] (typed pages)	(5) Style[5]	(6) Lag[6] (months)	(7) Miscellaneous[7]
409 Q.J. of Economics	Gen. ecs.	1;—	30m[r]	sMSH	4;14[r]	A 6.5%[r]
410 Q.J. of Experimental Psychology	Title	2;200m	14–38;19	sMSN*;8/75	10–15	—
411 Q.J. of Speech	Speech and communication	2;—	23–48	MLA	12.8[r]	A 16%[r]
412 Race; see Race and Class						
413 Race and Class	I:title	ni;—	8–20	sMSH	—	—
414 Radical America	I:Marxism, radical sociol.	ni;—	10–84	sMSH	—	—
415 Ramparts	Radical sociol.	ni;—	9–21	ni	—	—
416 Reading Improvement	I:title	2;120m	3–20	APA	—	—
417 Reading Research Q.	I:title	4;150m	18–84	sAPA	—	—
418 Reading Teacher	I:teaching of reading	3;—	8–20	sAPA	—	Read by elementary school reading teachers
419 Reading World	I:res. on teaching of reading	ni;—	6–23	APA	—	—
420 Regional Science and Urban Economics	I:res., title	3;100m	18–30	sMSN	12–14	—
421 Rehabilitation Counseling Bull.	I:title	3;150m	9–21	APA	—	—
422 Representative Research in Social Psychology	Social psych. methodology	3;125m	20m	APA*	—	—
423 Research in Education	I:title	ni;—	24m	sSA	—	—
424 Research in the Teaching of English	I:title	2;—	4–27	sAPA	—	—
425 Research Policy	I:res. policy, management, and planning	3;200	16–42	sMSH	—	—
426 Research Q.	I:res. on physical ed.	ni;200	9–28;14	sJASA*	—	—
427 Rev. of African Political Economy	I:title	2;200	40m	sMSH	—	—
428 Rev. of Black Political Economy	I:title	2;—	10–46	sMSH	—	—
429 Rev. of Economic Studies	Title; esp. by young authors	3;100m	21–99;52	sJASA	16;10	—
430 Rev. of Economics and Statistics	I:title	ni;—	24m	sAPA	15;7	—
431 Rev. of Educational Research	I:title	3;—	19–130	APA	5.5[r]	A 23%[r]

432 Rev. of Existential Psychology and Psychiatry	I:phenomenology and psych., esp. therapy	2;—	8–90	sMSH	—	—
433 Rev. of Income and Wealth	I:title	ni;250	12–75	sJASA	—	—
434 Rev. of Politics	Gen. politics	ni;—	16–55	sMSH	—	—
435 Rev. of Radical and Political Economics	I:title	6;100	24–46	Many	—	—
436 The Rev. of Regional Studies	Gen. regional studies	3;—	4–33	sMSH	1;—	—
437 Rev. of Religious Research	I:title	ni;125	14–28	ASA	3;2	A 21.5%r
438 Rev. of Social Economy	I:title	ni;—	13–27	sAPA	—	—
439 Revue Internationale de Psychologie Appliquée	Applied psych., esp. comp.	ni;500m	23–30	sAPA*	—	—
440 Rocky Mountain Social Science J.	Gen. soc. science	ni;—	15–35	sMSH	3;8r	A 25%r
441 Rural Sociology	Title	4;150m	24mr	ASA	3;—r	A 19%r
442 Scandanavian J. of Psychology	Gen. psych.	2;150m	7–38	sMSN*	—	—
443 School Counselor	I:res., theory on counseling	3;—	4–13;6	APA	—	Abstract not printed
444 School Rev.	Res., theory, philos. of ed., and related disciplines	2;"brief"; see (7)	18–40	sMSH	—	Read by teachers of science and mathematics
445 School Science and Mathematics	I:title	ni;—	5–22;7	sMSH*	—	—
446 Science	I:title	3;55m	12–30;20	sMSH;p. xv, 6/28/74	2;—	—
447 Science Education	I:title	2;—	6–25;13	sMSH	11–13	—
448 Science and Society	I:Marxist theory	ni;—	8–56	sMSH	3;3r	A 22%r
449 Science, Medicine and Man; see Ethics in Science and Medicine						
450 Science Studies; see Social Studies of Science						
451 Science Teacher	I:science ed.	ni;—	2–7	sMSH	—	Many nonprofessional readers
452 Scientific Am.	I:gen. science	ni;—	20–45	ni	—	
453 Scottish J. of Political Economy	I:title	2;—	11–25	sMSN	—	—
454 Signs	I:women	3;—	25–75	MSH	—	—
455 Simulation and Games	I:title	3;—	13–28	Sage	2;5r	—
456 Small Group Behavior	I:title	2;—	8–18	Sage*	2;5r	—
457 Social Compass	Socioreligious studies	2;175	40m	sMSH	—	—
458 Social and Economic Studies	Title:underdeveloped areas	2;—	28m	sJASA	—	—

Table 7.1 (*Continued*)

(1) Name of Journal[1]	(2) Topics[2]	(3) Number of Copies, Abstract[3]	(4) Article Length[4] (typed pages)	(5) Style[5]	(6) Lag[6] (months)	(7) Miscellaneous[7]
459 Social Education	I:teaching of soc. studies	ni;—	5–22	Many	—	—
460 Social Forces	Sociol.:esp. soc. structure and class	3;125m	12–37	sMSN	2;9r	—
461 Social Indicators Research	I:res., meth., theory, quality-of-life measurement	ni;150	20–75	Many	—	—
462 Social Policy	I:title	ni;—	14–53;21	sMSH	1,3r	A 35%r
463 Social Praxis	Gen. soc. science	3;200	9–93;19	sMSH	—	—
464 Social Problems	I:res., title	ni;150	16–35	ASA	—	—
465 Social Psychiatry	I:psychiatric disorders in relation to the soc. environment	3;125	20m	sAPA*	—	—
466 Social Research	Gen.:title	ni;—	20–44	sMSH	1,8r	A 24%r
467 Social Science	Gen.:title	ni;—	10–29;12	Many	—	—
468 Social Science Information	Gen.:title	ni;—	16–64	Many	—	—
469 Social Science and Medicine	I:title	2;400m	9–82	sMSH	—;6	A 12%r
470 Social Science Q.	Gen. sociol., pol. science	3;—	15–25,20	sMSH	2;6r	—
471 Social Science Research	Gen.:title	3;150m	7–46	sMSN	—	—
472 Social Service Rev.	I:soc. welfare	ni;125m	15–42	sMSH	—	Many readers are social workers
473 Social Studies	I:teaching soc. studies	2;—	5–20	sMSH	—	For teachers and administrators
474 Social Studies: Irish J. of Sociology	Sociol., esp. of Ireland	ni;—	18–38	Many	2;3r	A 63%r
475 Social Studies of Science	I:title	4;—	20–40	sMSH	—	—
476 Social Theory and Practice	Important, controversial soc. and pol. issues	2;—	17–40;20	MSH	—	—
477 Social Work	I:title	3;—	16m	sMSH	3;6r	Read by many social workers
478 Society	I:applied soc. science	ni;—	12–59	ni;see (7)	—	References are in text
479 Society and Leisure	Sociol. of leisure, ed., and culture	2;200m	20m	Many	—	—

No. / Title	Description					
480 Socio-Economic Planning Sciences	I:title, quantitative analysis	2;125	17–41;26	sJASA*	5–12	—
481 Sociologia Ruralis	Rural sociol.:esp. European	ni;—	16–36	Many	1;4r	A 20%r
482 Sociological Analysis	Sociol. of religion	ni;—	6–48	sMSN	—	A 28%r
483 Sociological Analysis and Theory	Sociol.:res. and theory	2;—	20–44	sMSH	1;4r	A 17%r
484 Sociological Focus	Gen. sociol.	3;150m	13–40;20	ASA	2;5r	A 7%r
485 Sociological Inquiry	Gen. sociol.	3;60	18–56	sMSN	2;5r	A 10%r
486 Sociological Methods and Research	Title	3;175m	24–80	Sage	2;5r	—
487 Sociological Q.	Gen. sociol.	3;125	15–32	ASA	1;3r	A 17%r
488 Sociological Rev.	Gen. sociol.	ni;—	14–26	sMSH	—	A 21%r
489 Sociologus	Empirical ethnol.: sociol. and psych.	ni;150	18–32	Many	3;7r	—[18]
490 Sociology	Gen. sociol.	3;150m	17–52	Many	—[18]	A 10%r
491 Sociology and Social Research	I:title	3;150m	15–24	ASA	3;—r	A 22%r
492 Sociology of Education	Title	3;100m	22–67	ASA	4;6r	sf $15a
493 Sociology of Work and Occupations	I:title, esp. comp.	3;125	19–46	Sage	1;6r	—
494 Sociometry	Theory, res.:soc. psych.	1;—	16–35	ASA*	—	—
495 Soundings	I:soc. science, humanities, religion	ni;—	15–31	MLA	—	—
496 Southern Economic J.	Gen. ecs.	ni;—	23–77	sJASA	—	—
497 Studies in the Anthropology of Visual Communication	I:title	3;75m	24–72	sMSN	—	—
498 Studies in Art Education	I:title	4;—	10–24	sAPA	—	—
499 Studies in Comparative Communism	I:title	3;—	13–53	sMSH	—	—
500 Studies in Family Planning	I:title	ni;—	20m	sMSN	2;6r	A 42%r
501 Studies in History and Philosophy of Science	I:title	2;—	100m	sMSH	—	—
502 Studies in Philosophy and Education	I:title	ni;—	13–41	sMSH	—	—
503 Suicide	I:title	3;100	20m	sAPA	6;9	A 33%r
504 Swedish J. of Economics	Gen. ecs.	2;100m	5–39	sAPA	—	—
505 Synthese	I:epistemology, methodology and philos. of science	ni;—	12–61	sJASA	—	—
506 Teacher's College Record	Gen. ed.	2;—	20 max.	sMSH	2;5	—
507 Teaching Political Science	I:title	2;—	14–40	Sage	—	—
508 Teaching Politics	I:title	ni;—	8–20	sMSH	—	—
509 Teaching Sociology	I:title	2;—	30m	Sage	2;5r	—

Table 7.1 (*Continued*)

(1) Name of Journal[1]	(2) Topics[2]	(3) Number of Copies, Abstract[3]	(4) Article Length[4] (typed pages)	(5) Style[5]	(6) Lag[6] (months)	(7) Miscellaneous[7]
510 Technological Forecasting and Social Change	I:title	3;200m	17–62	sJASA	2–10	—
511 Technology and Culture	I:title	ni;—	12–57	sMSH	3;7ʳ	A 25%ʳ
512 Telos	Critical sociol.	2;—	25–137	sMSH	—	—
513 Tesol Q.	Res.:teaching English to native speakers of other lang.	ni;200m	20m	sMSN	—	—
514 Theory and Decision	I:philos. and methodology of soc. science	ni;150	23–62	Many	—	—
515 Theory and Society	Theory underlying soc. science	2;—	13–53	Many	—	—
516 Theoretical Linguistics	I:title	1;100	28–50	sMSN	—	—
517 Theory into Practice	Ed.:theory and application	ni;—	15–25	sAPA	—	—
518 Town Planning Rev.	I:title, and related res.	2;—	32m	sMSH	1;9ʳ	A 22%ʳ
519 Training School Bull.	Training retarded persons	ni;100	4–27	APA*	—	Read by teachers of the retarded
520 University of Chicago School Rev.; see School Rev.						
521 Universities Q.; see New Universities Q.						
522 Urban Affairs Q.	I:title	3;—	30m	Sage	2;5ʳ	—
523 Urban Anthropology	Res.::title	2;200m	24–50	sMSN	2;5ʳ	—
524 Urban Education	Title	2;—	25m	Sage	—	—
525 Urban League Rev.	Res. to affect policy	ni;—	12–18	sMSH	2;5ʳ	—
526 Urban Life	I:urban ethnogr.	2;—	19–40	Sage	—	—
527 Urban Rev.	I:issues and ideas in public ed.	ni;—	12–34	sMSH	—	—
528 Urban Studies	Res.:urban and regional	3;120m	60m	sMSN	7–11	—
529 Virginia Social Sci. J.	Gen. soc. science	ni;—	11–28	sMSH	—	—
530 Vocational Guidance Q.	I:role of work in human lives	3;30	12m	APA	—	—
531 Wage-Price Law and Economics Rev.	I:title	2;—	20–40	sMSH;vol. 1, #1, 1975, p. 7	—	—

532	Western Political Q.	Gen. pol. science	2;150m	11–65	sMSH	—	—
533	Western Sociological Rev.	Gen. sociol.	3;100m	27–43	sASR	—	—
534	Women's Studies	I:title	3;150m	60m	ni	3;12^r	—
535	Working Papers for a New Society	I:policy studies	ni;—	23–52;30	sMSH	—	—
536	World Affairs	I:int. conflict	2;—	17–52	sMSH	—	—
537	World Politics	I:int. relations, comp. politics	2;—	40m^r	sMSH	1;9^r	A 12%^{r}
538	Young Children	I:title	ni;—	9–37	APA	—	—
539	Youth and Society	I:title	3;—	10–54	Sage	2;5^r	—
540	Zygon	I:relation of science and religion	3;—	22–45	sMSH	—	—

Source. Unless otherwise noted, data are from 1973, 1974, and 1975 issues of the journals.

1. Alphabetization is by word, ignoring "a," "an," and "the." "Am. = American; Aust. = Australian; Br. = British; Bull. = Bulletin; Can. = Canadian; J = Journal; Q. = Quarterly; Rev. = Review. For the correct way to cite journal titles in manuscripts of articles and books to be submitted for publication, see Sections 8.77 to 8.81.

2. Abbreviations used in column 2 are: adm. = administration; anthrop. = anthropology; behav. = behavior; bus. = business; clin. = clinical; comp. = comparative; crim. = criminology; cult. = cultural; dev. = development, developmental; ec. = economic; ecs. = economics; ed. = education, educational; ethnogr. = enthnographic; ethnol. = ethnology; exp. = experimental; gen. = general; hist. = history; I = interdisciplinary; ind. = industrial; inf. = information; int. = international; lang. = language; ling. = linguistics; lit. = literature; math. = mathematics, mathematical; med. = medical; meth. = methods; nat. = national; philos. = philosophy; pol. = political; psych. = psychology, psychological; res. = research; rev. = reviews; soc. = social; sociol. = sociology; stat. = statistics, statistical; tech. = technology. Title = journal's title indicates its subject matter.

3. In column 3 the entry *before the semicolon* is the number of copies of each article that you must submit for evaluation. The abbreviation "ni" means no information was given. In such cases, submit two copies. The entry *after the semicolon* is information on abstracts; a dash indicates that no abstract is required. A number by itself indicates that the journal's style requires an abstract of approximately that number of words. In general, do not submit an abstract that is more than 10 percent longer or 40 percent shorter than that number. An "m" means that the number of words shown is the maximum that the journal's style permits. In such cases, an abstract usually may be as much as 40 percent shorter, but it may not be longer.

4. Assumes 250 words per page, including abstract, notes, tables, illustrations, references, and appendixes. Two entries separated by a dash show the range of lengths (low and high). Entries following a semicolon show the modal length of articles. An "m" indicates that the journal's instructions explicitly limit articles to the stated number of pages; exceptions to stated limits are rare. Most counts were obtained by estimating lengths of articles in several issues. Superscript "r" shows that the source of information is Rhoades (1974); "t" shows that the source is *Teacher Education Forum* (1973).

5. Classification of style is based largely on the method used for documentation. APA = American Psychological Association; ASA = American Sociological Association; *JASA* = *Journal of the American Statistical Association*; many = journal shows many styles and states no preference; MLA = Modern Language Association; MSH = *A Manual of Style's* (1969) humanities style; MSN = *A Manual's* natural-science style; SA = *Suggestions to Authors*; Sage = Sage journal style; Tur = Turabian (1973). Lowercase "s" shows that a journal's style is similar, but not identical, to that indicated by the subsequent letters. An asterisk shows that the journal always or nearly always publishes articles that follow the data-analysis outline (see Sections 2.24–2.40 for details). I discuss editorial styles in Chapter 8.

Entry of a date (e.g., on *Am. Anthropologist*) shows that instructions on style are not printed in every issue; however, they are printed in the issue for the date shown. Numbers before the slash represent months; Sp = spring, Su = summer, F = fall, W = winter. Instructions are normally printed either in the front of the journal (on the inside cover or somewhere between it and the first page of the first article) or in the back (between the end of the book reviews and the back cover or on back cover). In some cases, the only information given is the editor's address.

6. When two numbers are separated by a semicolon, the first figure is the average number of months that elapse between submission of an article and the time a decision is made. The second figure is the average number of months that elapse between acceptance of a final draft and publication. When two numbers are separated by a dash, the two indicate the *range* of time (low to high, in months) that elapses between submission of an article and, if accepted, its publication. A single number is the *average* number of months elapsed between submission and publication. Figures marked with a superscript "r" are taken from Rhoades (1974). Figures marked with a superscript "t" are taken from *Teachers Education Forum* (August, 1973). Unless otherwise noted, all other entries are based on dates of submission and acceptance given with each article in the journals involved.

7. "R" or "A" preceding a percentage shows the approximate percentage of articles rejected or accepted. Superscript "r" shows that the source of information is Rhoades (1974). "Pub. ch." shows that the journal's editor charges a fee for publishing all or part of some articles. Consult the journal's instructions for details. "Write first" means: before you submit an article, write the journal's editor, describe the article briefly, and ask if submission would be appropriate. The letters "sf" mean submission fee. When two fees are given, the first applies to members of the association sponsoring the journal; the second, to nonmembers. When one fee is given, "n" shows that the fee is required only of nonmembers. An "a" shows that the fee is required of all authors. Fees are normally nonrefundable.

8. Bidwell (1974, p. 1072).

9. *American Psychologist* (1975, p. 419).

10. Zelditch (1975, p. 12).

11. Mayhew (1975, p. 13).

12. Use American Institute of Physics style for abbreviation of physical units.

13. From acceptance (usually receipt of final manuscript) to publication.

14. Nisbet (1974, p. 221).

15. From submission to decision.

16. See journal for special style instructions.

17. Over three years (Jackson 1975, p. 13).

18. No data; reviewing process suspended from 9/74 to 7/75 to reduce backlog of articles (Kitsuse 1975, p. 13).

CHAPTER EIGHT

Preparing Scholarly
Articles for Submission
to Journals[1]

INTRODUCTION

8.1   You now have a final draft of an article. You have also chosen the journal in which you want to publish it. This chapter gives step-by-step instructions on styling, typing, organizing, and mailing the article.

Definition of Editorial Style

8.2   Editorial style refers to rules for mechanical details such as preparing references and headings, documenting information, and presenting equations. Some styles also require a specific outline, or format. Editorial style usually does not include prescriptions for writing style. To determine editorial style,

○ Check Table 7.1, column 5, and the journal's instructions. Note 5 of Table 7.1 shows the usual locations for instructions.

8.3   In the absence of instructions or as a supplement to scanty or confusing instructions,[2]

○ Infer style from the appearance of printed articles in the most recent issue of the journal.

However,

○ Remember that such inferences may be misleading. For example, many journals print notes at the bottom of the pages to which they refer (literally, as footnotes). Yet the journals' editors nearly always require authors to collect their notes separately at the end of the manuscript.

Proper style and accuracy are important.

☐ Some journals will return without refereeing an article that has been improperly prepared.
☐ Some referees are favorably influenced by an article that looks like it "belongs" in the journal to which its author has submitted it.

The Seven Basic Styles

8.4 Social- and behavioral-science journals commonly use one of seven styles. Most of the other styles resemble one of the basic seven. Table 8.1 shows the styles, the abbreviations I use for them, the users, and the locations of examples.[3] Unfortunately, many journals that claim to follow a style do not follow it in every detail. Therefore,

○ Always check the journal and obtain instructions.
○ Either obtain a copy of the journal or photocopy some pages that show headings, subheadings, tables, illustrations, and references.
○ Give your typist this sample material and a copy of the instructions.

When given instructions and examples, typists usually ask fewer questions and type the manuscript more accurately. A few journals request that authors write and describe their arti-

**Table 8.1   Common Styles by Categories, Abbreviations, Users, and
Location of Examples of Documentation and Reference Lists**

Style	Abbre-viation	Used by Journals in	Examples in This Book
Name (Date) Documentation			
American Psycho-logical Association	APA	Anthropology, education, linguistics, psychiatry,	Chapters 1–7 and 9–17. Sections 8.42–8.45, 8.79, 8.81. Table 8.2.
American Socio-logical Association	ASA	psychology, social psychology, sociology	Figures 8.9–8.10, 8.12–8.13
Manual of Style, natural science	MSN		
Sage Journals	Sage		
Suggestions to Authors	SA		
[#] Documentation			
Journal of the American Statis-tical Association	JASA	Economics, mathematics, statistics	Sections 8.46–8.48, 8.79, 8.81. Figure 8.11
Superscript Numbers and Footnotes			
Modern Language Association	MLA	Business, history, linguistics, political science	Chapter 8. Sections 8.49–8.51, 8.77, 8.81
Manual of Style, humanities	MSH		

Sources.   See note 3, Chapter 8.

cles before sending them. If your chosen journal is one of these,
write before you have the article typed.

General Remarks on Chapter 8

8.5   In the following sections,

☐ I give specific instructions that hold for all styles.
☐ For all instructions that vary, I give general rules and
checklists for items that vary.

These instructions are not necessarily appropriate for doctoral
dissertations and class papers (see Sections B.2 and B.3). Use

them for such manuscripts only with your instructor's permission. These instructions are for authors and typists, but I have addressed them to authors since many must type their own articles. As you will note (e.g., in Section 8.9), I have written this chapter as if publication were guaranteed (see Section 8.3 for the reason). Two principles govern most styles: simplicity and consistency. In general, whenever you must make decisions about editorial style with no guidance from a journal's instructions, choose the simplest of the available alternatives and then use it consistently.

GENERAL TYPING INSTRUCTIONS

8.6 The following instructions hold for every page of every article.

8.7 Requirements for Paper. *The original ("ribbon") copy:*

○ Never use "erasable" bond.
○ Use paper of appropriate quality. *Sixteen-pound paper is the minimum acceptable.* Some editorial styles, for example *JASA* and MLA, require 20-pound bond paper.
○ If you are reproducing all copies from a master, use the highest-quality paper that will produce clear, dark copies. Avoid spirit masters, such as Ditto, which often produce light and unevenly printed copies.
○ Type or reproduce on only one side of each page.
○ Check size of paper. American styles usually require paper of $8\frac{1}{2} \times 11$ inches. British styles, such as SA, usually require ISO-size A4, 210×297 millimeters (approximately 8.2×11.6 inches).

All other copies:

○ If reproducing from a master, use the highest-quality paper that will give a clear, dark copy.
○ If typing on bond, check requirements for copies. Many

styles require photo- or xerographic copies rather than carbon copies.

8.8 Requirements for Typewriter Ribbon and Pitch.

○ If typing on bond, use a new black ribbon. Some styles require that originals be typed with a carbon ribbon.

○ Clean type face before starting to type. Follow the typewriter manufacturer's instructions, or ask a local typewriter serviceman for instructions.

○ Use the same type of pitch (spaces per inch) for the entire manuscript. *Pica* type has *10* spaces, or characters, per inch; *elite* has *12*.

8.9 Requirements for Lines and Margins.

○ Check line length. For example, APA, ASA, and SA styles require that typed lines never exceed 6 inches in length.

○ *Left and right margins.* For manuscripts with no equations or symbols in the text, 1 inch on each side is the minimum allowed. For manuscripts with symbols or equations, $1\frac{1}{4}$ inches on each side is the minimum allowed. Some styles require that the left margin be $1\frac{1}{2}$ inches; the right, 1 inch.

○ *Top and bottom margins.* One inch each is the minimum allowed. Some styles require 2 inches each.

○ Use the same margins on every page.

Editors need adequate margins so they can write typesetting instructions. They need consistent margins so they can estimate accurately the length of the printed document.

○ *Hyphens.* Use no hyphens at the ends of typed lines. Each hyphen in that position must be marked to indicate whether it is integral to a hyphenated pair of words or is simply dividing a word and should thus be deleted if the word can be completely set on one line.

Avoiding the hyphens makes copy editing, typesetting, and

proofreading easier. When you or your typist must choose between leaving a very short line (typing completely on the next line a word that would normally be divided) and typing into the margin, choose the short line.

8.10   Requirements for Spacing.   *Vertical spacing:*

○ Double-space between *all lines* of all title pages, abstracts, text pages, quotations, equations, notes, tables, illustrations, appendixes, bibliographies, and indexes.
○ NEVER single-space unless a journal editor explicitly says you may.

EXCEPTIONS:

○ *Triple-space* above and below blocked, indented quotations; above first-order headings (defined in Section 8.31), and above second-order headings unless there is no text between the heading and the immediately prior first-order heading (in such cases, double-space).
○ Begin approximately *2 inches from the top of the page:* the title on the abstract page and first page of text, and titles of all sections that begin on separate pages, such as notes, lists of references, bibliographies, and appendixes.
○ *Quadruple-space* between those titles and the first line of text, notes, references, bibliographies, or appendixes.
○ Follow the journal editor's instructions if you are preparing camera-ready copy (see also Sections 8.67 and 8.68).

Copy editors cannot edit lines that are single-spaced. Typesetters have difficulty reading single-spaced lines. *Horizontal spacing:*

○ *Indent five spaces* to begin a paragraph.
○ *Single-space* after words, commas, and semicolons.
○ *Single-space* after a colon if what follows is part of the preceding sentence. For example:

Elsewhere use, respectively: *that is, for example,* and *and so on.*   [1]

○ *Single-space* after a period, question mark, or exclamation mark only if it is within, and does not mark the end of, a sentence. For example:

Is it here? was his question.   [2]

○ *Double-space* after periods, question marks, and exclamation marks that signal the end of a sentence.

○ *Leave no spaces* between the letters of words, or between dashes and the words preceding and following the dashes. For example:

decision-making process   [3]

Her goal—to finish the work—seemed unattainable. [4]

8.11 Requirements for Symbols and Accents.

○ *Handwrite symbols and accents* unless your typewriter is equipped with them. Editors and typesetters may misinterpret typed approximations. For example, a single quotation mark can be either a grave or an acute accent; a χ (chi) may be an X.

○ To prevent misunderstanding, with the first appearance of a symbol, handwrite the name in the margin, and encircle it. For example:

⟨chi⟩   χ   ⟨sigma⟩   Σ

○ Repeat the name with each use if the manuscript also uses other, similar letters or symbols, such as x, X, and χ.

CAUTION: Some styles also require that you underline symbols. For example, X̲, not X.

8.12 Requirements for Spelling.   In general,

○ For American journals, follow *Webster's Collegiate Dictionary*.

○ For British journals, follow the *Oxford Dictionary*.

○ Section 5.72 lists other useful dictionaries.

8.13   Requirements for Capitalization.   For titles and short titles,

○ Capitalize the first and last words; the first word after a colon; all nouns, pronouns, verbs, adjectives, and adverbs; and all prepositions that contain more than four letters.

EXCEPTION.   Titles in bibliographies, lists of references, and footnotes sometimes follow different rules. See Sections 8.50 and 8.76 to 8.81.

○ For information on other aspects of capitalization, see Porter Perrin's *Guide and Index to English*[4] or any other good book on English grammar.

8.14   Requirements for Use of Numbers or Words.

○ Section 5.53 tells when to use numerals and when to use words for numbers.

8.15   Requirements for Separate Pages.   In general, items on the following list begin on separate pages.

EXCEPTION.   Items marked with an asterisk are sometimes combined with other items.

○ The cover sheet.* See also Section 8.19.
○ The abstract.* See also Section 8.26.
○ The first page of text.* See also Sections 8.28 and 8.29.
○ Each table.
○ Each illustration.
○ Captions.* See also Section 8.70.
○ The notes.
○ The list of references.
○ The bibliography.
○ Each appendix.

Headings and subheadings do not necessarily begin on separate pages, although they sometimes naturally occur that way.

8.16   Requirements for Parts of Articles and Order of Parts.

○ Learn what parts of an article your chosen journal requires. Section 8.15 lists the most common parts. Some journals also require that reference notes (see Section 8.72 and 8.73), identifying references (8.74 and 8.75) and acknowledgment notes (see Section 8.57) be separated from other notes. Some journals omit one or more of these parts, and some combine parts. For example, journals following Sage style often do not require an abstract. Journals following MLA style often combine the title page and the first page of text.

○ Learn how the parts should be organized. For example, *JASA* style prescribes: cover sheet, abstract, text, tables, illustrations, notes, list of references, appendixes. APA style prescribes: cover sheet, abstract, text, reference notes, list of references, notes, tables, illustrations, captions, appendixes.

Some styles prescribe no order. In such cases:

○ Use this order: cover sheet, abstract, text, notes, references, tables, illustrations, captions, appendixes.

8.17   Requirements for Numbering Pages.   When assigning a number to each page,

○ Determine the order of parts, as described in Section 8.16.
○ Learn which pages are counted. For example, *JASA* style counts every page. APA style counts all except the cover sheet and the illustration pages. ASA style begins counting with the first page of text. In the absence of instructions, count every page except the cover sheet.
○ Learn which pages are numbered. In general, do not type a number on the cover sheet, the abstract page, or the first page of text.

EXCEPTION.   In APA style, type 1 and 2 in the upper, right-hand corner of the abstract page and the first page of text, respectively.

○ In general, place the first page number in the upper, right-hand corner of the *second page of text*. In *JASA* style, this number is 4; in APA style, 3; in ASA style, 2.

○ Number the third and subsequent pages of text in consecutive arabic numerals following the number on the second page.

○ Learn whether tables and illustrations receive page numbers as well as identifying numbers (see Sections 8.62 and 8.71). For example, APA style requires page numbers for tables but not for illustrations. *JASA* style requires page numbers for both.

INSTRUCTIONS FOR PREPARING A COVER SHEET (TITLE PAGE)

8.18   Figures 8.1 to 8.3 illustrate instructions for cover sheets. All three are photoreproduced from typed pages to show exactly how your typed pages should look.

8.19   General Requirements for Cover Sheet.

○ For styles that require a separate cover sheet, follow the illustrations in Figure 8.1.

○ For styles that combine the cover sheet and the first page of text, follow the illustrations in Figure 8.2.

○ In the absence of instructions from the journal, prepare a separate cover sheet.

○ Always include title, by-line, and date.

○ Always check for possible inclusion of running head, current address, acknowledgment, or abstract (not shown in Figure 8.1; see Section 8.26). A running head (running headline, running title, abbreviated title, short title) is a short version of a title. Printers normally use it at the top of columns or pages after the first page of an article or book chapter.

○ Follow rules for capitalization in Section 8.13.

○ Do not underline.

Center the Title from Right to Left: (Title)

Just Like This   (Line 2 of title)

John Q. Author   (Author's name)

University of Anywhere   (Author's affil.)

A Shortened Title   (Running head)

Month Year   (Date)

John Q. Author   (Current address)

Department of ?

University of Anywhere

City, State, Zip Code

Country

Thanks for funding and other help.   (Acknowledgments)

Figure 8.1 Example: separate cover sheet. Required by APA, ASA, *JASA*, SA, and Sage styles. The running head, current address, and acknowledgments are optional—not required by all styles.

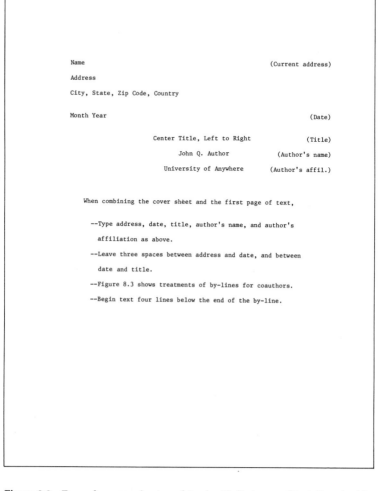

Name   (Current address)

Address

City, State, Zip Code, Country

Month Year   (Date)

                    Center Title, Left to Right   (Title)

                             John Q. Author   (Author's name)

                        University of Anywhere   (Author's affil.)

    When combining the cover sheet and the first page of text,

        --Type address, date, title, author's name, and author's

          affiliation as above.

        --Leave three spaces between address and date, and between

          date and title.

        --Figure 8.3 shows treatments of by-lines for coauthors.

        --Begin text four lines below the end of the by-line.

Figure 8.2 Example: cover sheet combined with first page of text. Required by MLA, by many journals following MSH style, and by some other journals that do not use blind reviews.

8.20   Requirements for the Title.

○ Prepare an accurate, brief title. See Sections 3.2 and 3.3 for help. Avoid titles that lack accurate descriptors.
○ Center each line from left to right.
○ If the title has two lines, make the second line shorter than the first.

8.21   Requirements for the By-line.   Author's name and affiliation:

○ Type the name in proper form. Some styles require full first and last names and a middle initial (if you have one), or a first initial and the middle and last names. Some prefer one or two initials and a last name. Some styles indicate no preference.
○ If no instructions are given, use full first and last names and a middle initial.
○ If you have one or more coauthors, consult Figure 8.3 for variations in the by-line.
○ Check instructions on institutional affiliation. Some styles require that you list the institution currently employing you. Others prefer that you list the institution at which you did the research, if the two differ. In the absence of instructions, give current affiliation. In your letter of submission, ask about preferred policy.
○ In general, center the by-line from left to right.

8.22   Requirements for the Date.

○ Show month and year in which you submit the article to the journal.
○ Type the date flush with the left margin.

8.23   Requirements for Optional Items.

○ *Running head.* Check the permitted length. For example, APA style permits a total of 60 letters and spaces between

TWO OR MORE AUTHORS, SAME INSTITUTION

First A. Author, Second B. Author, and Third C. Author

University of Anywhere

THREE AUTHORS, TWO AFFILIATIONS

First A. Author and Second B. Author

University of Anywhere

Third C. Author

Important University

TWO AUTHORS, TWO AFFILIATIONS

First A. Author   Second B. Author

University of Anywhere   Important University

OR

First A. Author

University of Anywhere

Second B. Author

Important University

Figure 8.3 Example: variations in treatment of by-line.

words. SA permits 80. In general, center a running head from left to right on the page.

○ *Address.* Give your current business address. Most journals use that address when mailing proofs. Many print it with articles for the convenience of readers who want reprints. On coauthored articles, give address of author responsible for proofreading and sending out reprints. Type each line of the address flush with the left margin.

○ *Acknowledgment.* See Sections 8.56 to 8.59 for further instructions.

○ *Abstract.* See Sections 8.24 to 8.26.

INSTRUCTIONS FOR PREPARING ABSTRACTS (SUMMARIES)

8.24 Description and General Instructions.   Potential readers and indexing and abstracting services use abstracts and summaries to catalog articles. Journal editors use them when they choose referees. Some styles—for example MLA and Sage—do not always require an abstract. To determine whether an abstract is required,

○ Check column 3 in Table 7.1, the journal's instructions, or several articles in the most recent issue of the journal.

○ In the absence of instructions, submit an abstract of approximately 125 words.

Figure 8.4 shows how a typed abstract should look.

8.25 Requirements for the Content of an Abstract.

○ Be specific. Do not just list the topics you discuss. For example, in Figure 8.4 "Comparison of the earnings differences shows most draftees with earnings equal to or below those of nonveterans" states a specific finding. In contrast, a statement such as "Comparison showed earnings differences between draftees and nonveterans" is not specific.

The Civilian Earnings of White and Black Draftees

and Nonveterans

Abstract

The impact of military service as a career contingency affecting adult

economic status is examined with a national probability sample of men

given preinduction exams by Selective Service in the early 1950s.

Civilian earnings in 1964 of former draftees and three types of

nonveterans are compared after controlling race, region of employment,

academic achievement, and years of education. Comparison of the

earnings differences shows most draftees with earnings equal to or below

those of nonveterans. After the probable negative effect of service on

draftee earnings has been removed, the remaining earnings difference is

discussed. The operation of selection factors that bias earnings

comparisons is evaluated. [A common] hypothesis [regarding the

military's effect as a "bridging environment"] is not supported.

Figure 8.4 A sample abstract. Reprinted from Phillips Cutright, "The Civilian Earnings of White and Black Draftees and Nonveterans," *American Sociological Review* **39** (June 1974), p. 317, by permission of Phillips Cutright and the American Sociological Association.

○ For a research report, state the problem, method, results, and conclusions.

○ For a review or a theoretical article, state the topics covered, the central thesis, the sources used (such as personal observation, published literature), and conclusions.[5] For an article that presents a new theory or method, describe its essence.

○ Be brief. For example, APA requires an abstract of 100 to 175 words for a research report, and an abstract of 75 to 100 words for a review or a theoretical article. ASA style limits abstracts to 150 words. *JASA* style requires 100 words or less; SA style, 100 to 200 words. When in doubt about length, submit an abstract of about 125 words.

○ To determine the length of an abstract, see column 3 in Table 7.1, the journal's instructions, or the abstracts for several articles.

○ To test the abstract's accuracy and completeness, check its content against that of the paragraph concluding your introduction (see Section 2.26) and that of the summary to your article (see Section 2.40).

8.26   Requirements for Typing an Abstract.

○ Type the abstract on a separate page.

EXCEPTION.   A few journals require that the abstract be typed on the cover sheet. In such cases, find out *where* on the cover sheet to put it. In the absence of instructions, type it below the by-line.

○ In general, center the title of the article from left to right, approximately 2 inches from the top of the page, as in Figure 8.4.

EXCEPTION.   Some styles, for example APA, omit the title. In such cases, type "Abstract" approximately 2 inches from the top of the page, and a word or two from the title in the upper, right-hand corner above the page number.

○ Type the abstract as one blocked paragraph. That is, begin each line of typing, including the first, flush with the left margin.

INSTRUCTIONS FOR PREPARING TEXT

8.27   General Requirements for Text.   Check the text of the article for:

- ○ *Organization and content.* Use the criteria in Sections 5.2 to 5.16. Also check the journal's preferred topics to be certain the article is appropriate. See Sections 7.8 to 7.16 for help.
- ○ *Accurate documentation.* Use the criteria in Sections 3.23 to 3.33.
- ○ *Clarity.* Use the criteria in Sections 5.18 to 5.34.
- ○ *Grammatical correctness.* Use the criteria in Sections 5.36 to 5.55.
- ○ *Brevity.* Use the criteria in Sections 5.56 to 5.62.
- ○ If the article is for a general audience, check *readability.* Use the criteria in Sections 5.65 to 5.69.

8.28   Requirements for First Page of Text.   *Separate cover sheet:*

- ○ Begin the first page of text on a separate sheet of paper.
- ○ Type the title approximately 2 inches from the top of the page, centered from left to right.
- ○ Do not type your name on this or any subsequent page.
- ○ Begin the text four lines below the last line of the title.

8.29   *Cover sheet and first page of text combined:*

- ○ Follow the instructions in Figure 8.2.
- ○ Do not place your name on any page other than the first page of text unless the journal's editor explicitly tells you to do so.

8.30   General Requirements for Typing Text.

○ Follow the general instructions in Sections 8.6 to 8.17.
○ For articles prepared according to APA style, type one or two words of the title over each page number.

INSTRUCTIONS FOR PREPARING HEADINGS AND SUBHEADINGS

8.31 Content of Headings and Subheadings

○ Use headings to show topics at the first, second, and third levels of importance in your outline. These are, respectively, first-order, second-order, and third-order headings.
○ Make them no longer than half a typed line.
○ Make them topical and grammatically parallel. Sections 2.3 and 5.6 show how to construct and revise headings and subheadings.
○ Follow instructions for spacing in Section 8.10.

8.32 Aspects of Style that Vary.   Always check:

○ The kinds of heading permitted.
○ The level of importance that each expresses.
○ Placement on the page.
○ Capitalization.
○ Underlining.
○ Punctuation at end.
○ Numbering.

Figure 8.5 shows how typed headings and subheadings should look.

8.33 General Typing Requirements.   In general, as Figure 8.5 shows,

○ *First-order headings.* Center from left to right on a separate line. Capitalization varies.

```
                                APA
                        First-Order Heading

Second-Order Heading

        Third-order heading.


                                ASA
                        FIRST-ORDER HEADING

Second-Order Heading

        Third-order heading.


                                JASA
                1.   FIRST FIRST-ORDER HEADING

1.1  First Second-Order Heading Under Heading #1


                                MLA
                I.   First First-Order Heading

Second-Order Heading


                               Sage
                       FIRST-ORDER HEADING

SECOND-ORDER HEADING

Third-Order Heading

        Fourth-Order Heading.
```

Figure 8.5 Examples of headings and subheadings. Note that MLA gives no rules for capitalization and underlining. Also, first-order heading can be the number by itself.

EXCEPTION.   Some journals, such as *American Journal of Sociology*, place first-order headings flush with the left margin.

○ *Second-order headings.* Type on a separate line flush with the left margin. Underscore, and capitalize following Section 5.54.
○ *Third-order headings.* Type as paragraph leaders. Place a period at the end of the heading. Underline, and capitalize only the first word unless one or more of the others is a proper noun.
○ Do not number headings.

8.34 Watch for Exceptions. For example, as Figure 8.5 shows,

○ For Sage journals, you may use four orders of headings. Capitalization of fourth-order headings follows Section 8.13.
○ For MLA style, number first-order headings with sequential roman numerals.
○ For *JASA* style, use only two orders of headings and number them sequentially by sections.
○ Not shown in Figure 8.5 but common: for articles under 20 pages in length, some journal styles prescribe only two orders of headings: side headings for first-order, and paragraph leaders for second-order, headings.

INSTRUCTIONS FOR PREPARING QUOTATIONS

8.35 Cautions for Use of Quotations.   In general,

○ Avoid long, direct quotations.

They are usually longer than a paraphrase would be, and sometimes you must obtain permission to use quotations totaling more than 50 words from one source. For discussion of when to use quotations, see Section 5.57. For help in obtaining permissions, see Sections 12.43 to 12.50.

8.36   Requirements for Typing Quotations.   In the absence of other instructions, for *quotations that are less than five typed lines in length,*

○ Integrate the quotation into your text.
○ Use quotation marks at the beginning and at the end of the quotation.
○ For American journals, use double quotation marks; for British journals, single ones.
○ For American journals, place periods and commas inside the quotation marks, and question marks and exclamation points outside. Place question marks and exclamation points inside the quotation marks only if they are part of the quotation.
○ For British journals, place all punctuation *outside* the quotation marks.
○ For further detail on the relationship of quotation marks to punctuation, see Perrin's *Guide and Index to English,*[6] or any other good book on English grammar.

For *quotations that are longer than seven typed lines,*

○ Block the entire quotation seven spaces from the left margin.

   EXCEPTION.   Some styles, for example APA, block quotations five spaces from the left margin.

○ Indent five additional spaces to show beginnings of paragraphs only for the second and subsequent paragraphs.
○ Use no quotation marks around the quotation.
○ Follow the rules for spacing in Section 8.10.

For quotations that are *between five and seven lines in length,*

○ Block only the quotations you want to emphasize.

8.37   Omissions, Changes, and Emphasis.   For all quotations,

○ Use an ellipsis, three periods with a space at the beginning and a space after each, if you omit words from within a quotation. See Section 5.8 for an example.

○ *Do not use an ellipsis* if you omit the beginning of a sentence or paragraph at the beginning of a quotation, or the end of a sentence or paragraph at the end. Simply punctuate as your text requires.

○ Place any needed punctuation before the ellipsis. For example, if you omit the last words in a sentence, place the period after the last word before the ellipsis. Leave one space, then type three periods with one space after each. See Section 5.8 for an example.

○ *Use brackets* to show any changes you make in the wording of a quotation, or any words that you add. See Sections 5.8 and 5.9 for examples.

○ Underline and explain the source of *emphasis in a quotation.* Underlining tells a printer to set the underlined words in italics. Following the end of the quotation state, in parentheses: (emphasis added) or (emphasis in original) or (Smith's italics). Or, make the same statement in a footnote without parentheses. Use the same kind of designation throughout the manuscript. For an example, see Section 3.24.

○ For instructions on documentation, see Sections 8.45, 8.48, and 8.49.

INSTRUCTIONS FOR PREPARING EQUATIONS

8.38   Aspects of Style That Vary.   Always check:

○ Whether equations are numbered. In general, if you have more than one equation, number them.

○ If numbered, whether in parentheses or brackets, and whether the number is placed flush with the left margin or the right. Flush right is more common.

○ If numbered, whether in sequential arabic numerals or by section. For example, 1, 2, 3, 4, or 2.1, 2.2, 2.3, 3.1. ASA style uses sequential numbers. *JASA* style requires numbering by sections.

8.39   Reference to Numbered Equations

○ In text, refer to the equations by number.

8.40   Requirements for Typing Equations.   In general,

○ Begin each equation at least seven spaces from the left margin.
○ Follow Sections 8.10 and 8.11 for instructions on spacing and use of symbols.
○ Place identifying numbers within parentheses or brackets. Type flush with the margin. For example:

$$[1]$$
$$[2.2]$$
$$(4.1)$$

○ Choose mathematical notations that will not complicate typesetting. For example, bars, tildes, and carets may have to be handset. In these examples, the right-hand expressions are easier than the left-hand ones to set in type.

Avoid These Expressions	*Use These Expressions*
$e \; \dfrac{-y^2 + z^2}{b^2}$	$\exp \left[-(y^2 + z^2)/b^2 \right]$
$\dfrac{\cos \dfrac{1}{y}}{\sqrt{b + \dfrac{c}{y}}}$	$\dfrac{\cos (1/y)}{(b + c/y)^{1/2}}$

INSTRUCTIONS FOR DOCUMENTATION

Description and General Instructions

8.41 Close documentation characterizes scientific writing. Sections 3.23 to 3.35 tell what to document and how to collect and organize information needed for documentation.

☐ As Table 8.1 shows, method of documentation is a particularly visible and important aspect of editorial style.

For example, if you are submitting an article to a journal that uses superscript numbers and footnotes for documentation, do not use a name (date) system simply because it is more convenient for you. Doing so suggests that you cared too little to check style, or that your article has already been submitted to, and rejected by, a journal that uses a name (date) system. Both may be true, but why advertise the situation? For all styles,

○ Check rules for citing unpublished documents. Some journals forbid such citations.
○ In the absence of other instructions, use *forthcoming* in place of a date for books that have been accepted but not published. Use *in press* for articles that have been accepted but not published. Use *unpublished* in place of a date for unpublished manuscripts, even if they have been submitted to a publisher for evaluation. If a multivolume work has not been completed, give the date of the first volume, followed by a dash.

Name (Date) Documentation

8.42 Description. Some styles—for example APA, ASA, MSN, SA, Sage—require authors to document facts and ideas by showing either a name or a name and a date in the text and giving a list of references at the end of the document. For example, see documentation in Chapters 1 to 7 and 9 to 16 of this book. When using this method for documentation,

○ Use no numbered notes solely for documentation. Notes with documentation must also include a substantive observation. For example, see note 1 of Chapter 7 in this book.

8.43 Aspects of Style That Vary. Name (date) styles have few practices in common. Before beginning to type, check the items listed below. For examples, see Table 8.2. The roman numerals identify the boxes in the table. Check:

○ Use of name alone when list of references shows only one document by an author. Examples in boxes I and II of Table 8.2.

○ Use of only name and a lowercase letter when list of references shows more than one document by an author. Examples in boxes VII and VIII.

○ Use of initial with last name when reference list contains two or more authors with the same last name. Examples in boxes I and II of Table 8.2.

○ Punctuation between name and date when both elements are within parentheses. For examples, see even-numbered boxes.

○ Punctuation between date and page number. Examples in boxes II to VII.

○ Use of *and* or *&* between names. Examples in boxes V to X, XIII, and XIV.

○ Use of brackets to isolate date when part or all of a reference is enclosed within parentheses along with a short comment. Examples in boxes XV and XVI.

○ Order of references when two or more references are enclosed within a pair of parentheses. Two orders are common. One is to list names alphabetically by last name of first author: (Alpha, 1963; Beta, 1956; Zeta, 1960). This order is the most useful one if you are listing several dates for one or more authors. The second order is by date, earliest first: (Beta, 1956; Zeta, 1960; Alpha, 1963). Journals' instructions often do not say which they prefer. In such cases, infer from the order of citations in several articles. If both orders are used in any given issue of a journal, use whichever suits you best.

○ Use of page numbers *only* for direct quotations (e.g., *Social Forces*; box IX).

8.44 When three or more scientists have coauthored an article, some styles require that you substitute "et al." for the names of all authors after the first. Look for the following variations on use of "et al." with the first author's name:

○ Always used. See boxes IX and X.
○ Used only for second and subsequent citations of a document. For first citation, use names of all authors. See boxes IX to XII.
○ Not used unless there are four or more coauthors. See boxes XI and XII.
○ Italicization of "et al.": *et al.* See boxes IX and X.

Regardless of style requirements,

○ Do not use "et al." if the resulting citation would be identical to citation of another document. For example, Adams, Berk, and Conley (1973) and Adams, Berk, and Berkowitz (1973) would both be abbreviated to Adams et al. (1973).

8.45 General Typing Requirements.

○ Punctuate citations within the sentences to which they are attached. For example:

That finding is clear (Jones 1974).   [1]

"That finding is clear" (Jones, 1974).   [2]

NOT

That finding is clear. (Jones 1974)   [3]

"That finding is clear." (Jones, 1974)   [4]

○ Use lowercase letters attached to the date to distinguish two or more documents with the same author(s) and dates. See

Table 8.2 Forms and Examples of Name (Date) Documentation

Condition	Name Outside Parentheses		Name and Date Inside Parentheses	
	Form	Style	Form	Style
1 author	I Jones (1974) J. Cole (1971)[a] Jones	 Most Rare; Social Forces	II (Jones, 1975) (J. Cole, 1975) (Jones 1975) (J. Cole 1975) (Jones)	 APA, ASA, SA, Sage MSN Rare; Social Forces
1 author, with page number	III Jones (1975:3) Jones (1975, p.3) Jones (3)	 APA, ASA, SA, Sage MSN Rare; Social Forces	IV (Jones, 1975:3) (Jones 1975:3) (Jones 1975, p.3)	 APA, ASA, SA, Sage —[b] MSN
2 authors	V A and B (1975) A and B (1975, p.3) A & B (1975:3)	 APA, ASA, Sage MSN SA	VI (A and B, 1975:3) (A and B 1975, p. 3) (A & B, 1975:3)	 ASA, Sage MSN APA, SA
2 or more documents: same author, same date	VII A (1975a, 1975b) A and B (1975a, 1975b) A (1975a:3) A (1975a, p.3) A & B (1975a, 1975b) A (a,b)	 Most APA, ASA, MSN, Sage APA, ASA, SA, Sage MSN SA Rare; Social Forces	VIII (A, 1975a, 1975b) (A 1975a, 1975b) (A and B, 1975a, 1975b) (A and B 1975a, 1975b) (A & B, 1975a, 1975b) (A:a,b)	 APA, ASA, SA, Sage MSN ASA, Sage MSN APA, SA Rare; Social Forces

	(left column)	(right column)
3 authors	**IX** A et al. (1975, 1976)[c] APA: Second and subsequent documents; ASA, Sage: always A et al. (1975)[c] A, B, and C (1975) A et al. (79) SA APA, first citation; MSN always Rare; *Social Forces*	**X** (A et al., 1975, 1976)[c] APA: second and subsequent; ASA, Sage: always (A et al., 1975)[c] (A, B, and C 1975) (A, B, & C, 1975) SA MSN APA: 1st citation
4 or more authors	**XI** Same as IX A, B, C, and D (1975) A et al. (1975)[c] APA, ASA, SA, Sage MSN: 1st citation MSN: second and subsequent	**XII** Same as X (A, B, C, and D 1975) (A et al. 1975)[c] APA, ASA, SA, Sage MSN: 1st citation MSN: second and subsequent
2 documents	**XIII** A (1975) and B (1975) A and B (1975) and C and D (1975) A & B (1975) and C & D (1975) A and B Most APA, ASA, MSN, Sage SA Rare; *Social Forces*	**XIV** (A, 1975; B, 1975) (A, 1975; B 1975, 1976) (A and B, 1975; C and D, 1975, 1976) (A & B, 1975; C & D, 1975) (A and B 1975; C and D 1975) (A:a,b; B:a,b) APA, ASA, SA, Sage MSN ASA, Sage APA, SA MSN Rare; *Social Forces*
Parenthetical comment added to documentation	**XV** A (1975; a useful . . .) A ((1975); a useful . . .) APA, ASA, SA, Sage Rare; *American Journal of Sociology*	**XVI** (A, 1975; a useful . . .) (A, 1975; a useful . . .) (A (1975); a useful . . .) APA, ASA, SA, Sage MSN Rare; *American Journal of Sociology*

Note. Style abbreviations are in Table 8.1. From box V on, authors' names are designated by letters to minimize crowding between columns. The journals named use the rare styles.
[a]See third instruction, Section 8.43.
[b]This form is almost never used.
[c]See Section 8.44.

boxes VII to VIII. In general, assign letters in the order in which you cite the documents. For example, 1975a is the first document you cite, 1975b the second, and 1975c the third.

EXCEPTION. A few journals prefer letters assigned in alphabetical order as established by the titles of documents cited. This order disregards order of citation.

○ Within parentheses, use a comma to separate dates (or, for *Social Forces*, lowercase letters) for two or more documents by the same author. See boxes VII to X.

○ Within parentheses, use a semicolon to separate the works of one author from the works of another. See box XIV.

[#] Documentation

8.46 Description and General Instructions. Some styles—for example *JASA*—require authors to show documentation by inserting a bracketed or parenthesized number in the text.

○ Always check whether brackets or parentheses are required. Brackets are more common. A very few journals—for example, *American Journal of Orthopsychiatry*—use neither. Instead, authors place the numbers as superscripts on lines of type. The numbers look just like the superscript number 7 at the beginning of section 8.49. If you refer to more than one document, use a separate number for each.

○ Always check whether a name may be used with the number, either inside or outside the brackets or parentheses. If you use the author's name with superscripted numbers, write the text to include the name.

Section 8.48 shows examples.

8.47 Assignment of Numbers. Unlike documentation with superscript numbers and notes (see Sections 8.49 to 8.51), the number is *not* established by the order in which the citations occur. To establish a number for each document,

○ Complete a draft of the manuscript.
○ Every time you cite a document, leave two to seven bracketed or parenthesized spaces in your line of typing (to insert a number, and possibly a page number, later). For journals using superscripts, simply leave space for the numbers. If you use page numbers, place them in the text, in parentheses.
○ Insert penciled, sequential arabic numerals, beginning with *1*. Take the reference card from your reference file (described in Section 3.34) and pencil the same arabic numeral at the top. When you are through, some cards may have more than one numeral.
○ Reorder the cards alphabetically.
○ Number and type in alphabetical order. Use Figure 8.11 as a guide.
○ Enter the alphabetical-order numbers in the spaces you left in the text. The penciled, sequential numbers will allow you to match cards and spaces quickly.
○ Erase penciled numbers and return cards to file.

8.48 Requirements for Typing. In general,

○ Check punctuation. Citations may be punctuated either within or outside the sentences involved. Sentences [20], [23], and [25] below show documentation *outside* punctuation.
○ Type citations as in the following examples. In each group I show bracketed citations first; parenthesized, second; superscripted, third.

> *One citation to document a statement:*
>
> | Jones [2] found it. | [1] |
> | See Jones [2, p. 5]. | [2] |
> | We know that (2). | [3] |
> | We know that (2, p. 5). | [4] |

We know that.[2]	[5]
We[2] (p. 5) know that.	[6]

For two documents:

Jones [2] and Smith [4] found it.	[7]
We know it [2,4].	[8]
We know it [2 and 4].	[9]
We know it [2, p. 5; 4, p. 8].	[10]
Jones (2) and Smith (4) found it.	[11]
We know it (2, 4).	[12]
We know it (2 and 4).	[13]
We know it (2, p. 5; 4, p. 8).	[14]
Jones[2] and Smith[4] found it.	[15]
Jones[2] (p. 5) and Smith[4] (p. 8) found it.	[16]
We[2,4] (p. 5; p. 8) know it.	[17]

For documents with three or more authors:

Jones et al. [3, p. 4] found it.	[18]
We know it [3, p. 4].	[19]
"We know it." [3, p. 4]	[20]
Jones et al. (3, p. 4) found it.	[21]
We know it (3, p. 4).	[22]
We know it. (3, p. 4)	[23]
Jones et al.[3] found it.	[24]
"We know it."[3] (p. 4)	[25]

EXCEPTION.   A few styles require that et al. be underlined: *et al.*

Superscript Numbers and Footnotes

8.49 Description. MLA, MSH, Turabian, and many specialized styles of documentation—for example, of congressional and other legal documents—use superscript numbers and footnotes to show documentation.[7] In text, the citation looks exactly like the 7 at the end of the previous sentence.

EXCEPTION. A few styles require that the number in text *not* be superscripted but instead be typed on a line with text, inside brackets or parentheses. In such cases, place the brackets or parentheses with number *outside* the period at the end of a sentence.

The note itself resembles the notes to this chapter. Some journals print notes at the foot of the pages on which they occur. Others collect and print them at the end of the article.

8.50 Requirements for Typing. In general,

○ Type the notes on a separate page, entitled "Notes." Follow the requirements for spacing in Section 8.10.

  EXCEPTION. Some styles require a triple space between one note and the next.

○ Type author's name in normal order. First and last names and middle initial are usually preferred. For example, see note 7.
○ Integrate, by order of occurrence, all notes—whether for documentation, observation (Sections 8.53 and 8.54), or acknowledgment (8.56 to 8.59). Assign sequential arabic numerals beginning with 1.
○ NEVER type any note at the foot of the page on which the superscript number occurs unless the journal's editor explicitly tells you to do so.
○ Avoid Latin terms such as *op. cit., loc. cit., ibid.* Instead, use author's last name and a short title. For example, see note 5 of this chapter. With a short title, the reader can locate the full reference more quickly than if he or she has only the Latin term.

8.51 Aspects of style that vary.   Always check:

○ Order of elements required for documentation (listed in Sections 3.28 to 3.33).
○ Omission of elements.
○ Punctuation between elements.
○ Abbreviation of journal names, usually according to a specific list.
○ Capitalization of titles.

For details and examples, see Sections 8.77 and 8.81.

Unusual Systems of Documentation

8.52   For help on unusual systems of documentation, see Section 8.80.

INSTRUCTIONS FOR PREPARING SUBSTANTIVE NOTES

8.53 Description.   Substantive notes are observations other than documentation that may be important to some readers but would interrupt the flow if incorporated into the text. For example, see note 2 of this chapter. Sometimes substantive notes are combined with documentation. For example, see note 9 of this chapter.

○ Use as few substantive notes as possible, particularly with name (date) and [#] styles of documentation.

Notes interrupt the reader and increase the difficulty of typesetting.

8.54 General Typing Requirements.   *For styles that use superscript numbers and footnotes* for documentation:

○ Use the notes to this chapter as examples.
○ Follow the instructions in Sections 8.50 to 8.51.

8.55 *For styles that use name (date) or [#] for documentation:*

○ Collect all notes at the end of the article, numbered in sequence as they occur. Reference notes (see Section 8.72 to 8.73) and acknowledgments (8.56 to 8.59) are sometimes included.

○ Type the notes as a unit, beginning on a separate page entitled "Notes." Follow the instructions for spacing in Section 8.10.

   EXCEPTION.   Some styles require a triple space between the end of one note and the beginning of the next.

○ Never type a note at the bottom of a page of text unless the journal's editor explicitly tells you to do so.

○ For notes that include documentation, follow the example in note 1, Chapter 7. Modify the form of the citation if necessary, following the instructions in either Sections 8.43 to 8.45 or 8.48.

○ In text, insert a superscript number at the point where you want to make the note. If possible, place the numbers at the end of a sentence. For example, see placement of superscript 7, Section 8.49.

INSTRUCTIONS FOR PREPARING ACKNOWLEDGMENTS

8.56   Uses for Acknowledgment Notes.   Formal acknowledgment is a courtesy.

○ Use an acknowledgment note to thank fund-granting agencies, research assistants, collegial readers of drafts, editorial consultants, and other persons and institutions who have helped you with an article. Figure 8.6, a fictitious note, lists some of these parties.

○ Also use the acknowledgment note to state whether your article is based on a dissertation, or has been previously presented at a meeting of a professional association.

○ Follow the requirements for spacing in Section 8.10.

The Title of the Paper

Acknowledgments

I wish to acknowledge assistance from NSF Grant GS-99999 and from State University's Institute of Social Research. I want to thank the students, teachers, and administrators at Elementary School for their cooperation, and S. Q. Student for help with programming. The criticisms of John Smith, A. Good Researcher, and The Journal's referees improved the paper. A. N. Editor provided editorial help. An earlier version of this article was presented at the meeting of The Scientific Society, New York (August 1974). This article is based on research reported in a dissertation submitted to University of Anywhere in partial fulfillment of requirements for the Ph.D. degree. I wish to thank my Chairman, Professor William Smith James, for his help. The author is professor of psychology at Great State University. Requests for reprints should be sent to Professor I. M. Author, Department of Psychology, William Smith Hall, Great State University, City, State, Zip Code.

Figure 8.6 A sample acknowledgment note.

8.57 Aspects of Style That Vary. Always check:

○ *Mailing address.* Some styles, such as APA, require that you include your mailing address.
○ *Present position and place of employment.* Some styles, such as *JASA*, require that you state your present position and place of employment.
○ *Placement.* Common locations for the acknowledgment note are:
On the cover sheet, as in Figure 8.1.
On a separate page, following the cover sheet.
On a separate page, immediately following text.
On the "Notes" page, four lines below the heading.
○ *Form of name.* If possible, give all names in the same way. For example, always give last name and two initials. Often, though, the persons named prefer different forms. In such cases, use the form that each person prefers.
○ *Use of parentheses around dates.*

8.58 Check for preferred typing form. The following forms are common.

○ Exactly like a paragraph of text.
○ Exactly like an abstract, as in Figure 8.6.
○ As a numbered footnote—usually the first one.
○ As a note preceded by an asterisk, as in ASA style.
○ As two paragraphs rather than one. Most commonly, the second paragraph includes author's current position, place of employment, and address.

8.59 In the absence of instructions,

○ Follow the illustration in Figure 8.6.
○ Place the page in the manuscript following the title page and preceding the text. If there is no separate title page, place the acknowledgment page immediately after the text.

INSTRUCTIONS FOR PREPARING TABLES

8.60   Chapter 3 describes use of tables (Section 3.4), construction of tables (3.5 to 3.7), and definitions of parts in a table (3.8 to 3.19). In general, a single-spaced table in elite type on paper that is $8\frac{1}{2} \times 11$ inches wide, with 1-inch margins on all sides, will just about fill a printed page that measures 6×9 inches. Tables longer than one page, such as Table 7.1 in this book, can be extended onto another page. Tables that are too wide for one page can sometimes be set vertically on two pages, but that is the physical limit for typeset tables.[8]

8.61   General Instructions.

○ Exclude tables that show only raw data or analyses of variance, or that have fewer than eight entries (see Sections 3.4 and 3.5).

○ Eliminate peripherally related or extremely detailed data.[9]

○ In the text, refer to each table. Delete any that you do not mention.

○ Refer to tables by their numbers. Do not refer to them as "above" or "below," because compositors cannot always position them exactly as you would like.

EXCEPTION.   Occasionally you may refer to a table that is much farther back, or much farther forward, in your article. In such cases, "above" or "below" may help your reader. For example, in this chapter I sometimes refer to Table 7.1 "above" because it is in a previous chapter.

8.62   General Typing Requirements.

○ Place each table on a separate piece of paper. Never type tables on the same pages with text unless the journal editor explicitly tells you to do so.

○ Type an indicator into the text to show where the table or figure belongs. Double-space above and below the indicator. For example:

> [Table 1 about here]
> (Table 1 about here)

> ---
> Table 1 about here
> ---

You may type the indicator either between paragraphs or between lines of a paragraph.

○ Begin typing number and title 1½ inches from the top of the page.

○ Number main-text tables sequentially, in order of appearance, with arabic numerals.

○ Check need for page number as well as table number.

○ Double-space between *all lines*.

○ Leave at least three spaces between columns.

○ In text refer to tables by number, not by title. For example:

In Table 3 . . .	The data show (Table 3) . . .
(APA, ASA)	
In table 3 . . .	The data show (table 3) . . .
(MSH, MSN)	

Table Number and Title

8.63   Look for variation in treatment of table number and title. See Figure 8.7 for examples.

○ *Numbering of appendix tables.* Two systems are common: sequential capital letters beginning with *A*, and sequential numbers followed by a prime sign. For example:

Table A, Table B
Table 1', Table 2'

○ *Treatment of number.* Does it stand by itself as in *JASA* style, or is it preceded by "Table," as in Table 8.1? If the latter, is "Table" completely capitalized as in MSN and MSH? Is the number an arabic or a roman numeral? Arabic is more common. Is the number centered from left to right on the page,

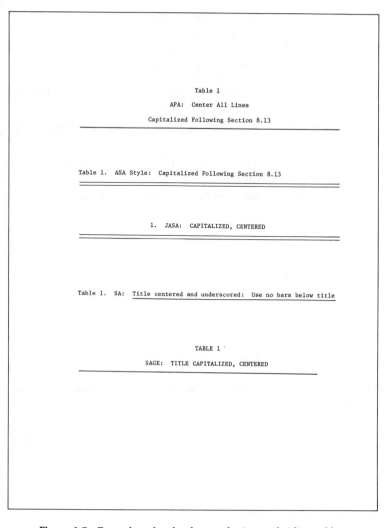

Figure 8.7 Examples of styles for numbering and titling tables.

as in Table 8.1, or is it typed flush with the left margin, as ASA style requires?

○ *Placement of title.* Is each line of the title centered from left to right beneath the number, as in Table 8.1? Is it typed on a line with the number, beginning at the left margin, as ASA style requires?

○ *Capitalization of words in title.* Is each word completely capitalized, as Sage style requires, or are words capitalized following Section 8.13, as ASA style requires? Or, as SA requires, only the initial word and any word immediately following a colon?

○ *Underline.* Is the title underlined, as SA style requires?

○ Does a line (rule) or two lines separate the number and the title from the body? ASA style requires double top rules, close together, as in Tables 8.1 and 8.2; Sage requires one, as in Table 1.1; SA, none.

Body of a Table

8.64 Vertical and Horizontal Lines.

○ Check requirements for use. For example, most styles *prohibit vertical lines.* Most permit horizontal lines but request that they be *kept to a minimum.* SA requests no lines.

○ Check requirements for drawing lines. For example, most journals accept lines drawn in black ink or typed with a black ribbon, but APA journals prefer that lines be drawn in pencil so they can be changed easily.

○ When in doubt, *use no vertical lines.* Use horizontal lines only beneath column heads and beneath the body. Draw lines using a pencil and a ruler. The journal's editor will add more lines if they are necessary. Numbers neatly nested in boxes may be aesthetically appealing to some authors, but they provide many journal editors with their most persistent nightmares.

The rules in tables in this chapter are somewhat more typical of tables in journals. The rules in tables in the remaining chapters are somewhat more typical of tables in books.

8.65   Row Stubs and Column Headings.

○ Check capitalization. In general, only the first letter of the first word in each heading is capitalized, but some styles—such as MSH and MSN—follow the rule in Section 8.13, particularly for column headings.

○ Check treatment of second and subsequent lines. They may be either centered beneath the first line, begun directly beneath the first letter of the first line, or directly under the second letter of the first line.

○ In the absence of instructions, capitalize only the first letter of the first word in each row stub. Follow Section 8.13 for capitalizing column headings and boxheads. For row stubs, indent second lines one space from the left margin. For column headings, center second and subsequent lines below the first. For example, see treatment of column heads and row stubs in Table 8.2.

Notes to a Table

8.66   Look for variation in treatment of notes.

○ Check division between body and notes. Most styles require a line between these two elements.

○ Check the order for source, general, and specific notes. In the absence of instructions, follow the model in Figure 3.1.

○ Check capitalization and underlining of "Source" and "Note." When in doubt, follow the pattern in Figure 3.1.

○ Check the designation of specific notes. In general, follow the pattern in Figure 3.1. However, some styles require that you designate notes to tables with lowercase letters or with a system of asterisks, daggers, double daggers, and so forth (see note 1, Chapter 3).

○ Check indentation. In general, begin typing notes flush with the left margin, as in Figure 3.1. However, some journals require that you indent the first line. In such cases, check the number of spaces required for the indentation.

○ Check superscription. In general, type "Source" and "Note" on a line with what follows. Superscript the specific-note designations one-half space.

Photoreproduction of Tables

8.67 To reduce printing costs, many journals require authors to supply tables and illustrations that are "camera-ready"—properly prepared for photoreproduction. Rules for preparation are often quite rigid.

8.68 The general rules are:

○ Prepare clean, neat tables.
○ Use an electric typewriter with clean typefaces. If possible, use a carbon ribbon.
○ For every table use the size of type that the journal requires. *JASA* style requires elite type. Others may require pica.
○ Check requirements for widths of tables. That is, how many elite (or pica) spaces wide the tables may be.
○ For each table, count the number of left-to-right spaces needed. Determine this figure by counting the number of letters and spaces required by the headings of each column (or by the widest entry, if one or more entries is wider than the heading), plus at least 2 spaces between each column.
○ Then space the table to fit the prescribed width. For example, if a table requires a minimum of 55 spaces and the style requires 38- or 80-space tables, then type the table exactly 80 spaces wide—no more, no less.

INSTRUCTIONS FOR PREPARING ILLUSTRATIONS

8.69 Sections 3.20 to 3.21 describe the general purpose and preparation of illustrations, and give specific instructions for graphs.

8.70 General Instructions. For all illustrations,

○ Place each on a separate piece of white drawing paper that measures 8½ × 11 inches.

EXCEPTION.   Some styles require larger paper.

○ Use black india ink.

○ Do not type letters; do not write freehand letters unless you are a professional artist. Use a lettering stencil (e.g., Leroy or Wrico) or a letter-transfer device, such as Artype, Instantype, or Chartpak.

○ Minimize the number of lines.

○ Use circles, triangles, and squares, either filled or unfilled, to indicate points on curves or lines and locations of people, houses, and so forth.

○ Use a *legend* (the approximate equivalent of notes to a table) to explain all lines and symbols. For examples of legends, see Figures 8.1, 8.2, 8.4, and 8.5.

○ With particularly difficult illustrations, seek help from a draftsman or a specialist in audiovisual aids.

○ Give each illustration a separate *caption*—number and title. For examples, see Figures 8.1 to 8.14.

○ Number illustrations individually, in sequential arabic numerals, from the first to the last.

EXCEPTION.   Some styles require that you number appendix illustrations with either letters or numbers and prime signs. For example:

Figure A, Figure B, Fig. A, Fig. B.
Figure 1′, Figure 2′, Fig. 1′, Fig. 2′.

○ Type captions and legends for all illustrations on a separate page. For example:

Fig. 1. The caption   (MSH, MSN)
Fig. 2. The caption   (MSH, MSN)

Figure 1. The caption.   (APA, ASA)
Figure 2. The caption.   (APA, ASA)

EXCEPTION.   Some styles require *each* caption, or caption and legend, either on the illustration itself or on a separate page.

○ At the top of each illustration, lightly write, in pencil, "top."
○ On the reverse side write lightly, in pencil, your name, the number, and a word or two from the manuscript's title to identify the illustration.
○ Refer to each illustration in text and provide a location note. Double-space above and below the indicator. For example:

(Figure 1 about here)

Figure 1 about here

○ In text refer to illustrations by number, not by title. For example:

In Figure 3 . . .	The trends (see Figure 3) . . .
(APA, ASA)	
In figure 3 . . .	The trends (see figure 3) . . .
(MSH, MSN)	

8.71 Aspects of Style That Vary.   Always check:

○ *Style for preparing number and title.* In particular, check capitalization and underlining. Possible variations are the same as for numbers and titles of tables (described in Section 8.63).
○ *Style and placement of legend.* Common placements: either immediately following the caption or in open space in the body of the illustration.
○ *Need for a page number* in addition to figure number.
○ *Instructions for preparing and mailing photographs.* Often you will have to write the editor for this information.[10]

INSTRUCTIONS FOR PREPARING REFERENCE NOTES

8.72 Uses for Reference Notes.   Some styles—for example APA—require that authors use reference notes when they cite

letters, papers presented at meetings, and other materials that
are not widely and easily available to readers of an article.

8.73   General Typing Instructions.

○ Follow the requirements for spacing given in Section 8.10.
○ Order the elements, punctuate, and capitalize exactly as you
  do the documents in your list of references, footnotes, or
  bibliography.
○ For an example of reference notes in APA style, see Figure
  8.8.
○ Insert and number the reference-note page immediately after
  the last page of text.
○ Refer to reference notes in text by author's last name and
  note number. For example,

  Smith (Note 3)
  Snow (Note 4)

refer to the third and fourth notes in Figure 8.8.

INSTRUCTIONS FOR PREPARING IDENTIFYING REFERENCES

8.74   Uses for Identifying References.   If you are submitting
your article to a journal that uses blind-review procedures
(described in Section 10.14),

○ Remove from your list of references all items that might
  identify you as the author of the article being reviewed.

Doing so will speed the process of evaluation. Examples of
identifying documents are:

○ Your doctoral dissertation, if its title closely resembles the
  title of your article or if you cite it as the source of more
  detailed information on background, method, or a specific
  finding.

Reference Notes

1. Lastname, A. B. Unavailable manuscript. Manuscript submitted for publication, 1975.

2. Lee, C. D. Personal letter. 1974.

3. Smith, A. F. Unpublished results. Mimeo, State University, Department of Sociology. Used with the author's permission. 1975.

4. Snow, O. P. Paper given at meeting. Paper presented at the meeting of the American Association of Paper Givers, City, Month 1974.

Figure 8.8 Example: reference notes in APA style.

○ Unpublished articles and project reports.
○ Letters.
○ Citations like: "The writer has already shown (Smith, 1975) . . . ."

8.75   General Instructions.

○ Type such notes on a separate page, entitled "Identifying References."
○ Number them sequentially in alphabetic order.
○ Follow the requirements for spacing in Section 8.10.
○ Order the elements, punctuate, and capitalize exactly as you do the documents in your list of references.
○ In text, cite only the note number. For example:

They found it (identifying note 1).

○ Use no name.
○ Insert the page immediately after the cover sheet.

INSTRUCTIONS FOR LISTING DOCUMENTS

8.76   General Instructions. List bibliographic data on documents in a separate section of the manuscript. Follow the instructions for spacing in Section 8.10.

EXCEPTION. Some styles require a triple space between documents. Check Sections 3.27 to 3.33 for lists of data required for each kind of document. Presentation of this information— order of facts, capitalization, italicization, punctuation, and so forth—is a major characteristic that distinguishes one editorial style from another.

8.77 For styles that use *superscript numbers and notes,* such as MSH and MLA, the notes usually provide all the data needed. The general characteristics of documentation in these styles are:

☐ Numbers in sequence, according to position in manuscript.

☐ Name in normal order.

☐ Article titles placed within quotation marks, and book titles italicized. Capitalization follows Section 8.13.

☐ Date near the end of each reference.

☐ Commas rather than periods between the elements in the reference.

☐ Page numbers preceded by "p." or "pp."

8.78 A few journals that use notes for documentation also require a bibliography—a list of documents only. Most do not because printing is costly, and the necessary information is in the notes. For instructions, consult the journal and Sections 3.36 and 12.33.

8.79 For styles that use *name (date) and [#] documentation,* the list of references includes only documents cited. The bibliography of this book lists documents in MSN style (except for treatment of continued numbers). The basic characteristics of MSN style are:

☐ Names reversed, last name and initials only, followed by period.

☐ Order alphabetical, by author's last name.

☐ Date follows name, followed by period.

☐ Article and chapter titles have no quotation marks; capitalization only of first word and first word after a colon.

☐ Second and subsequent lines indented three spaces.

☐ Page numbers:[11] if the first number is less than 100, or is 100 or a multiple of 100, use all digits. For example:

4–11; 83–84; 100–106; 700–716

If the first number is more than 100 (in multiples of 100) but less than 110, use only the changed part for the second digit. For example:

208–9; 306–7

If the first number (in multiples of 100) is more than 109, use the last two or three digits as needed. For example:

264–66; 206–365; 1165–281

For lists of documents in other styles and distinguishing characteristics, see Figures 8.9 to 8.13. For all name (date) and [#] styles,

○ List every document cited. Conversely, cite every document listed. To be sure you have done so, check citations in the finished manuscript with documents in the list.
○ Order documents alphabetically, by last name of author. Follow instructions in Section 3.34.
○ If you have unpublished documents, follow the instructions in Section 8.41.
○ In name (date) citation, if you have two or more documents for the same author and date (or *in press* or *forthcoming* or *unpublished*), assign lowercase letters to the date. Instructions are in Section 8.45.

8.80   For details on less common styles of documentation, for example of congressional and other legal documents,

○ Consult the journal's instructions. Often it will suggest a specific style sheet.
○ Examine the form of citations in several articles in the most recent issue of the journal.
○ Consult *A Manual of Style*, Chapters 15 and 17.

8.81   Aspects of Style That Vary.   For each document in all three categories of documentation, check the following items for possible variation:

○ *Numbering:* required (*JASA*) or not; with brackets (*JASA*) or not.
○ *Name:* completely capitalized (as in Sage style) or initial capital letters only (as in ASA); initials plus last name only

References

Author, S. J. A chapter in a book. In C. P. Excellence (Ed.), A book
    of readings. City: Publisher, 1974.

Authoress, A. T. A monograph. City: Publisher, 1974. (a)

Authoress, A. T. A second monograph. City: Publisher, 1974. (b)

Researcher, A. C., Jones, C. D., & Smith, A. B. Report. (USPHS Tech.
    Rep. No. 175) City: Agency, 1974.

Student, A. G. A dissertation. Unpublished doctoral dissertation,
    University Name, 1974.

Student, A. G. Dissertation (Doctoral dissertation, University Name,
    1977). Dissertation Abstracts International, 1977, 38, 4082A-4083A.
    (University Microfilms No. 59-13, 281).

Student, S. K., & Coauthor, S. P. An article title. A Journal, 1974,
    32 (Month or Number, within parentheses, only if paging is by issue,
    not by volume), 341-349.

DISTINGUISHING CHARACTERISTICS

Names: reverse order, initials only; & between names of
        coauthors.

Dates: at end of reference; ordered from earliest first to latest.

Article and chapter titles: no quotation marks, capital letters
        only on first word and first word after colon.

Book titles: underscore; capitalize like article titles.

Page numbers: complete.

Second and subsequent lines: indented three spaces.

Figure 8.9   Examples and characteristics of APA-style references.

```
                              References

Author, A. Tenured, C. D. Jones and A. B. Smith

    1974a    A Monograph.  City [well known]:  Publisher.

    1974b    Report on Research.  City:  Sponsoring Agency.

Authoress, A. B. and Samuel P. Coauthor

    1974     "A chapter in a book."  Pp. 201-21 in Collector P.

             Excellence (ed.), A Book of Readings.  City [not well known],

             State [abbreviated]:  Publisher.

Student, Susie K.

    1974     A Doctoral Dissertation.  Unpublished doctoral dissertation,

             University of Anywhere.

Student, Susie K. and Samuel P. Coauthor

    1974     "An article:  an example."  A Journal 32 (Month or Number if

             paging is by issue and not by volume):341-9.

    1975     "A paper."  Paper presented at A Conference (Month year).
```

DISTINGUISHING CHARACTERISTICS

Names: reverse order on first name only; not repeated on second and subsequent references.

Dates: double-spaced beneath name, on line with titles; ordered from earliest first to latest.

Article and chapter titles: use quotation marks; capitalize only first letter of first word and proper nouns.

Page numbers: for chapters, immediately after title, preceded by "Pp."; for articles, at end, normally preceded by colon and no spaces; as brief as possible.

Figure 8.10   Examples and characteristics of ASA-style references.

References

[1] Author, G. Tenured, A Monograph, City: Publisher, 1974.

[2] Authoress, A. T., A Book, Revised ed., City: Publisher, 1976.

[3] Researcher, A. Contract, "A Report," City: Agency, 1974.

[4] Researcher, Andrew C., "A Report," Series No. 88, Institute for the Study of Social Change, University of Anywhere, 1974 (mimeographed).

[5] Student, A. Graduate, "Any Dissertation," Unpublished Ph.D. dissertation, Graduate School of Business [Arts and Sciences, etc.], University of Anywhere, Month 1974.

[6] Student, A. Graduate, and Samuel P. Coauthor, "A Chapter," in C. P. Excellence, ed., A Book, City: Publisher, 1974, 341-9.

[7] Student, Susie K., et al., "An Article Title: An Example," A Journal, 32 (Month 1974), 341-9.

DISTINGUISHING CHARACTERISTICS

Numbers: assigned, within brackets, after alphabetization.

Names: reverse order on first name only; *et al.* for second and subsequent authors when three or more persons are coauthors; followed by comma.

Publishers' names: in full, not in short form, for example John Wiley and Sons, not Wiley.

Page numbers: all at end, as brief as possible.

Dates: placed near end.

Figure 8.11   Examples and characteristics of *JASA*-style references [#].

References

Author, A. T. (1974). <u>A Monograph.</u> City: Publisher.

Authoress, A. T. (1975). <u>A Book.</u> City: Publisher.

Researcher, A. C. (1974a). <u>A Report of Completed Research</u>. City: Agency That Put Out Report.

Researcher, A. C. (1974b). An article. <u>A Journal</u> 32, 270–274.

Student, A. C. & Coauthor, S. P. (1974). A chapter in a book. In C. P. Excellence (ed.), <u>A Book of Readings.</u> City: Publisher.

Student, S. Q. (1974). <u>A Doctoral Dissertation.</u> Ph.D. Dissertation. City: University of Anywhere.

Student, S. Q., Smith, A. B., & Jones, C. D. (1975). <u>A Book.</u> City: Publisher.

DISTINGUISHING CHARACTERISTICS

Names: all reversed, initials only, & in place of *and*.

Dates: immediately after name, same line, within parentheses, followed by period; ordered from earliest first to latest.

Article and chapter titles: no quotation marks; capitalize only first word and first after colon.

Book titles: underscore.

Journal names: abbreviate (see SA booklet); underscore.

Page numbers: complete.

Second and subsequent lines: indented two spaces.

Figure 8.12 Examples and characteristics of SA-style references.

References

AUTHOR, A. T. [ed.](1974) A Monograph. City: Publisher.

RESEARCHER, A. C. (1974) A Report on Research. City: Agency.

STUDENT, A. G. (1974) "A dissertation." Ph.D. dissertation. City:

   State University.

STUDENT, S. Q. and S. P. COAUTHOR (1974a) "A chapter," pp. 204-221 in

   C. P. Excellence (ed.) A Book of Readings. City: Publisher.

---(1974b) "An article in a journal." Amer. J. 32 (Month):341-349.

DISTINGUISHING CHARACTERISTICS

Names: reverse only first name, initials and last name only,
            capitalize completely; no period after a second name,
            or after [eds.] or (eds.); for second and subsequent
            documents by author, use dashes instead of name.

Dates: within parentheses, not followed by period; ordered
            from latest first to earliest.

Article, chapter, and dissertation titles: use quotation marks;
            capitalize only first word, first after colon, and proper nouns.

Page numbers: for chapters, follow "pp.," immediately after
            title; for articles, at end following colon and no space.

Journal names: in 1975, some journal names were abbreviated.

Figure 8.13   Examples and characteristics of Sage-style references. (This style closely resembles that used by Academic Press journals.)

(APA), two names plus an initial (ASA), or no pattern; normal order (MSH), or reversed order (last name first) for first author (ASA) or all authors (APA); & (APA) or *and* (ASA) between names of authors; use of *et al.* for second and subsequent authors (see Section 8.44); use of dashes or a short line to replace author's name for second and subsequent listings by the same author (Sage).

○ *Punctuation* between items. For example, author's name may be separated from the date or title by a comma (MSH), a period (MSN), a colon (some British styles), a semicolon (rare), or a space and an open parenthesis (SA).

○ *Date:* order—from earliest to latest (ASA, SA), or latest to earliest (Sage); placement either immediately after the name (ASA) or near the end of the reference (APA, MSH); location on the same line as the previous item (most common) or on a separate line from the previous item (ASA); surrounded by parentheses (SA, Sage); followed by punctuation (MSN uses a period, ASA and Sage use none).

○ *Titles of articles and chapters in books:* omitted or not; capitalization (contrast *JASA* and MSH with APA and ASA); enclosed within double or single quotation marks (ASA, but not APA); subsequent punctuation within quotation marks (most American styles) or outside (most British styles).

○ *Titles of books:* capitalization; underlined (as by APA) or not (ASA); followed with a period (ASA), comma, or space and open parenthesis (MSH).

○ *Editions:* 2d ed. (MSH, MSN) or 2nd ed. (APA).

○ *Ed. and eds.:* placed before or after the editor's name; placed within or outside parentheses or brackets.

○ *Journal titles:* capitalization; underlined (APA, but not ASA); abbreviation (SA, but not APA).

○ *For journals, information on volume, issue, and date:* all three required or some omitted, and under what circumstances; punctuation before and after each element; use of parentheses (normally, month or number or both, and sometimes year, are enclosed within parentheses).

○ *Page numbers for chapters in books:* required (ASA) or not (APA); if so, placed after title of chapter (ASA) or at end of reference (*JASA*); preceded by "pp." or "Pp." (ASA), or colon or comma (*JASA*).

○ *Page numbers for journal articles:* required (usually); preceded by "pp." or by comma or colon.

○ *For all page numbers:* expressed as briefly as possible, for example 341–9 (ASA) or not, for example 341–42 (MSN).

○ *For books, information on city, state, publisher:* all three required or some omitted; items separated by comma or colon (colon followed by two spaces is most common punctuation between city and publisher); enclosed by parentheses (MSH) or not (ASA); followed by a comma or period. In general, use brief form of publisher's name; for example: Wiley, not John Wiley and Sons.

○ *Second and subsequent lines:* indented (APA), blocked (ASA), or flush with left margin.

When instructions are not explicitly given,

○ Look through the journal for examples of the kind of document you are citing.

INSTRUCTIONS FOR PREPARING APPENDIXES

8.82   For instructions, see Section 3.22 and appendixes to articles in the journal to which you are submitting your manuscript.

INSTRUCTIONS FOR OBTAINING PERMISSIONS

8.83   If you quote more than 50 words from any one source, or use any photograph, table, or illustration that is either owned or copyrighted by someone else, read Sections 12.43–12.50.

INSTRUCTIONS FOR FINAL PREPARATION AND SUBMISSION

Proofreading and Correcting

8.84 Proofread carefully for typographical and factual errors. Follow the instructions in Section 11.32. Do not delegate this task to others. Be particularly careful to:

○ Look for common typographical errors, such as *filed* instead of *field*; *casual* instead of *causal*; *or* instead of *of*.
○ Check whether different language has been used to designate identical phenomena. See Sections 5.19 to 5.21 for help.
○ Check the numbers in tables against their original sources.
○ Check page references and bibliographic data against their original sources, or against individual index cards taken from the original sources. See Sections 3.27 through 3.34 for help.
○ Check quotations against their original sources, or against an index card copied from the source.
○ Insert figures that must be hand lettered, for example $<$ or $>$.

Most manuscripts are retyped several times, and errors creep in easily. When you make corrections,

○ Do not handwrite them. Always use a typewriter.

If a correction involves inserting one or more words on a completely typed page, either retype the page or insert the typed correction above the line and use a caret ($\wedge$) to indicate position. For minor errors use a correction fluid, such as Liquid Re-Type. Paint over the error, let the fluid dry, and retype correctly. This method usually covers better than correction paper and does less damage to the paper than complete erasing.

Duplicating the Article

8.85   For general instructions, see Section 8.7. Then:

○ Find out how many copies the journal needs. See Table 7.1, column 3.

○ Check each page of the journal's copies for clear printing.

○ Check the number of other copies needed. In general, make one for each colleague who has assisted you, and retain at least one for your file. Many journals *do not return manuscripts*. Even if the article is accepted for publication with no changes, you may need the file copy for correcting galley and page proofs.

Submitting the Manuscript

8.86   Organize parts of the manuscript as the style requires. See Section 8.16 for guidelines. Prepare a brief letter of submission and place that on top of the copies to be submitted. If you are submitting to a journal that has more than one section—for example, *JASA* or the *Journal of Experimental Psychology*—be certain you are submitting the article to the appropriate section. Also, check on, and include if necessary:

○ A return-addressed, stamped, 9 × 12 envelope for return of the manuscript. (Section 10.20 explains why. Some journals never return manuscripts, even with an envelope.)

○ A postcard, addressed and stamped, whose return will acknowledge that the manuscript has arrived.

8.87   Mail the manuscript either first class, or third class with a first-class letter enclosed. Manuscript rate is usually unsatisfactory because you must send the letter separately. If you wish to guarantee an acknowledgment, use first-class mail and register or certify the parcel. Send photographs according to the journal editor's instructions.

Preparing a Record Card

8.88   On a 3 × 5 card,

○ Record the article's title, date of submission, and journal's name.

○ Use the card from now on to record the manuscript's history. Eventually you will record the name of the journal in which it was published, the volume and number, and page numbers.

If more than 12 weeks pass without word about the manuscript's status,

○ Write a polite letter of inquiry. See Section 11.2 for details.

Using a Checklist

8.89   Figure 8.14 is a checklist. Attach a copy of it to each manuscript and check off items as you do them. The list will help you monitor the manuscript's progress.

SUMMARY

8.90   I begin this chapter with a list of general typing requirements (Sections 8.6 to 8.17). I then discuss instructions for preparing cover sheets (8.18 to 8.23), abstracts (8.24 to 8.26), text (8.27 to 8.30), headings and subheadings (8.31 to 8.34), quotations (8.35 to 8.37), equations (8.38 to 8.40), documentation (8.41 to 8.52), substantive notes (8.53 to 8.55), acknowledgments (8.56 to 8.59), tables (8.60 to 8.68), illustrations (8.69 to 8.71), reference notes (8.72 to 8.73), identifying references (8.74 to 8.75), references (8.76 to 8.81), and appendixes (8.82). I also give instructions on permissions (8.83) and on final preparation and submission of a manuscript (8.84 to 8.89).

1. Typed in proper form.
2. Pages properly ordered and numbered.
3. Illustrations prepared in camera-ready form (if required).
4. Pages proofread.
5. Errors corrected.
6. Manuscript duplicated in acceptable manner and in sufficient copies for journal, author's files, and colleagues.
7. Letter of submission prepared.
8. Letter attached to appropriate number of copies of manuscript.
9. Stamped, self-addressed 9 × 12 envelope (if required).
10. Stamped, self-addressed acknowledgment card (if required).
11. 3 × 5 card prepared.
12. Mailed:

>   First class _____
>   Third class _____
>   Certified____
>   Registered _____
>   Date _____

13. File this form with author's file copies.

Figure 8.14   Checklist for completion of manuscript preparation.

NOTES TO CHAPTER 8

1.   Documentation in this chapter is different from that in all others. This change, normally a poor practice for book authors, was made to provide examples of superscript numbers and footnotes. The style is MSH (except for treatment of page ranges; see Section 8.79), defined in Table 8.1. The tables are also styled differently to provide additional examples (explained in Sections 8.63 and 8.64).

2.   Writing to a journal's editor often elicits a style sheet by return mail, but most style sheets, including those regularly published in every issue of some journals, leave many details unclear.

3.   The data sources used for these styles are: American Psychological Association, *Publication Manual*, 2d ed. (Washington, D.C.: APA, 1974); "Notice to Contributors," rev. ed., *American Sociological Review* (Washington, D.C.: American Sociological Association, 1976); *Journal of the American Statistical Association*, "JASA Style Sheet" (Washington, D.C.: American Statistical Association, n.d.); Modern Language Association of America, *The MLA Style Sheet*, 2d ed. (New York: MLA, 1970); University of Chicago Press, *A Manual of Style*

(Chicago: University of Chicago Press, 1969); Standing Committee on Publications of the British Psychological Society, *Suggestions to Authors*, rev. ed. (London: Cambridge University Press, 1971); Sage Publications, "Journal Editorial Style, Sage Publications" (Beverly Hills, Calif.: Sage Publications, n.d.).

4. Fifth ed. (Glenview, Ill.: Scott, Foresman, 1972), pp. 499–501.

5. APA, *Publication*, p. 15.

6. Pp. 554, 684–686.

7. Kate L. Turabian, *A Manual for Writers of Term Papers, Theses, and Dissertations*, 4th ed. (Chicago: University of Chicago Press, 1973).

8. University of Chicago Press, *A Manual*, pp. 273–274.

9. Sometimes you may deposit these with a national retrieval center, for example the National Auxiliary Publication Service (NAPS); APA, *Publication*, p. 119. Paid for by users, this is a service of the American Society for Information Science. It is for supplementary material, such as extensive calculations and detailed drawings, that cannot be included economically in a printed article, or may interest only a few readers. If you use such a service, indicate that fact in an acknowledgment note. NAPS's address is: ASIS/NAPS, c/o Microfiche Publications, 305 East 46th Street, New York, N.Y. 10017.

10. See University of Chicago Press, *A Manual*, Chapter 11; and APA, *Publication*, pp. 50–55, for more details on illustrations, definitions, and different methods of preparation.

11. This treatment of page ranges is also true of MSH.

CHAPTER NINE

Notes, Short Reports, Comments, Responses to Comments, Review Articles, and Book Reviews

INTRODUCTION

9.1 In addition to articles, journals publish notes, short reports, comments, responses to comments, review articles, and book reviews. This chapter describes and gives instructions for these kinds of publication. For help in writing them, see Chapters 2 to 6.

NOTES

Description of Notes

9.2 Notes are short articles. Editors and referees evaluate them as they do articles. Some journals print them in a section entitled "Notes." Other journals intersperse them with regular articles. Unlike most articles, many published notes were not originally planned as such. Instead, they are the slimmed-down versions of articles on which referees have recommended publication—but only if the authors reduce the length. The author's choice is usually to reduce or not to publish, and most prefer to publish. Many notes are research reports, often on topics that have limited importance or will interest only a few readers. For example, a report on the political values of persons holding Ph.D. degrees in English would probably attract only a few readers.

Value of Notes

9.3 Many scientists and their deans look with distain on notes as if length were the only indicator of quality. Nevertheless, many notes report the necessary, bit-and-piece puzzle-solving that constitutes normal-science research (see Kuhn 1970). As such, they should be published to prevent duplication of the research.

When to Write a Note

9.4 Consider writing a note if you have replicated past research, replicated past research with one change in variables, or clarified one aspect of a theory or method. On such topics, readers' interest is primarily in the implications of your work. Apply the following criteria to your topic:

○ Can you omit most of the introduction to the manuscript by citing one or two previous documents?

○ For a research report, can you omit most of the method section in a similar manner?

If so, you will find that you can give almost as much attention to results and implications in a 12-page note as in a 20- or 25-page article (see Table 5.1). You may also find that notes have one advantage over articles:

☐ Many journals have substantially shorter publication lags for notes than for articles.

Instructions for Writing a Note

9.5 When preparing a note,

○ Choose a journal following the instructions in Chapter 7.

○ Follow the guidelines for style in Chapter 8.

○ Consult the journal for any special instructions. The most common rule is a strict limit of 10 to 12 typed pages (250 words per page), including notes, documentation, tables, and illustrations.

SHORT (BRIEF) REPORTS

Description of Short Reports

9.6 Short (brief) reports are very short articles. They are usually refereed for acceptability. The shortest ones are expanded abstracts with emphasis on results and implications. In psychology, such reports often describe simple or preliminary experiments, extensions, replications, and so forth (APA 1974, p. 112). In economics and statistics, they often add one or two equations to a particular method.

9.7 Some journals, particularly in psychology, set aside a special section for brief reports. For example, see the *Journal of Consulting and Clinical Psychology*. Others, such as the *Journal of the American Statistical Association*, intersperse the reports with articles of normal length. Some journals present each report on a single page in very small type, usually accompanied by a note that encourages readers to write the author for further details. Because they often fit into the small amounts of space left after an editor has chosen an issue's major articles,

☐ Short reports often have even shorter publication lags than do notes.

Instructions for Writing a Short Report

9.8 When writing a short report,

○ Choose a journal following the instructions in Chapter 7.
○ Follow the guidelines for style in Chapter 8.
○ Consult the journal for any special instructions. The most common rule is a strict limit of 2 to 6 typed pages (250 words per page), including notes, documentation, tables, and illustrations.

COMMENTS AND RESPONSES TO COMMENTS

Description of Comments and Responses

9.9 Most journals publish comments and responses to comments, usually in a separate section. A comment is a direct response to an article that the journal has published. When an article's author responds—often in simultaneous publication with the comments of critics—the exchange becomes a debate. The purpose of both comments and responses is to sharpen intellectual issues. Editors usually referee unsolicited comments for acceptability. An author's right to respond to critics is often assumed.

Comments

9.10   Four Ways to Use Comments.   Use comments to:

○ *Point out errors*. Sometimes these are misprints, but they also may be genuine errors. Always check a journal's statement of *errata* to be certain a correction has not already been made.
○ *Question presuppositions*. An author's point may hold if you grant certain assumptions, but there is good reason to question them.
○ *Criticize procedure*. For example, method X is not appropriate for studying topic Y in country Z.
○ *Disagree with interpretation*. For example, an author has interpreted the data in a table one way. You have a different, equally plausible interpretation.

9.11   Organization of Comments.   If you have comments in all four categories, your outline might look like [1]:

I. Errors   [1]
    A. First error
        1. Statement
        2. Reason why statement is wrong
    B. Second error
        1. Statement
        2. Reason why statement is wrong
II. Wrong assumptions
    A. First incorrect assumption
        1. Statement
        2. Reason why assumption is incorrect
    B. Second incorrect assumption

1. Statement
2. Reason why assumption is wrong
III. Criticisms of procedure
   A. Statement of procedure
   B. Reason why procedure is wrong
   C. Acceptable alternative (optional; brief statement, and only if space permits)
IV. Wrong interpretations
   A. First incorrect interpretation
      1. Statement
      2. Reason why interpretation is wrong
      3. Alternative interpretation
   B. Second wrong interpretation
      1. Statement
      2. Reason why interpretation is wrong
      3. Alternative interpretation

If you do not have comments in each of the four categories,

○ Delete whichever categories you do not need and renumber the roman numerals accordingly.

9.12 Beginning, Ending, Headings, and Tone. In general, you will need only a sentence or two of introduction and a sentence for closing. If you have comments in only one category, you probably will not need headings. If you have comments in more than one category,

○ Create first-order headings from topics at the first level of importance in your outline. See Section 5.6 for help in writing headings.
○ If your manuscript is longer than 10 pages, create second-order headings from topics at the second level of importance.

9.13 Overall, strive for polite, clear confrontation.

○ Comment on specific points.

○ Do not discuss arguments not presented in the original article.

○ Write clearly. Avoid details. Avoid technical language not present in the article (see Sections 5.19 and 5.20).

○ State each argument only once. If you repeat, limits on space will force you to eliminate other arguments you might usefully have made.

○ Avoid detailed support of arguments. You lack space to describe 10 supporting studies or 5 theories. Simply mention one or two as examples. If you consider all the evidence to be crucial, write a note or an article instead of a comment and submit that to the journal instead.

The spirit of good debate is best served when the participants balance the excitement of the conflict with restraints that prevent overargumentation. Ironically, beating an argument to death with too much logic or data may cause readers to lose interest and thus defeat your purpose.

9.14 Instructions for Writing the Manuscript. When writing the manuscript,

○ Follow the guidelines in Sections 9.12 and 9.13.

○ For style, follow the guidelines in Chapter 8.

○ Consult the journal, or correspondence from the editor, for special instructions.

○ Prepare the cover sheet as in Figure 8.1, with the following difference: several spaces above the title, give bibliographic data for the article you criticize. For example:

Comment on: I. M. Author, "An Article," *A Journal* 38(1977): 110–120.

○ Length: 2 to 6 typed pages (250 words per page), including notes, documentation, tables, and illustrations.

Responses to Comments

9.15 If you are an author responding to comments on your article, you might organize your response in:

○ An outline exactly like [1], but written as a rebuttal.
○ An outline exactly like the one you used for your article.
○ An outline that orders topics by the damage they do to your
  argument in the article.

An outline for the third option might look like [2]:

  I. First major damaging argument   [2]
 II. Second major damaging argument (and so forth)
III. Minor arguments
    A. First minor argument
    B. Second minor argument (and so forth)

The value of this outline is that refuting damaging arguments
gives the greatest amount of support to your case. By treating
each damaging argument as a topic at the first level of importance, you focus readers' attention on your treatment of it.
When you reach the minor arguments, your outline will rein-
force your statement about their relative lack of importance. If
you wish, you might state that you are refuting them not because they are crucial but because you wish to be thorough.
Outline [2] also has a practical advantage. Sometimes an editor
will require that you reduce the length of a response. With
outline [2], you can easily cut the entire last section and substitute a brief summary. The first and third options work particularly well if you are responding to comments by more than one
critic.

9.16   When writing the manuscript,

○ Follow the guidelines in Section 9.14.
○ Length: up to 12 typed pages (250 words per page), including
  notes, documentation, tables, and illustrations.

REVIEW ARTICLES

Description of Review Articles

9.17 A review article gives an extensive, detailed survey of a specific aspect of a science, usually for a specific period of time. Well-known scholars usually write review articles, sometimes at the invitation of a journal's editor. They are nearly always longer than research articles. A few journals, such as *The Psychological Review*, publish only reviews. More commonly, journals set aside part of each issue for one or more review articles. A variant on reviews is the "state of the field" issues published by some journals—for example, *The Sociological Quarterly*. In such issues comprehensiveness results from a coordinating editor's choice of contributors and articles.

Instructions for Preparing a Review Article

9.18 When you write a review article,

○ Pay special attention to clear writing. One purpose of review articles is cumulation of research and theory. Since many readers use these articles to frame their own thinking about research, lack of clarity can have a broader impact than it might in a research article.

○ Give a clear summary of research and theory in the area you are reviewing. Use general concepts, illustrated with specific observations.

○ List specific problems that need study.

○ Suggest appropriate methods.

○ Predict directions for the future.

○ Expect an exceptional amount of documentation. For a 70-page review article, you might easily cite between 100 and 400 documents (Menzel, Jones, and Boyd 1961, p. 126).

○ If you are writing an uninvited article, choose a journal following the instructions in Sections 7.8 to 7.17.

○ Follow the guidelines for style in Chapter 8. Consult the journal for special instructions.

Sometimes you will find an outline like [3] useful.

I. Introduction   [3]
II. Summary of theory and research
   A. Theoretical argument #1
      1. Central concepts
      2. Relevant research
   B. Theoretical argument #2
      1. Central concepts
      2. Relevant research
   C. Theoretical argument #3 (and so forth)
III. List of specific problems needing study
   A. Problem #1
      1. Statement of problem
      2. Reason why study is needed
      3. Suggested method for study
   B. Problem #2
      1. Statement of problem
      2. Reason why study is needed
      3. Suggested method for study
   C. Problem #3 (and so forth)
IV. Directions for the future
V. Summary

BOOK REVIEWS

Description of Book Reviews

9.19 Journals publish book reviews to help scientists decide whether they want to read the books reviewed. Normally, journal editors invite scholars to review a book or a group of related books, although some editors accept volunteer reviewers. Reviewers usually receive a complimentary copy of the book from the journal in which the review will be published. When seeking a reviewer for a book, journal editors normally try to avoid persons known to have a conflict of some sort with the book's author (Hirsch, Kulley, and Efron 1974, p. 10). In general, editors choose reviewers who hold lower status in the profession than the authors whose books they review (Hirsch, Kulley, and Efron 1974, p. 15).

9.20 Some journals—for example, *Contemporary Psychology* and *Contemporary Sociology*—publish only book reviews. More commonly, journal editors set aside part of every issue for reviews. In addition to regular book reviews, usually between 500 and 1500 words in length, many journals also publish *review essays*, which are detailed reviews of a single book; *review symposiums*, in which two or more reviewers discuss a single book[1]; and *survey reviews*, in which one reviewer discusses several books on similar topics. (Some journals use different names for these categories.) In general, essays and symposiums are reserved for books that journal editors believe to be important contributions to scholarship.

Instructions for Reviewing Monographs

9.21 Some journal editors give reviewers precise instructions on topics to discuss, order of topics, and number of words alloted to each. In the absence of such instructions, try using outline [4] or a modification of it when reviewing a monograph:

I. Summarize the book's scope, content, organization,   [4]
originality and probable importance to scholarship,
and describe the author's style. Summarize by chapters
if the book is an edited collection.

II. Evaluate the author's qualifications to write the book.

III. List the groups for whom the author wrote the book.

IV. Evaluate other aspects of the book. Document with one or
two examples:

A. Appropriateness for its intended audience
B. Thoroughness with which it accomplishes its stated
task
C. Accuracy of method, research, and citations
D. Adequacy of index
E. If part of a series, its place in the series

9.22 It is difficult to separate a summary of content from evaluation. In general,

○ Try to allot from 60 to 80 percent of a book review to evaluation. The more familiar an author's general topic, the less space you need to give to pure summary.
○ Treat topics II and III briefly.
○ Avoid notes and references, especially to your own work. The purpose of a review is only to summarize and review the book in question.
○ Do not try to include every item in outline [4] in every book review. Choose items to fit the particular book and journal.

Instructions for Reviewing Textbooks

9.23   When evaluating a textbook, try using outline [5]:

I. Evaluate comprehensiveness, scope, and substance.   [5]
   A. Is factual information current, clear, accurate, and complete?
   B. Are all necessary topics covered?
   C. Are any unnecessary topics covered?
   D. Does the author cite all major contributions to the topics being discussed?
   E. Is the bibliography thorough, but not padded?
   F. Will the book's breadth of information be acceptable as a review (introduction, survey, discussion) of the topic in question?
   G. What assumptions does the author make about students' prior training and level of sophistication, and instructors' needs?
   H. Will the book's adequacy be obvious to potential users?
II. Evaluate the author's qualifications.
   A. Has he or she written previous textbooks?
   B. Is he well-known for work on the topic about which the textbook was written?
   C. Has he taught courses like the ones for which he wrote the book?

III. List the courses for which the author wrote the book.

IV. Evaluate the book's appropriateness for those courses.

    A. Will the book engage the reader?

        1. Are the illustrations understandable?

        2. Are they drawn from real life?

        3. Are central ideas applied to contemporary social concerns?

        4. Will the student feel "written down to," or bored by a mass of facts and figures?

        5. Is the book readable? See Sections 5.65 to 5.69 for help.

    B. Is the book's framework clear and consistent?

        1. Does it unite the entire manuscript?

        2. Is the organization logical?

        3. Does the author point out alternate frameworks and their advantages or disadvantages, along with reasons for choosing this particular framework?

        4. Are theoretical interpretations properly supported by data, and are data discussed in light of theory?

        5. Have data and theory been separated clearly, so students can tell fact from theory?

        6. Does the author point out unanswered questions?

    C. What is the book's intellectual payoff?

        1. Will students gain a perspective on the book's topic?

        2. Will they gain statistical and methodological skills?

        3. Will they learn to use major concepts and to discuss them intelligently?

        4. Will they develop a proper skepticism toward weak data and oversimplified explanations?

        5. Will they develop a sense of significant questions, and of ways to investigate them?

        6. Will students feel a sense of having mastered the material and of having had their abilities fairly challenged?

In general, observe the cautions in Section 9.22.

Instructions for Survey Reviews and Review Essays

9.24 If you are writing a *survey review* of several books on similar topics, you might review each book separately following outlines [4] or [5] over and over, or you might prefer to review the books simultaneously. For example, if you were reviewing several monographs, your outline might look like [6] (based on [4]):

  I. Summarize . . . .   [6]
      A. Book 1
      B. Book 2
      C. Book 3 (and so forth)
 II. Evaluate the author's . . . .
      A. Book 1
      B. Book 2
      C. Book 3 (and so forth)
III. List . . . .
      A. Book 1
      B. Book 2
      C. Book 3 (and so forth)
 IV. Evaluate other aspects . . . .
      A. Book 1
      B. Book 2
      C. Book 3 (and so forth)

In general, observe the cautions stated in Section 9.22.

9.25 A *review essay* usually gives all the information in outline [4] and much more. In fact, you may not need to observe the cautions given in Section 9.22. When written skillfully, survey reviews and review essays can give valuable summaries of the intellectual areas to which the books' (or book's) topic belongs.

General Instructions for All Reviews of Books

9.26 When you review a book or books,

○ Consult Chapter 8 for general instructions on typing.
○ Consult the journal's instructions, or the instructions sent by

the editor, for: prescribed length; exact form for typing, and location of, bibliographic information on the book(s) you are reviewing; and location of your name and institutional affiliation.

In the absence of specific instructions,

○ Type bibliographic information double spaced, at the top of the first page, beginning 2 inches from the top. Include author's or editor's name, title and subtitle, translator (if any), city and state, publisher, date, and price, in that order.
○ Begin typing the review four spaces below the bibliographic information.
○ Type your name at the end, last name flush with the right-hand margin. Below your name type your institutional affiliation, and then the date.

SUMMARY

9.27 In this chapter I give descriptions of and guidelines for notes (Sections 9.2 to 9.5), short (brief) reports (9.6 to 9.8), comments and responses to comments (9.9 to 9.16), review articles (9.17 and 9.18), and several kinds of book reviews (9.19 to 9.26). I give sample outlines for comments and authors' responses to them, review articles, and book reviews.

NOTE TO CHAPTER 9

1. I do not discuss review symposiums separately in this chapter. From the reviewer's perspective, the review is an ordinary review of a single book. The fact that the review is published with one or more other reviews of the same book is important only if the editor has requested that the reviewer examine one particular aspect of the book and exclude others.

CHAPTER TEN

The Problems and Promises of Journal Publishing

THE DIFFICULTY OF GETTING ARTICLES PUBLISHED

Submission Rates and Publication Lags

10.1 To many authors, journal editors are irritating obstacles in the struggle to get published. Because they represent the journals they edit, editors take the brunt of authors' irritation. The irritations are all too real. As Chapter 8 shows, submission requirements are numerous and detailed, and they usually differ from one journal to the next. Simply obtaining a description of editorial style can be difficult. Long publication lags are endemic—up to five years, and rarely less than eight months from submission of an article until, assuming acceptance, it is published. During 1974 and 1975, the editors of two well-known journals declared a moratorium on reviewing articles until they could reduce their backlogs.

High Rejection Rates

10.2 Rejection rates are high, and the most prestigious journals have the highest rates.[1] For high-rejection journals, the general principle governing acceptance seems to be, "When in doubt, reject; in low-rejection journals, when in doubt, accept" (Zuckerman and Merton 1971, p. 78). A major question, as *Nature* (1971, p. 3) has pointed out, is: Do we praise the high-rejection journals for their toughness, or despise them for rendering such poor service to contributors? There are many reasons for high rejection rates. A common complaint by journal editors in the social and behavioral sciences (e.g., see Freeman 1972) is that many articles submitted have been written by nonprofessionals. Most people would never write about a recent experience with the motor of a car and then submit it to a journal in physics, but they *will* write about a personal experience with a church group and submit the result as an article in the sociology or psychology of religion. Another reason is that many manuscripts are abysmally prepared. McCartney (1973c, p. 2) commented that only a third of the manuscripts received by his journal would meet even minimal standards for a course in freshman English composition. Some manuscripts are prepared in inappropriate editorial styles. Some are typed on several different machines, and some are even submitted with pages scotch-taped together. Finally, many articles are submitted to journals for whom the content is inappropriate. Any of these conditions may elicit an immediate rejection from a journal's editor (see also Section 11.4).

Ratio of Potential Authors to Available Pages

10.3   Careful authors can prevent rejection for any of these reasons. What they cannot avoid, however, is the pressure from the increasing demand for space in journals. At least in the past, social and behavioral scientists have been handicapped (relative to the physical sciences) by a decline in the ratio of available pages in prestigious journals to the number of persons in the discipline (Zuckerman and Merton 1971, p. 79). Increases in the number of social and behavioral scientists and in the number of articles they write have not been matched by an increased amount of space in which to print articles. For some journals, the average length of articles is also increasing, further cramping the available space.

Reports of Referees

10.4   The scholar who has surmounted these obstacles and received a decision on an article is sometimes frustrated by the reports of referees. Journals rarely accept articles in their original form, and incorporating referees' comments and recommendations into an acceptable revision can be difficult. Occasionally, though not often, referees' reports are inaccurate and even capricious.[2]

10.5   These difficulties are partly caused by problems that plague most journals. When authors understand the problems, they can often find satisfactory ways to deal with them and thus resolve their own difficulties.

RISING EXPENSES

General Costs

10.6 At one time, journals were largely owned by societies and supported through members' dues. After World War II as grant-supported research expanded, journals began to depend on subventions—page charges—and reprint sales. Still later, library subscriptions became another prime source of support. As grant funds have become less plentiful, journals have increased the price of institutional subscriptions in an attempt to replace the funds that page charges used to supply. The time may soon come when many libraries are unable to support all the subscriptions they have carried, and among the first to go will be some of the highly specialized journals that serve small readerships and have no revenue other than library subscriptions (Abelson 1974).[3]

10.7 Today, many journals are still owned by nonprofit associations, but many are also owned by commercial enterprises. For example, Sage, Macmillan, and North-Holland all publish more than one journal. The commercially owned journals support themselves through funds from subscriptions, advertising, submission charges, and subventions. In general, they must be profitable or they will be modified, sold, or discontinued. The journals sponsored by nonprofit organizations must balance their expenses with funds received from subsidies, subscriptions, advertising, submission charges, subventions, and contributions. When choices must be made, the subsidies sometimes permit these journals to choose high-quality articles over ones that might sell more issues.

10.8 The journal editor must pay for routine office expenses, as well as for preparing and printing issues. Among the obvious costs—some of which have been rising much faster than the rate of inflation—are editing, printing, paper, and postage for mailing issues. Among the less obvious expenses are postage for correspondence, stationery, a typewriter, and secretarial help. Most journals have modest offices, and many a journal is housed only in its editor's departmental office. Some editors have no secretaries; of those who do, many have only quarter- or half-time help. The editor, usually unpaid (some receive honoraria for their services), often spends 40 or more hours each week processing manuscripts and preparing issues, in addition to teaching and doing research. Referees also are usually unpaid.

10.9 In recent years, increases in costs have far outstripped increases in revenues. Also, the number of manuscripts submitted has increased. For example, between 1973 and 1974, the number of manuscripts received by the *American Psychologist* increased from 395 to 607; by the *Journal of Applied Psychology*, from 369 to 500 (*American Psychologist* 1974, p. 474; 1975, p. 619); by the *American Sociological Review*, from 629 to 696 (Zelditch 1975). As a result, journal editors have had increasing work loads without concomitant increases in staff and office space. Authors have felt the effects of this pressure in unanswered letters, refusal to acknowledge receipt of manuscripts, refusal to return manuscripts, increasing publication lags (see, e.g., McCartney 1975; Schwartz 1975), and decreasing number of pages devoted to articles.

The Costs of Processing a Manuscript

10.10   Overall Cost.   In 1975, estimates of the cost of processing ranged between \$35 and \$60 per manuscript *received* (not necessarily accepted for publication). Thus a journal, such as the *Journal of Applied Psychology*, that receives 500 manuscripts in a year spends between \$17,500 and \$30,000 on processing alone. Viewed from this perspective, the \$10 and \$15 nonrefundable submission charges shown in Table 7.1 seen eminently resonable. Even the highest charges probably do not cover the cost of processing.

10.11   Initial Checking of Manuscripts.   When a manuscript arrives, an editor[4] checks it for appropriate content, correct style and requisite number of copies, and may mail an acknowledgment card. Often, the manuscript is rejected immediately if the content is obviously unscholarly or inappropriate (see, e.g., Schwartz 1975, p. 65). Some editors will also reject manuscripts if the style is inappropriate, for example, if the author has used name (date) citation for documentation when the journal requires superscript numbers and notes. (Both methods are discussed in Sections 8.41 to 8.52. Some journals include a warning about this practice in their instructions to contributors.) Usually the editor returns the manuscript with the letter of rejection only if the author has included a stamped, self-addressed envelope. Some editors will send an improperly styled manuscript out for review but will not act on a referee's recommendation of acceptance until the author has prepared the manuscript properly. The journal's staff will not do this job for an author.

10.12 Some editors will not process further a manuscript for which they have too few copies. They will request that the author send more. The rest will continue processing but will not photocopy the manuscript. Instead, they will send the manuscript to only one referee at a time, thus lengthening the time before a decision is made, and will not keep a backup copy to guard against loss. The frequent requirement of four or five copies is quite understandable to authors who know that the journal editor uses one copy, someone on the editorial board may use a second (and intentionally save stamps by not returning the manuscript when notifying the editor of suggested referees), two copies go to referees, and a fifth remains in the office.

10.13 Choice of Referees. The editor, often helped by assistant editors and editorial board members (see Section 10.29), then examines surviving manuscripts for possible referees—usually at least two. After selecting referees, some editors (e.g., at *Science*) telephone to ask the referees whether they are willing to undertake the job and return the evaluation within a specified period. Some editors write instead of telephoning, and enclose an abstract. This practice prevents manuscripts from being sent to unwilling referees, who may also forget to return them or notify the journal of their unwillingness. However, writing the letter and waiting for a response take time, so many editors simply send a polite letter and the manuscript, and request the manuscript's immediate return if a review within, say, four weeks is impossible.

10.14   Evaluation Procedure.   Manuscripts refereed by the editor or by an editorial board are usually evaluated most quickly. Those refereed without anonymity can usually be sent to referees as soon as they have been chosen. Manuscripts that are blind-reviewed, or refereed anonymously, require more work. Unless an author has removed identifying references (see Sections 8.74 to 8.75), the editor or his staff must do so. Sometimes this means only removing the cover sheet, but the editor must still read the manuscript to ascertain that it contains no other identifying material. Sometimes he or she must cut out references with scissors or put tape over them. Then he must catalog the manuscript for identification when it returns from the referees.

10.15   Evaluation may take between two weeks and several months. If a referee refuses a job, the editor must choose another referee. If a referee is slow, some journal editors write a reminding letter, but others lack the time and will do so only if prompted by an anxious author. The correspondence involved probably costs at least $5 per letter in stationery, stamps, secretarial time, and maintenance on machinery. Once received, if the initial evaluations of a manuscript are not similar, an editor may seek another opinion.

10.16   Decision and Notification of Authors.   When all evaluations have been received, the editor makes a decision and writes a letter to the author. Often he attaches copies of the evaluations. Sometimes he writes a form letter, and sometimes he offers an evaluation of his own. Some editors write letters to thank referees, sometimes enclosing copies of their letters to authors and of other referees' evaluations. At this point, unconditionally rejected manuscripts exit from processing unless the author protests the decision. Sections 11.5 to 11.7 describe when and how to protest.

10.17 A very few manuscripts (for most journals, under 13 percent) are unconditionally accepted and put into production. The remaining manuscripts receive conditional decisions. The authors usually revise and resubmit the manuscript. The editor then reevaluates it, sometimes requesting help from the original referees and sometimes selecting new ones. Eventually the manuscript is unconditionally accepted or rejected. The whole process is lengthy. The dates for first (second, third, and later) submissions that some journals routinely print with each article show that processing rarely takes less than 4 months. More commonly, processing takes from 8 to 18 months and may take as many as 36.

10.18 An Example. Schwartz (1975, p. 65), describing processing by the *American Journal of Sociology*, broke the process into four stages: (1) time elapsed between a manuscript's arrival from a contributor and its assignment to a referee, (2) referees' reading time, (3) time elapsed between a manuscript's arrival from the second referee and the editorial board's final decision on it, and (4) the time it takes to communicate this decision to the author. Between these stages is the time required to prepare and mail the manuscript several times. Schwartz (1975, pp. 71–73) found that between 1968 and 1972, the mean time required for stage 1 was 2.2 weeks; for stage 2, 8.0 weeks; for stages 3 and 4 combined, 7.4 weeks. Of the 7.4, Schwartz estimated that 5.2 weeks were required by stage 4. Schwartz also found that the total waiting time for manuscripts had risen from 13.3 weeks in 1970 to 24.4 weeks in 1972 (p. 74). Most of this increase affected stages 3 and 4, in which the mean processing time rose from 4 weeks in 1968 to 12 weeks in 1972 (p. 75). Schwartz also found that the longer the manuscript, the longer the processing time (p. 83). These findings are for only one journal, but they describe time required by stages in a general process and thus give an idea of the amount of time generally needed for processing. Schwartz argued (p. 78) that once a backlog of work has reached a certain point, it generates activities (e.g., inquiries about delayed manuscripts) that will further increase the backlog (e.g., answering the inquiries further delays other work).

The Costs of Producing a Finished Article

10.19 Once accepted, a manuscript is assigned to a future issue and is edited, checked, set in type, proofed, and printed. Sections 11.28 to 11.36 describe this process. During production, a journal incurs costs for editing, printing, and mailing proofs. The editor may incur additional expenses by corresponding with the author if the latter alters the manuscript substantially or is unhappy about any aspect of production. He may incur further expenses if the author fails to meet any of the production deadlines (see Section 11.30).

Responses to Rising Expenses

10.20 Journal Editors' Responses.   The editors have met rising costs with numerous changes in procedure. Not all journals have made all the changes listed below, but most have tried one or more.

☐ Require a nonrefundable submission fee. See Table 7.1, column 7. Besides providing revenue, this change may reduce the number of manuscripts submitted by nonprofessionals.

☐ Limit the length of manuscripts. Exceptions are rare—for example, for a presidential address to an association.

☐ Acknowledge receipt of a manuscript only if the author has enclosed a stamped, self-addressed postcard. This simple change saves the cost of stamps, cards, and preparation.

☐ Return manuscripts only if the author supplies a 9 × 12 self-addressed, stamped envelope. This change saves the cost of postage, envelopes, and preparation.

☐ Require proper editorial style.

☐ Refuse to return manuscripts, even with an envelope.

☐ Require multiple copies. This change saves copying charges and the time needed to make copies.

☐ Request editorial board members and referees to return only suggestions and evaluations, not manuscripts.

☐ Enforce exclusive-review policies (described in Sections 11.15 to 11.20).

☐ Require authors to prepare their manuscripts for blind reviewing.

☐ Make greater use of notes, short (brief) reports, and even letters. For example, see Mayhew (1974); also Sections 9.2 to 9.8.

☐ Request a subvention (from an author's grant funds) to cover part or all of the cost of publication. The subvention is not mandatory and does not affect acceptance of an article. Some editors use subventions to increase the number of pages in an issue, and then move ahead in the queue of accepted manuscripts the article for which the subvention has been paid.

☐ Require a subvention to pay part or all of the costs of publishing an article. Some journals require authors to pay for printing tables and illustrations, but not text.

☐ Require authors to submit illustrations and tables in camera-ready form. This change saves on typesetting costs.

☐ Increase the costs of subscriptions and advertising.

☐ Increase the number of pages devoted to advertising.

☐ Encourage authors to place exceptionally long or complex tables with an information service such as NAPS (see Section 8.61 and note 9) that will supply copies on request for a fee.

☐ Use computers to compose each issue. Computer technology can reduce both cost of composition and time required for the process. Kachergis (1976) describes the benefits for one journal.

10.21 In some instances (e.g., Scholars Press, described in Miles 1976; and Canadian Consortium for Scholarly Publications, described in Wagner 1976), scholars have formed their own presses. Scholars in many geographical locations serve as referees, editors, and even salesmen. The presses use cheap forms of reproduction, often from camera-ready copy, and have few advertising and distributing costs. The presses pass their savings to customers in the form of low prices on journals and books.

10.22 Authors' Responses. Authors can help both themselves and the journals by taking the following actions with each manuscript:

○ Check carefully a journal's substantive focus before submitting a manuscript. See Sections 7.8 to 7.17 for help.

○ Do not submit manuscripts similar in content to articles you have already published (see Jackson 1974).

○ Submit an article to the appropriate editor or section of a journal. For example, *JASA* has more than one section, and the *Journal of Experimental Psychology* is now four, more specialized journals (see Table 7.1).

○ Do not submit manuscripts with highly specialized subject matter to journals that publish only articles with wide general interest.

○ When the subject matter permits, write a note or short report instead of an article (see Jackson 1973). For help, see Sections 9.2 to 9.8.

○ Prepare the manuscript in proper editorial style. See Chapter 8 for help.

○ When writing an article, respect stated limits on length (listed in Table 7.1).

○ For journals that use blind reviews, prepare the manuscript accordingly. See Sections 8.74 and 8.75 for help. Tell the editor, in your letter of submission, that you have done so.

○ Prepare a clear, descriptive title (see Sections 3.2 and 3.3) and abstract (8.24 and 8.25). These will help the editor to choose appropriate referees.

○ If you think appropriate referees will be difficult to choose, suggest persons who are not colleagues and who have not read the manuscript as you prepared it.

○ Send a clean, neat, complete manuscript, in the appropriate number of copies (see Jackson 1973, p. 14).

○ Submit the manuscript to only one journal at a time. See Sections 11.15 to 11.20 for discussion.

○ Enclose a stamped, self-addressed acknowledgment card, or send your manuscript by certified or registered mail.

○ Send a stamped, self-addressed envelope if you wish your manuscript returned.

Taking these steps will prevent the irritation of having a manuscript returned for reasons that you could have avoided. They will also shorten the time you need to wait before receiving a decision.

10.23 More generally, also consider taking the following actions:

○ If you have a research grant, pay the requested page charges.

○ Routinely include page charges in every application for a research grant.

○ Subscribe to journals instead of paying for photocopies of articles.[5] Consider joint subscriptions with several colleagues. In the long run, such action may save some journals (see Abelson 1974).

○ When you agree to referee a manuscript, write a clear, objective report, make specific suggestions, and return the evaluation promptly (see McCartney 1975).

MAINTAINING QUALITY IN ARTICLES

Importance of the Referee System

10.24 Referees help to maintain quality in articles (Zuckerman and Merton 1971, p. 66). Journals that do not use referees are viewed with suspicion. Sometimes the editors are the only referees (journals in psychology long relied solely on senior editors or on the editors and members of editorial boards). Other times editors request help from scholars not officially connected with a journal but whom the editor chooses (perhaps in consultation with an editorial board) for their familiarity with various specialty areas. Because the goal of refereeing is to restrict publication to works that are both scientifically sound and useful (Ziman 1968, p. 111), many scholars see referees as gatekeepers who are impossible to please and whose comments are nearly always wrong. One author remarked that referees are "the people you love to hate."

10.25 Such judgments are not borne out by data. Two scientists, acting independently, rarely diverge much in their opinions on the value of a potential publication (Polanyi 1946, p. 51; Backman 1972, p. 26; McCartney 1973b, p. 443). Referees may offer different reasons for their recommendations, but about 70 percent of the time the judgments on whether to publish are remarkably close.

Characteristics and Choice of Good Referees

10.26 Characteristics. Ideally, referees are competent, appropriate, and efficient. *Competent* referees have a broad knowledge of issues, contemporary research, and common methodologies within a specialty. Additional competence— theoretical, methodological, or empirical (in another specialty)—is a bonus. Competent referees can make judgments and then detail their reasons (McCartney 1973d, p. 146). Some editors find that mature, experienced scholars are no more competent than new ones (e.g., see McCartney 1973d, p. 287).[6] Indeed, some editors find that the younger referees are actually more competent, especially in their knowledge of methods and formal theoretical criteria.

10.27 *Appropriateness* refers to whether a referee knows well the subject matter of a particular manuscript. Also, he or she should not be a colleague of the author's, someone mentioned in the acknowledgments (or, sometimes, an author of a cited document), or someone known to object on principle to the issue, theory, or method on which the manuscript is based (see McCartney 1973d, p. 287–288).

10.28   *Efficiency* refers to the speed with which a referee returns an evaluation. Most editors prefer to have comments returned within 2 or 3 weeks, but certainly within 12. See Sections 11.2 and 11.21 to 11.23 for further discussion and suggestions. To increase efficiency, some journals have expanded their pools of referees and given each member fewer assignments (e.g., see Short 1972, p. 26).

10.29   Choices.   Journal editors try to choose referees so that as a group, they represent the work in a discipline or specialty. In selecting referees, an editor draws from many pools: past and present colleagues, assistant (or deputy) editors' and editorial board members' past and present colleagues and acquaintances at other institutions, persons who have given papers at meetings, past contributors to the journal, and so forth.

10.30   To select the referees for a particular manuscript, a journal's editor may ask for suggestions from those on the editorial board who are active in the special area that the manuscript seems to represent. Naturally, the longer an editor manages a journal, the greater becomes his or her knowledge of specific referees and their particular strengths and weaknesses. Those who are consistently slow or who return poor reviews are usually dropped from lists of possible referees (see McCartney 1973d, p. 287). A frequent problem is the difficulty of assuring anonymity. Some scientists' research is well enough known that a disguise is virtually impossible. In such cases, editors are particularly concerned to select referees who will act without bias even though they will probably guess the author's identity.

Description of Aspects Evaluated

10.31   Most editors send each referee a letter requesting evaluation by a certain date, an evaluation form, and a manuscript. The referee types the evaluation on the form but does not sign it. Usually the form requests one of three or four recommendations. For example: publish as is, publish with changes (specified), or reject. More detailed: publish (major contribution, sound); warrants publication if space is plentiful; acceptable with minor modifications; revise and resubmit (with suggested changes specified); or reject. Some forms ask referees to evaluate the adequacy of documentation. Some request evaluation of writing style. The most frequent comments on writing criticize excessive length and the need for extensive copy editing. Some editors are distressed when they encounter potentially publishable manuscripts that are too poorly written to be rescued (see Freeman 1972). For further discussion of evaluation forms and of typical patterns of referees' comments, see McCartney (1973b, 1975, pp. 499, 521, 533).

Decisions on Manuscripts

10.32 Decisions are an editor's responsibility. Editors who use referees are not bound by their recommendations. Some editors will accept an article over two negative recommendations, or reject over two affirmative, if they feel that there is reason to do so. Editors feel most comfortable if their decisions are based on detailed referee comments, and they tend to avoid referees whose past reports give few reasons for their recommendations. In general, given the shortage of space, editors tend to accept articles that receive the most favorable comments. Within this category they prefer papers that will require the least editing. Once a decision is made, the editor notifies the author, usually stating the reasons for the decision and often including copies of the evaluations.

Other Functions of the Referee System

10.33 Some editors see refereeing not only as an aid to making editorial decisions but also as a factor that contributes to the education of the authors (see Short 1972, p. 26). Inevitably, as McCartney (1973b, p. 440) noted, some authors consider it gratuitous of the editor to assume that the author will find referees' comments *useful* (see also Short 1973). However, the editors seek detailed comments, pass them along to authors, and genuinely hope that the comments will help the author produce a better manuscript, even though it may eventually be published by a journal other than theirs. They like to hear from pleased authors (see Hill 1973, p. 14), and sometimes forward the praise to the referees. Ultimately, on occasion and on request, an editor may put in touch with each other a referee and an author with strong mutual interests (see, e.g., Short 1974, p. 12).

10.34 One editor recounted the story of a well-known scholar's response to the referees on one of his manuscripts. Both referees had returned unfavorable evaluations, and the editor had rejected the manuscript. Later the scholar thanked him for the comments, indicating that the manuscript had been hastily written, and then suggested that the referees be encouraged to conduct research in the area of study addressed by the manuscript, for he had found their comments to be excellent. The editor's basic point was that though few scholars like to have either their ideas or their prose tampered with, both are usually better off for the experience.

SUMMARY AND SUGGESTED RESOURCES

10.35 In this chapter I discuss the difficulty of getting an article published (Sections 10.1 to 10.5), the pressure caused by rising costs (10.6 to 10.9), the details that accompany the processing of a manuscript (10.10 to 10.18), the journal editors' attempts to meet their budgets (10.20 and 10.21), and some steps that authors can take to help (10.22 and 10.23). I then discuss the journals' system for maintaining quality—the nature, importance, and functions of the referee system (10.24 to 10.34). Often, when authors examine difficulties in getting published from the perspective of difficulties that plague journals, they can find workable solutions to their own problems. Authors interested in more detail on journals in education should read Silverman and Collins (1975), *The "Gatekeeper" Role in Educational Journal Publishing*. For a more general discussion, see DeBakey's (1976) *The Scientific Journal: Editorial Policies and Practices* and O'Connor and Woodford's (1975) *Writing Scientific Papers in English*. Also, the quarterly journal *Scholarly Publishing* sometimes prints articles of general interest to both authors and journal editors.

NOTES TO CHAPTER 10

1. In 1967 the average rejection rates for widely circulated journals were (Zuckerman and Merton 1971, p. 76): anthropology, 48 percent; economics, 69 percent; history, 90 percent; linguistics, 20 percent; mathematics and statistics, 50 percent; political science, 84 percent; psychology (excluding experimental and physiological), 70 percent; experimental and physiological psychology, 51 percent; sociology, 78 percent. By 1972, the mean rejection rate for seven prominent journals in sociology had risen to 86 percent (McCartney 1973a, p. 600). Table 7.1 gives rates for specific journals in 1973 and 1974. Articles sent to inappropriate journals are rejected at even higher rates (Garvey, Lin, and Nelson 1970).

2. Some scientists, much aware that they are both the referees and the refereed, find much truth in Pogo's words: "We have met the enemy and he is us!"

3. In the early 1960s, *Science*'s support came 60 percent from advertising, 32 percent from members, and 8 percent from nonmembers and libraries. By 1974 the balance had shifted to: 36 percent from advertising, 39 from members, 22 from nonmembers and libraries, and 3 from other sources (Abelson 1974).

4. In this chapter I refer to "the editor" for the sake of brevity. Secretaries and assistant or deputy editors, if available, help with many of these tasks.

5. It is illegal to photocopy copyrighted material, but copying machines are routinely placed in many libraries. Garfield (1975) has suggested that libraries charge a fee for copying copyrighted material and return a portion to the publisher through a copyright clearinghouse, such as that operated by the Institute for Scientific Information (ISI).

6. To evaluate a new referee's competence and appropriateness, some editors pair a referee being used for the first time with one whose capabilities are well known.

CHAPTER ELEVEN

Between Authors and Journal Editors

INTRODUCTION

11.1 Authors want journals to publish their articles. Journal editors want to publish the highest-quality issues possible while not overspending their budgets. Most of the time compromise is necessary. Compromises and mutual responsibilities are the topics of this chapter.

RESPONSES TO DELAYED DECISIONS

11.2 Authors become understandably annoyed when they do not receive an editorial decision within 12 weeks or so after submission of an article. In this situation, write a letter like the following one:

Dear _____:

On [date] I sent you a copy of [title] to consider for publication. I received an acknowledgment indicating that you had received the manuscript on [date, usually stamped on the card], but I have received nothing since. I would appreciate knowing that the manuscript has not been lost or mislaid, and that you will soon make a decision. In the event a loss has occurred, I will be happy to supply more copies.

I look forward to hearing from you at your earliest convenience.

Sincerely,

Few editors object to a polite inquiry after 12 weeks have passed. Indeed, the American Sociological Association (ASA) now requires the journals it sponsors to report to authors at the end of 12 weeks even if a decision cannot yet be made. Some journal editors regularly remind overdue referees of expected evaluations, but others will do so only if prompted by authors.

RESPONSES TO EVALUATIONS AND DECISIONS

Unconditional Acceptance

11.3 *Unconditional acceptance* occurs less than 15 percent of the time and poses no problems.[1]

Unconditional Rejection

11.4 Reasons. Rejection is usually for one of four reasons: inappropriate subject matter (see Sections 10.2 and 10.22), improper use of statistics or methodology, inaccurate theory or interpretation, or controversial findings (Garvey, Lin, and Nelson 1970, p. 1171). The first three reasons are far more common than the last, and the first most common of all.[2]

11.5 Responses to Rejection. If your manuscript has been rejected for inappropriateness,

○ Choose another journal. For help, see Sections 7.8 to 7.17.
○ Change the editorial style if necessary (see column 5, Table 7.1), and then submit the manuscript to the second journal.

If your manuscript has been rejected for any other reason, you can make one of two responses:

○ Choose another journal (see above).
○ Protest the decision.

To help you decide which is appropriate, ask a colleague to read the manuscript and the evaluations. See Sections 6.5 to 6.10 for help. Particularly with the better journals, erroneous evaluations are not common. Referees who do them with any frequency soon find that their services are not needed (a good reason for making justifiable complaints). If your manuscript was rejected despite some favorable remarks, it may be that your conclusions need greater emphasis, or that your arguments would benefit from a different organization.

11.6 If you protest,

○ Write a letter. Never telephone. The editor will need time to review the manuscript before responding to you.
○ Make certain the errors are clear and easy to demonstrate, as when a referee has misunderstood a statistical manipulation and you can cite a source that proves your point.
○ List the errors and reject them point by point.

11.7 If the editor agrees to reevaluate the manuscript, you might suggest the names of several persons whom you believe to be competent referees. Choose persons who have not read earlier drafts. Some editors will choose one referee from your list and one from some other source.

11.8 If you submit the manuscript to another journal, do not enclose the evaluations from the previous journal. However, some editors like to know of prior submissions so that, by corresponding with the editor of the previous journal, they can avoid choosing the same referees. Check the journal's *Instructions to Contributors* for a statement of such a policy.

11.9 The most perplexing rejection is one received despite *favorable* evaluations. If the rejection is due to poor writing, you may be able to persuade the editor to reevaluate after you have rewritten the manuscript. However, it sometimes happens that other manuscripts received more favorable evaluations than yours did, and the editor has chosen to publish those manuscripts rather than yours. Decisions of this sort are becoming more common as journal editors reduce the size of their issues in an effort to meet their budgets. In general, if you receive such a rejection,

○ Submit the manuscript to another journal, perhaps one that is less widely known or more specialized than the one from which you received the rejection. If necessary, change the style. See column 5 of Table 7.1 and Chapter 8 for help.

Conditional Acceptance; Revision and Resubmission

11.10   Reasons to Revise and Resubmit.   If you receive either a conditional acceptance with a request for minor alterations or a request to revise and resubmit, in general,

○ Do not submit to a different journal.

○ Try to meet all of the suggestions and then resubmit the manuscript to the journal that requested the revision.

Lag and rejection rates for most journals are discouragingly high. Also, if you choose instead to submit to a different journal, it is unlikely that its editor will accept the article for publication with no changes. Perhaps most important, if the manuscript *is* eventually published "as is," it will seldom be as good as further revision could have made it.

11.11   Responses to Referees' Comments.   If, when revising, you find a point at which you feel a referee has misunderstood you and you cannot see why,

○ Ask a colleague to evaluate both the manuscript and the referee's comments. Lacking your closeness to the manuscript, a colleague can often find the real problem and suggest a solution. See Sections 6.8 to 6.12 for an example and further help.

11.12   Editors often require authors to shorten their manuscripts, sometimes by as much as a third or a half. Many authors find such requests distressing and even outrageous. They know that short articles are often valued less than long ones. Also, some authors have recently completed dissertations in which they described, discussed, and criticized all documents they cited. To them, using briefer references seems intellectually dishonest. However, if everything ever written on a topic had to be recapitulated for every article on a related topic, academe would be drowning in literature. Also, referees rarely suggest cutting substantially when doing so would severely impair a presentation. *You* might like to say more, but your readers will probably get the same message, and they may even absorb more if you write less. Given the scarcity of space in journals, cutting increases the likelihood that your article will be published. For help in deciding what to cut,

○ Examine the referees' and editor's suggestions.
○ Consult Sections 5.56 to 5.62.
○ Consult with a colleague or editorial consultant if you need further help. See Sections 6.4 to 6.12.

Resubmission of a Manuscript

11.13 When you are ready to resubmit a manuscript, write the editor a polite, covering letter.

○ State how you met the various criticisms.
○ Note any suggestions you did not follow and give the reason.

The editor may then evaluate the manuscript himself, send it to the original referees, or choose new referees (who may or may not be sent copies of the original evaluations). The outline for the letter might look like [1]:

   I. First suggestion   [1]
      A. Referee's comment
      B. Your response
  II. Second suggestion
      A. Referee's comment
      B. Your response
 III. Reevaluation of manuscript
      A. Method preferred
      B. Reason for preference

Even if your manuscript is rejected, it will be better and stronger for having been carefully revised. Eventually, another journal may accept it for publication. One of the ironies of publishing is that journals often publish articles whose quality owes much to the referees of another journal.

11.14 Record your course of action and its outcome on the 3 × 5 card you prepared when you first submitted the manuscript. See Section 8.88.

ETHICAL QUESTIONS

Exclusive-Review Policies

11.15 Description of Policies. Most journals print a statement like the following:

☐ "The _____ regards as unacceptable submission of a manuscript to a professional journal while that paper is under review by another journal."

The editors assume that submission of a manuscript clearly implies a commitment to publish in that journal. Editors who discover (often through their referees) that a manuscript has been submitted to at least one other journal will withdraw the manuscript from processing. A few journals, for example *Sociological Methods and Research*, permit multiple submission. However,

☐ They expect right of first refusal. That is, if the journal's editor decides to publish the manuscript, he or she expects the author to allow the journal to publish it.

11.16 Editors' Reasons for the Policies. The editors give many reasons for these policies:

☐ Careful processing costs time and money (see Sections 10.10 to 10.18). If more than one journal accept a manuscript, all except one will have wasted both time and money and have delayed the processing of other manuscripts.

☐ For some editors and referees, the only tangible reward for their work is the pleasure of seeing in print articles on which they have spent time.

☐ When two parties play a game, both agree to certain rules. The journals have stated their rules clearly, and they expect authors to abide by them.

☐ Copyright laws complicate simultaneous publication, which is a possible outcome when journals permit multiple submission. Also, space in journals is too scarce to waste on multiple publication.

11.17 Authors' Disagreements. Many authors disagree with these policies. Their careers depend on publication, and multiple submission increases an author's chances of receiving an acceptance. Not violating the policy may cost an author a job, promotion, or raise. More generally important, cumulation in science requires more rapid publication than is the case at present (McCartney 1974). The fundamental question, then, is: How to balance the journals' needs for exclusive review with the authors' and the academic profession's need for shorter lags?

11.18 Possible Solutions. Aware of both this basic question and of the fact that consistently slow evaluations may persuade authors to submit their future manuscripts elsewhere, many journal editors have tried one or more of the following remedies:

☐ Increasing their pools of referees and giving each one fewer manuscripts to review.

☐ Seeking a formal commitment from referees to return evaluations within a stated period of time.

☐ Making a progress report to authors 12 weeks or so after submission, even if refereeing has not been completed. This policy emphasizes an author's right to withdraw the manuscript at this point without prejudice (see Zelditch 1975).

☐ Encouraging authors who feel they are receiving unfair treatment to withdraw their manuscripts and then submit them elsewhere.

☐ Encouraging shorter manuscripts, which can be refereed and published more rapidly (see Sections 9.4 and 9.6, and Schwartz 1975, pp. 82–83).

☐ Building lists, in advance of need, of possible referees for manuscripts on very specialized topics.

☐ Encouraging authors to seek collegial criticism before submitting manuscripts (see Sections 6.3, 6.5, and 6.6).

☐ Encouraging, in graduate school, training in sound techniques of evaluation.

11.19 Some authors have considered another solution to this problem. When submitting a manuscript state, in a letter and on the title page, that "this manuscript is submitted for consideration for publication. If notice of your publication decision is not received within [number of days or weeks] from the date of your receipt of this manuscript, the author will consider the nonreceipt of notice as rejection" (see Smith 1975, p. 13). The author may then submit the manuscript to another journal.

11.20 Reasonable Expectations for Turnaround. Even for journals with complex processing procedures, on most manuscripts most authors should be able to expect decisions in 12 weeks or less. Manuscripts that receive different recommendations from referees usually take longer. Every new round of evaluations introduces an additional delay of 3 weeks or more into the evaluation process. For more detailed discussion of the exclusive-review policy, see McCartney (1974).

To Referee or Not to Referee

11.21 As a general rule, reject a request to referee a manuscript if any of the following conditions are true:

○ The author is a close friend.
○ You have read and criticized prior drafts of the manuscript.
○ You disagree strongly with the author's general intellectual perspective.
○ You cannot read the manuscript for at least two months.

○ You feel, for any other reason, that you cannot make an impartial evaluation.

Return the manuscript with a brief letter of explanation. If any of the first four conditions hold but you feel you may still be an appropriate referee, write a letter to the editor describing the situation and requesting advice.

11.22 If you receive for refereeing the same manuscript from two different journals,

☐ Notify both editors of the situation.
☐ Delay evaluation until each has responded.

11.23 If you receive for refereeing a manuscript that you have previously refereed for another journal (and on which you probably recommended rejection), you may be tempted to return it without further consideration. However, journals have different purposes and serve different audiences. Recommendations should be based not only on quality but on suitability for a journal and its audience. Also, the manuscript may have been revised and improved. Therefore,

☐ Consider differences in the journals and look for possible differences in content before deciding against a second detailed evaluation.

Journals' and Editors' Responsibilities to Authors

11.24 "Kindness." Some editors dislike hurting an author's feelings with an unconditional rejection, so they hold out the possibility of revision and resubmission even though, deep down, they know that the manuscript can never be made acceptable. Or, they will hold onto a marginally acceptable manuscript for months in the hope that space in which to print it will magically appear (it rarely does). The motive is understandable, but both actions waste the author's time. In the long run, the consequences are usually less kind than an initial rejection would have been.

11.25 Prior Commitments. Journals change editors frequently, and many journals have substantial backlogs of accepted articles. Editorial policies sometimes change when editors change, but new policies should not be allowed to affect commitments made by a previous editor. To reverse a decision simply because a manuscript's topic is unsuited to the new editor's plans is unfair to authors.

11.26 The Need for Detailed Guidelines on Editorial Style. Most journals require that manuscripts be prepared in specific styles, yet instructions are not easily available. Journals that regularly publish descriptions of editorial style and evaluation procedures help authors and save themselves many questions. Even more troublesome is the plethora of styles. At present, the only detailed, widely used style guide in the social and behavioral sciences is the APA's *Publication Manual* (1974). The most widely read journals in sociology use at least three different editorial styles. Journals in anthropology use similar styles, but they vary in details. In the long run, all journals in a discipline would receive better and more accurately prepared manuscripts if the journals' sponsors settled on one basic style, commissioned the preparation of a detailed manual such as the APA's,[3] and made it available at cost. The manual's detail would ensure consistency, and would remove the cost of printing instructions in each issue or of mailing instructions on request. In addition to guidelines on style, such a manual should give detailed instructions for referees and detailed descriptions of processing and evaluation.

11.27 Other Topics. For a discussion of obligations on documentation, see Sections 3.23 to 3.26. Relations with critics and coauthors are discussed in Sections 6.13 to 6.20. Acknowledgment of help is discussed in Sections 8.56 to 8.59.

AUTHORS' RESPONSIBILITIES ON ACCEPTED MANUSCRIPTS

Guidelines for Preparing the Manuscript for Production

11.28   After they accept a manuscript, some journal editors begin production immediately. However, most will let authors make one more revision. At this point,

○ Read the manuscript carefully.

○ Indicate permissions received, if any, in acknowledgments. Follow the instructions given in the letter that grants permission. In the absence of instructions, note receipt of permissions in the acknowledgment note. See Sections 8.56 to 8.59 and 12.49 for help.

○ Consider making any substantive changes that the editor or referees have suggested.

○ Edit for clarity, grammatical correctness, and brevity. See Sections 5.18 to 5.62 for help.

○ Type on high-quality bond (Section 8.7).

○ Proofread with exceptional care, out loud (see Sections 8.84 and 11.32). Most problems that arise during galley and page proofing could have been avoided if the author had done earlier proofreading carefully. Remember that *some journals charge authors for corrections in type that are not necessitated by printers' errors!*

○ Prepare tables and illustrations according to the editor's instructions. See Sections 3.4 to 3.21 and 8.60 to 8.71 for help.

○ Photocopy the manuscript.

○ Send copies of letters granting permissions. *Never* send your only copy of a permission letter.

○ Send as many copies as the editor requests, by the date requested.

○ Retain at least one copy of the manuscript for your files.

○ Send the manuscript by first-class mail.

○ Record the date sent on your 3 × 5 card (see Section 8.88).

The Copyright Permission Form

11.29   At this point or later, the editor will ask you to sign a form that gives the journal permission to copyright your article, usually as part of the contents of the issue in which it appears. Copyright is usually held by the journal and not by the author. Always be certain that:

○ The article will be copyrighted.
○ You retain the right to reprint the article or portions of it without charge.
○ You understand and approve of the procedure by which others may obtain the right to reprint your article or a portion of it.
○ If you have questions, ask them of the editor. Resolve them before signing any forms.
○ Return the form as soon as you have signed it.

The Production Schedule

11.30   From this point on, every step in production must be accomplished by a given date. Dates are set by printing schedules, and delays add to the cost of printing an issue. If you fail to meet a deadline, your article may not be printed in the issue for which it was intended. Sometimes it will be printed, but without corrections you might have wanted to make. The following sections describe all possible steps in production. For any given article in any given journal, your participation in one or more steps may be skipped. For your own convenience,

○ Ask the editor to send you a schedule of dates on which you will be sent edited manuscript to check, galley proofs, and page proofs.
○ Since you are usually expected to complete checking or proofreading within 24 or 48 hours of receiving the manuscript, plan not to be out of town on any of those dates.

Some editors interpret failure to respond by the specified date as indicating that you have checked or proofread and found no errors.

The Edited Manuscript

11.31 An editor checks your manuscript for nonsubstantive errors, makes corrections, and marks type for the printer. Because even moving a comma may alter meaning, some editors give authors a chance to check edited copy.

- ○ Enter all changes on your copy of the manuscript.
- ○ Notify the editor of changes you cannot accept. In general, do not restore the original. Try different wording. See Section 6.11 for reasons and help.

Once you have seen and approved copy, or implied approval by not making corrections, you are responsible for it. Subsequent changes that you make in either galleys or page proofs, even of errors made by a copy editor, will be charged to you.

Galley Proofs

11.32 Galley proofs are long pages of printed lines set exactly as they will appear in the journal except that the lines have not been divided into pages. The width of the printed line matches the width of printed lines in the journal. Illustrations and camera-ready copy usually are not included. Correct galleys from the typed manuscript, either your own copy or the journal's (some journals do not return the typescript). Proofread out loud following this procedure:

- ○ Read with a partner. The person with the typed manuscript reads out loud, including all punctuation. The other person reads the master set of the galleys, word by word, correcting all errors.
- ○ Check with extra care symbols, equations, numbers in tables, and the spelling of technical terms.

○ Use proofreader's marks to make corrections. See Figure 11.1 for the marks and examples of use.

○ Use a pencil, not a pen.

○ Use a different color than the copy editor is using.

○ Never write between printed lines.

○ Correct only printer's errors. Galley proofing is not an invitation to do further editing, even though most authors never complete the job without finding something they wish they had said differently.

○ Make other changes *only* if something is blatantly in error or if leaving the original wording might result in a lawsuit. If you proofread the final draft of the manuscript carefully (see Section 11.28), you will not have to correct anything other than printer's errors.

○ If you make a correction longer than half a line: type it on a separate sheet of paper, cut it out, tape it onto the galley page, and draw a neat arrow to show where it belongs. Mention such items in a separate note to the editor.

○ If you write on the galley proofs any words that are *not* to be set in type, *encircle them completely*.

○ Transfer all corrections to the second copy (author's copy) of the galleys, or photocopy the corrected galleys.

○ Write the editor a letter describing any problems.

○ Send the letter, the master set of the galleys, and the journal's copy of the manuscript by certified first-class mail.

Page Proofs

11.33 Page proofs contain printed lines whose length and width exactly match those on the printed page. For most journals, you will see either galley or page proofs, but not both.

○ Proofread page proofs following the instructions in Section 11.32. Read out loud from the typescript if you have not seen galleys. Read out loud from the corrected galleys if you proofread them earlier.

○ Mark errors exactly as you would in galley proofs.

Figure 11.1 Commonly used proofreader's marks and examples of use.

However, because length of pages has been set, corrections are far more difficult and costly in page proofs then in galleys. Therefore, even for printer's errors, if you must alter one or more words,

○ Substitute words and punctuation that occupy the same number of spaces as you had before. Resetting a few words in one line is far less expensive than having to reset several lines.

Reprints

11.34 With either the galley or the page proofs, you will usually receive an order blank for reprints.

○ Select the quantity you want.
○ Fill in the form.
○ Enclose a check for the proper amount.
○ Do not delay, expecting to order later. That is usually impossible.
○ Return the form with the proofs.

If you do not receive an order form with proofs, write immediately and inquire. Reprints usually do not arrive until at least a month after the article has been printed. When they arrive, give copies to colleagues who have helped you. Spouses and parents also appreciate copies.

Charges for Corrections

11.35 Journals that charge for some or all corrections in galleys, or that charge by the page for printing, render a bill before the issue is printed.

○ Pay it promptly.

Failure to do so may cause the editor to drop the article from the issue.

Errata

11.36 After publication, read the article. Occasionally errors slip through. Most journals will publish corrections of crucial errors—for example, those that make sentences or equations incorrect or meaningless. Journals rarely use *errata* to correct errors of less consequence, such as changes of punctuation that you may have marked in proofs but that the printer failed to correct in the type.

Comments

11.37 Watch for notes and comments on your article. You may be given a chance to reply at a later date. Sometimes the journal's editor will send you copies of comments and ask you to prepare a response that will be published simultaneously with the comments. If asked to prepare a reply, respond promptly. Too much delay will blur readers' memories of your article. See Sections 9.9 to 9.16 for help.

SUMMARY

11.38 In this chapter I discuss the compromises between, and mutual responsibilities of, authors and journal editors. I discuss inquiries about delayed decisions (Section 11.2), responses to evaluations and decisions (11.3 to 11.14), ethical matters such as exclusive-review policies (11.15 to 11.27), and authors' responsibilities for an accepted manuscript (11.28 to 11.37).

NOTES TO CHAPTER 11

1. Unless, as occasionally happens, you discover an error that destroys your analysis but was overlooked by the referees. In such circumstances, withdraw the manuscript.

2. The frequency of the first may explain the extensive "recycling" of social- and behavioral-science manuscripts through one journal after another.

3. As Chapter 8 shows and many authors know, even a five-page pamphlet is woefully inadequate.

Part Three

GENERAL INSTRUCTIONS FOR PREPARING A BOOK MANUSCRIPT

Monographs,
Textbooks, and
Edited Collections

CHAPTER TWELVE

General Instructions for Preparing a Book Manuscript

INTRODUCTION

12.1   Books are not overgrown articles. Certainly the most obvious difference between the two types of manuscript is in physical size, but that fact causes difficulties for which many writers are not prepared. Standard outlines (described in Sections 2.21 to 2.42) are usually inappropriate, so book writers must create their own. Drafting takes longer, and revising takes infinitely longer. Typing and reproduction are costly. Critics willing to read a manuscript for a book are harder to find, and locating a willing publisher can be the most difficult task of all.

12.2   Because it is lengthier than an article, a book also has wider scope and greater depth of topic. This fact usually means that an author is trying to choose an outline from among many viable possibilities (see Section 2.11). He or she is also trying to unite a larger body of material under a common theme (see Section 5.7). The devastating effect of added length is reflected in the proportion of signed contracts (approximately half) that are never fulfilled with a completed book.

MANAGING THE DIFFICULTIES OF LENGTH

Choosing a Technique for Drafting

12.3 When beginning to write a book,

○ Read Chapter 4 and choose a technique for drafting that suits you and your topic.
○ Try it on one or two chapters. If it is hard to use, try another.

The best technique is not necessarily the one you use for drafting articles. You may eventually find that you like working on only one chapter at a time, from first draft through final draft. Or you may work best when you have several chapters in different stages of preparation at the same time.

Organizing the Manuscript

12.4 To organize your manuscript and prevent loss of pages,

○ Purchase one or more notebooks that are 3 inches wide at the spine. Mark sections with dividers that measure $8\frac{1}{2} \times 11$ inches.

Make sections for the preface, acknowledgments, table of contents, each chapter, each appendix, bibliography, and index. If you change your organization of chapters, simply reorder the sections as needed. To make changes easy, use dividers with clear plastic tabs that hold removable labels. In the section for the acknowledgments,

○ Keep a list of people who help you with your research and writing. Include research assistants, computer programmers, typists, and others.
○ Keep a list of persons who criticize chapters for you.

Organizing Time and Keeping Track of Progress

12.5 To help you organize your time and keep track of your progress,

○ Draft a schedule. See Table 12.1 for an example.

Use the labels of the sections in the notebook as row stubs (Section 3.12 describes row stubs). For column heads (Section 3.17), use: first draft; R1, R2, R3, R4, R5 (for the five stages in revision; see Sections 5.2 to 5.64); check accuracy of references; type; proofread; copy; mail. Draw lines to form cells. At the intersection of each row and column, pencil in a proposed date for completion. You need not necessarily work on chapters in order. When a task is done, enter a completion date in pen.

○ Tape the table on the inside front cover of the first notebook.

CHOOSING AN EDITORIAL STYLE

Description of Styles

12.6 Most book companies have a "house" editorial style in which they want manuscripts prepared. These styles resemble those listed in Table 8.1 and described in detail in Chapter 8. Authors usually receive a style guide without charge when they sign a contract. Some guides, for example University of Chicago Press's *A Manual of Style* (1969, 546 pp.), completely explain all aspects of book production from grammar to printing. Others, for example Addison-Wesley's (1965), concentrate on manuscript preparation and thus are much shorter.

Choice of a Style

12.7 If you have signed or expect to sign a contract with a specific company,

Table 12.1 Sample Schedule for Writing a Book with Six Chapters

Section	Draft 1	R1	R2	R3	R4	R5	Check Refs.	Type	Proof	Copy	Mail
Preface	8/77										
Acknowl-edgments	8/77										
Contents	8/77										
1	1/77	8/77									
2	2/77										
3	6/77										
4	4/77										
5	5/77										
6	3/77										
A	7/77										
B	7/77										
Bibliography	7/77										
Index	12/78										

○ Use the company's style guide.

○ If you must deviate from the company's style, ask permission to do so and attach a list of deviations to the manuscript.

○ If you use another guide that is very different from your publisher's, obtain written permission from the publisher to do so. Attach a copy of the guide unless the publisher tells you that the production department already has a copy.

○ Also, ask about submitting copies of the first one or two chapters so that a copy editor can check style and make suggestions for changes. For both you and the company, such a check may save time on subsequent editing and proofreading.

There are excellent reasons for following your publisher's style if at all possible.

☐ The typographical needs of your book publisher probably differ from those of the journals with which you are familiar.

☐ Your book will be produced best and most efficiently if the production department can use the style with which its personnel are most familiar.

12.8 If you have not signed a contract,

○ Follow the University of Chicago Press's (1969) guidelines. Most other publishers take many of their guidelines from it.

○ Use the natural-science instructions (MSN; see Table 8.1) if you are in anthropology, educational research, linguistics, psychiatry, psychology, social psychology, or sociology.

○ Use the humanities style (MSH; Table 8.1) if you are in business, history, historical or philosophical education, or political science.

Answers to Questions About Style

12.9 If you have questions for which the style guide gives no answers,

○ Write a letter to your publisher with the questions and examples of possible answers.

○ If you have no publisher, choose among alternatives on the basis of *simplicity*. The simplest way usually costs less in time and money.

○ After making choices, follow them *consistently*.

○ Keep a list of all such choices for your own use. When you mail the completed manuscript, send with it a copy of the list.

INSTRUCTIONS FOR TYPING A MANUSCRIPT

12.10   When typing the manuscript, follow these general instructions for all pages (largely based on practices recommended and used in University of Chicago Press 1969). The instructions are written as if you were submitting the manuscript for production. Prepare it this way even if you are submitting it for evaluation. For additional details on submitting a manuscript for evaluation, see Sections 15.2 to 15.4. For additional details on submitting a manuscript for production, see Sections 17.1 to 17.3.

Paper, Typewriter, Margins, Paragraphs

12.11   All copies of a manuscript must be sturdy and easy to read.

○ *Paper.* For the original: use 16- or 20-pound paper that is $8\frac{1}{2} \times$ 11 inches. Never use "erasable" bond. Use xerographic copies rather than carbons. If you use masters, use mimeograph or multilith, and high-quality copying paper. Obtain your publisher's permission before using masters. Type or copy on only one side of each page.

○ *Typewriter.* Use a new black ribbon. Use the same size of type pitch (pica, 10 spaces per inch; elite, 12) throughout. Clean the typewriter keys before beginning.

○ *Margins.* Leave 1½ inches on the left; 1 inch top, bottom, right.
○ *Paragraphing.* Indent the first line of every paragraph five spaces from the left margin.

Spacing

12.12   Copy editors need plenty of space on pages to edit and to mark type for compositors.

○ NEVER SINGLE-SPACE LINES unless the publisher explicitly tells you to do so.
○ *Double-space* between all lines of all title pages, dedications, epigraphs, forewords, prefaces, tables of contents, chapters, quotations, equations, notes, tables, illustrations, bibliographies, appendixes, glossaries, indexes, lists of illustrations, and lists of tables.
○ *Triple-space* above center and side headings and above and below blocked, indented quotations and extracts.

   EXCEPTION.   Double-space above a side heading if a center heading immediately precedes it.

○ Leave *four spaces* between a chapter number and title and between the title and the beginning of the text; between the headings "Contents," "List of Illustrations," "List of Tables," "Foreword," "Preface," "Notes," "Bibliography," "List of References," "Appendix," "Glossary" and "Index" and the first line of text or the first line of the first entry in these sections.
○ Leave at least 3 *inches* between the top of the page and the first line of typing on the first page of the half-title page, title page, dedication, epigraph, table of contents, list of illustrations, list of tables, foreword, preface, each chapter, bibliography, list of references, glossary, each appendix, index.
○ Leave at least 2 *inches* between the top of the page and the heading "Notes."

Quotations, Equations, Symbols, Accents, Capitalization, Use of Numbers, Spelling

12.13 Guidelines for *typing quotations* are in Sections 8.35 to 8.37. Guidelines for *typing equations* are in Sections 8.38 to 8.40.

EXCEPTION.   Number equations sequentially by chapters: (12.1), (12.2), and so forth. Also, contrary to the practice of many journals, the book publisher may prefer to have equations typed in the form shown in the left-hand column of Section 8.40. Always check the publisher's style guide for instructions. Guidelines for *treatment of symbols and accents* are in Section 8.11; for *capitalization*, in Section 8.13; for *use of numerals and words*, in Section 5.53. For *spelling*, use *Webster's Third* or *Webster's Collegiate Dictionary*.

EXCEPTION.   British companies may require that you use the *Oxford Dictionary*. Section 5.72 lists other useful dictionaries.

Separate Pages and Page Numbers

12.14   Items That Start on a Separate Page.   Begin on a separate page: half-title page, title page, dedication, epigraph, table of contents, foreword, preface, each chapter, notes to each chapter, each table, each illustration, list of tables, list of illustrations, list of captions for illustrations, each appendix, bibliography or list of references, glossary, and index.

12.15   Page Numbers.   In general,

○ Place page numbers in the *upper right-hand corner* of the page.

  EXCEPTION.   For the first page of the table of contents, foreword, preface, each chapter, each appendix, bibliography or list of references, glossary and index, center the number in the margin at the bottom of the page.

○ DO NOT ASSIGN PAGE NUMBERS to illustrations and the list of captions.

○ Consult your publisher's style guide for instructions on whether to assign page numbers to tables. If you find no instructions, ask. Some publishers want tables interleaved with pages of text and numbered in sequence with text pages. Some want tables collected and numbered at the end of each chapter. Some want no page numbers. Some want tables to be separate from the manuscript.

12.16   *Page numbers for all except the final draft:*

○ For each chapter and appendix, number pages sequentially beginning with 1: 12-1, 12-2; 13-1, 13-2 (for chapters); A-1, A-2; B-1, B-2 (for appendixes).

12.17   *Page numbers on the final draft:*

○ *Front matter.* Beginning with the first page, number in sequential, lowercase roman numerals beginning with "i."
○ *For rest of manuscript.* Beginning with first page of first chapter, number in sequential arabic numerals from 1 through the last chapter, the appendixes, the glossary, and the bibliography.

The Text

12.18   *Headings and subheadings:*

○ Follow the examples for APA in Figure 8.5, but omit the underline.

If you need to number headings and subheadings, consult the publisher's style guide for instructions. In general,

○ Do not use the system for numbering outlines that is described in Chapter 2. It is cumbersome.
○ Consider using single or double enumeration.

Single enumeration (shown in Figure 8.5 as *JASA* style) requires arabic numerals beginning with 1 to show the first (second, third, etc.) main heads in a chapter. Use compound numbers for headings at other levels. For example:

 3.1   First subsection in main section 3.

 4.3.2   Second third-order topic in third subsection of main section 4.

Double enumeration adds the chapter number. For example:

 5.3.1   First subsection in main section 3 of Chapter 5.

For most scientific books, numbering to the second level of importance should be adequate.

Documentation:

○ For MSN, follow examples of documentation in all chapters of this book except Chapter 8. For MSH, follow examples in notes to Chapter 8 (except for page ranges; see Chapter 8, note 1) and instructions in Sections 3.27 to 3.36, 8.41, 8.49 to 8.51, 8.77, 8.78.

Hyphens:

○ Use no hyphens at ends of typed lines.
○ See Section 8.9 for reasons and instructions.

Notes

12.19 In general,

○ Number the notes for each chapter sequentially beginning with 1.
○ Collect them at the end of each chapter on a page entitled, for example, "Notes to Chapter 12." NEVER type them on pages with text unless the publisher explicitly tells you to do so.[1]
○ Number the pages of notes in sequence after the text pages of the chapters to which they refer.

EXCEPTION. Sometimes a publisher prefers that the

notes, typed separately for each chapter as described just above, be collected as part of the back matter, placed following the last appendix, and numbered in sequence after the last page of the last appendix.

○ For examples of notes in MSN style, see those to Chapters 2 to 7 and 9 to 16 of this book. For notes in MSH style, see those to Chapter 8. For proper treatment of page ranges in both styles, see Section 8.79.

Tables and Illustrations

12.20   In general,

○ Place each table and each illustration on a separate page.
○ NEVER type or draw onto pages with text unless the publisher explicitly tells you to do so.
○ Number each in sequence by chapters as is done in this book. For example, Table 8.1, 8.2, 8.3; Figure 8.1, 8.2, 8.3.
○ Place an indicator of position in the text. See Section 8.62 for examples.
○ Refer to tables and illustrations by number. See Section 8.62 for examples. Do not refer to them as being "above" or "below," because compositors cannot always place them exactly where you wish.

Sections 3.4 to 3.19 explain use and construction of tables and give definitions of parts. Sections 8.60 to 8.68 explain requirements of different styles. Sections 3.20, 3.21, 8.70, and 8.71 give similar guidelines for illustrations. Follow your publisher's style guide if its requirements differ from those described here.

12.21   For tables,

○ Use as few vertical and horizontal lines as possible. They are very expensive to set in type. The tables in all chapters except 8 have rules that are typical of tables in books.
○ Capitalize the title and column headings following the in-

structions in Section 8.13. Capitalize only the first word of row stubs. For an example, see Figure 3.1.

○ Check the publisher's requirements for placement and page numbering. See Section 12.15.

○ For treatment of notes, see the illustrations in Figure 3.1.

12.22   For illustrations,

○ Type and capitalize captions and legends (both are defined in Section 8.70) as shown in Figures 8.4 and 8.5 and other figures in this book. Section 8.70 shows examples of other styles for captions.

○ Place captions and legends in a separate list.

○ On the reverse side of each illustration write lightly, in pencil, the number and a word or two from the manuscript's title.

○ Keep the list and the illustrations separate from the manuscript.

EXCEPTION.   When submitting a manuscript for a publisher to consider for possible publication, you may prefer to interleave nonphotographic illustrations with the appropriate text pages. Some referees prefer not to have to search in separate piles for illustrations. If in doubt, ask the publisher for instructions.

○ Ask your publisher if the company has any special requirements for treatment and mailing of illustrations.

INSTRUCTIONS FOR FRONT MATTER

Half-Title and Title Pages

12.23   The half-title page shows only the main title. The title page shows the full title and the author's name and institutional affiliation (the by-line). On both pages,

○ Center the title from left to right.

On the title page,

○ Center the author's name also, and the institutional affiliation below the name. For an example, see the first four lines in Figure 8.1.
○ If you have a coauthor, see Figure 8.3 for arrangements of authors' names and affiliations. The order of names on the title page and in the contract you sign with a publisher should be the same.

Dedication and Epigraph

12.24   A *dedication* should fit on one or two lines of type.

○ Begin it with "To" ("Dedicated to" is redundant).
○ Center it from left to right.
○ Capitalize the first letter in proper nouns. For all other words, capitalize as you would in an ordinary English sentence.

An *epigraph* is a short quotation. Some writers prefer an epigraph to a dedication. In an epigraph,

○ Capitalize words following capitalization in the original text.
○ Give the source on the line following the quotation, using no parentheses or brackets. Use the author's name and the title of the work. You need no other bibliographic data.
○ In general, do not explain the relevance of an epigraph. If you feel you must, do so in the preface or in the introduction but never on the epigraph page.

If you use both a dedication and an epigraph, place them on separate pages, prepared as described above.

Table of Contents

12.25   The table of contents gives readers a brief outline of a book's content. The publisher's marketing department uses the table of contents when planning promotion for a book.

○ Draft the table of contents from copies of chapter outlines.
○ Include chapter and part titles and page numbers.
○ On the draft you submit to a publisher for production, do not show page numbers. Simply enter "000." You will fill in numbers when you receive page proofs.
○ For an example, see Figure 12.1.

It is not necessary to show first- and second-order headings, but most readers find them useful.

Lists of Illustrations and Tables

12.26 Prepare each list separately. Type the numbers and titles, or numbers and captions, exactly as they appear on the illustrations and tables. These lists are often omitted from books with very few or very many tables and illustrations. Sometimes they are printed, but in a briefer form than you provided. However,

○ Always submit lists. Even if they are not printed, the publisher may use them as a checklist to guard against loss.
○ For examples, see the lists printed in this book.

Foreword

12.27 A foreword is usually between two and four typed, double-spaced pages in length, and is written by someone other than the book's author. Most forewords are written either to praise a book or to establish a perspective on it.

○ Sign a foreword at the end. Type its author's name flush with the right margin, and his or her title below the name. Place the author's institutional affiliation flush left.

Preface and Acknowledgments

12.28 In the preface,

○ Explain why you wrote the book and what hopes you have for it.

Contents

Figure 12.1 Example of table of contents. An alternative practice: some publishers never list forewords, prefaces, acknowledgments, or other parts that precede the Contents. Also, they place the lists of illustrations and tables after the Contents and list both parts in the Contents.

○ Include acknowledgments of help you have received in research, and in writing and typing your manuscript. See Section 12.4 for help with acknowledgments.

○ If necessary, list permissions received to quote copyrighted and unpublished material. See Sections 12.43 to 12.50 for instructions.

○ Use no material that is essential to understanding the text of the book. For example, a review of literature belongs in the text and not in the preface.

○ Sign the preface if you wish.

○ When you prepare the preface, remember that potential readers will skim it when deciding whether to read the book. Also, your publisher will use it when preparing promotional material for your book.

If you have only acknowledgments to put in a preface, title it "Acknowledgments" instead of "Preface."

INSTRUCTIONS FOR TEXT

12.29   Check and correct the text for organization and content, clarity, grammatical correctness, brevity, and style. Use the criteria in Sections 5.2 to 5.64. If you are writing for any other than a highly specialized audience, check readability (see Sections 5.65 to 5.69). Check the accuracy of documentation. Also, ask your computer center about programs and equipment that would permit you to type and edit the manuscript on a computer terminal. Marilyn Frankenthaler (1976), a graduate student in Spanish with no experience in computer use, typed and edited her entire dissertation in Spanish on the computer. Using IBM's Administrative Terminal System (ATS/360), she was able "to execute major or minor . . . revisions, to correct errors in punctuation, spelling, words, sentences, . . . and to reorganize small or large sections of text without ever having to retype" the entire document. At each step in revision, she could instantly obtain neatly printed copy (Frankenthaler 1976, p. 61).

12.30   When proofreading the typed manuscript,

○ Check citations in text or notes with documents listed in the bibliography. Every document cited should be included in the bibliography.

○ If the bibliography is to list only documents cited, discard documents you did not cite.

○ Check for typographical errors (some common errors are described in Section 8.84).

○ Proofread out loud following the procedure in Section 11.32.

○ To make short corrections in the typed manuscript, use a correction fluid, such as Liquid Paper, to cover the error. Let the fluid dry and retype correctly.

○ To insert short sections, type the addition above the appropriate line and mark the spot where it belongs with a caret: ∧.

○ For complicated corrections and long insertions, retype the manuscript page. If the retyping gives you more than one page, assign the page number to the first page and the number plus letters to the subsequent pages: for example, 21, 21a, 21b, 21c, 22. On the bottom of page 21, type and encircle: (21a, 21b, and 21c follow) . On the bottom of 21c, type and encircle: (22 follows) .

○ An alternative procedure: leave the original page, for example 21, as is. Type the added material on one or more additional pages and number them 21a, 21b, and so forth. On the bottom of pages 21 and 21b (or the last page of the addition), type and encircle a note that tells what page follows: (21a follows)(22 follows). Use a caret (∧) on page 21 to show where the addition should be inserted. In the margin by the caret handwrite and encircle: (Insert pp. 21a and 21b here).

○ Avoid handwritten corrections. They are hard to read.

○ Avoid corrections in the margins. They hinder a copy editor.

INSTRUCTIONS FOR BACK MATTER

Appendix

12.31   Section 3.22 tells what to include in an appendix. If you have only one appendix, it may be designated, simply, "Appendix." For example, see Figure 12.1.

Glossary

12.32   Use a glossary if your manuscript contains many foreign words or technical terms.

- ○ Arrange words alphabetically. See Section 12.36 for guidelines.
- ○ Inquire about computerized alphabetization. If you type entries into a terminal, the computer may be able to alphabetize them for you.
- ○ Begin each word on a separate line.
- ○ Do not put periods at the ends of definitions unless at least one is a complete sentence. Then use a period after each one.

Bibliography

12.33   When preparing a bibliography,

- ○ Follow the general instructions in Sections 3.36 and 12.30.
- ○ To minimize errors, type directly from bibliography cards.
- ○ If you list both cited and uncited documents, group them separately. Title the cited documents "References." Title the uncited ones "Bibliography." You may wish to divide the latter into categories. For examples, see Section 3.36.
- ○ If you are writing a textbook or editing a large collection devoted exclusively to bibliographic items, you may wish to annotate some or all of the entries. Use only a sentence or two per entry. Each annotation should describe the most salient feature of the document for the reader.

Indexes

12.34 How to Begin. Begin the index when you start writing a manuscript. As you write,

○ Note various topics, each on a separate index card, and alphabetize them. Use 3 × 5 cards and a file box that is at least 8 inches deep.

○ For each topic, the index card should show a key word or term, a statement about that term (which may later become a subentry), and either a page number or beginning and ending page numbers. If your book is numbered by sections, as this one is and many bibliographies are, list either the section number or inclusive section numbers. Each card should contain information like that in the following three examples:

> Outlines
>> general functions   2.1-2.2
>
> Outlines
>> expression of topics   2.3-2.7
>
> Outlines
>> data-analysis   2.24-2.40

○ When the manuscript is complete, mark all potential index topics on each page, beginning with page 1 of the text and including information on tables and figures and in amplifying notes. Make a card for each new topic and add to the cards in your file.

○ Sort the cards and discard duplicates.

○ An alternative procedure: inquire about computer programs for indexing. If you have typed the manuscript on a terminal, you may need only to type in the specific items you want indexed. The computer will then search your manuscript for all occurrences of those items, list page numbers in sequence, and alphabetize entries. If you have not typed the manuscript on a computer, you may be able to type in the items and page numbers. The computer will then alphabetize items and arrange page numbers in sequence. Subsequent editing, such as changing manuscript-page numbers to printed-page numbers, may be typed into the terminal. When you are done, the computer will print a neat, errorless copy.

12.35   What to Include.

○ Index both topics and proper names. If you have many of both, index them separately. Otherwise make one index including both.
○ When in doubt about whether to index a given item, include it. You can easily delete it later if you change your mind.
○ Try to view the index from the reader's perspective, and include information accordingly. What information will readers need? What questions will they ask, and how? What breakdowns of information will be most useful?

12.36   How to Alphabetize.   For most works in the social and behavioral sciences, the most important aspect of organization is alphabetization. There are two methods: letter by letter up to the first comma, and word by word. For example:

> Education and psychology   [word by word]
> Educational psychology
>
> Educational psychology   [letter by letter]
> Education and psychology

In this book, Table 5.6 is alphabetized by letter, so "accordingly" precedes "a great deal of." Table 7.1 is alphabetized by word, so *Behavior Science Research* precedes *Behavioral Science*.

○ If you have computer assistance in preparing your index, use letter-by-letter alphabetizing. Also ask a programmer to tell you exactly how the program treats entries that are not letters such as spaces, hyphens, periods, commas, and semicolons.
○ For all indexes, if you are mixing names of persons and places, the names of persons precede names of places. For

example: *England, Laura* would precede a reference to the country of *England*.

○ For compound names, such as Smith-Jones, and names with particles, such as de sola Price, alphabetize following common practice in your discipline. For example, Derek de sola Price is usually alphabetized under *Price*.

○ For word-by-word alphabetizing, treat *Mc* and *M'*, which are abbreviated forms of *Mac*, as if they were actually spelled *Mac*. Similarly, treat *St.* in a person's name, for example June St. John or St. John Smith, as if the *St.* were spelled *Saint*.

12.37 How to Prepare Entries and Subentries. Each entry should include both a heading and either a page number or inclusive pages. Subentries are particular aspects of entries. For example:

> Textbooks, 000–000: definition of, 000; preparation of, 000; uses for, 000
>
> Standard outlines, 2.21–2.42; for data analysis, 2.24–2.40; for method and theory, 2.41–2.42

When preparing entries and subentries,

○ See to it that they have not only a logical but a parallel grammatical structure. For example, in the first example just above, *textbook* would follow the preposition at the end of each subentry: *definition of textbook*. In the second example, the subentries are subcategories.

○ Do not use the same word in two different senses. For example, do not use *American* as both a noun and an adjective.

○ Prepare entries in the same style. The examples above are in *run-in* style. *Indented* style is shown in the following example:

> Standard outlines, 2.21–2.42
> for data analysis, 2.24–2.40
> for method and theory, 2.41–2.42

12.38 When to Use Cross-references. If a reader might look for a topic under a name different from the one you choose,

○ Prepare an entry under the alternative name. Follow it with a period and *"See* _____." For example:

> Fourfold table. *See* 2 × 2 table

○ If you have information on a topic under two related headings, at the end of each heading refer the reader to the other heading. For example:

> Format, 000–000.
> *See also* Outline

EXCEPTION.   If the related entry is less than a line long, do not use *"See also."* Instead, include the related entry and page numbers as a subentry of the other entry.

CAUTION.   Index styles vary. Check your publisher's style guide. For example, some publishers would prefer that the entries just shown be listed as follows:

> Format, 000–000
> *see also* Outline
> Fourfold table, *see* 2 × 2 table

12.39   How to Prepare Cards.   To prevent misreading, type the index cards. You may want to use a special platen for index cards and long strips of perforated 3 × 5 cards rather than separated ones. These speed typing.

12.40   How to Edit.   After the index is completed, edit the cards for consistency and completeness.

○ Look especially for instances in which you used two or more terms for the same phenomenon, such as *tribe* and *nation* as a collective reference to the same set of Indians. Use only one term and put all references after it. If duplicate terms occur often, check Sections 5.19 to 5.21. Your writing may lack clarity.

○ Be certain you have all necessary cross-references, and none that are superfluous.

○ Complete editing *before you receive page proofs.*

12.41   When and How to Add Page Numbers.   When you receive page proofs,

○ Write the page-proof page numbers on the typed manuscript pages. Use the copy on which you marked index items (see Section 12.34). Each time a new printed page begins, mark the exact spot on the manuscript page. In general, a printed page will include between 1½ and 2 manuscript pages.

○ Next, beginning on page 1 of the typed manuscript, take out the index card for each entry in turn. At the bottom of each card list the printed-page numbers. If some of the original page numbers were on adjacent pages, they may now be on the same printed page.

EXCEPTION.

○ If you number entries, paragraphs or sections as I did in this book, you may index completely from the typed manuscript, using section numbers instead of page numbers.

12.42   How to Type a Final Draft.

○ Type directly from cards.

○ Ask your publisher for instructions. You may have to use a special kind of paper, or lines of specified lengths, that would be improper for the rest of the manuscript.

○ In the absence of instructions, type entries across the page. NEVER type in double columns.

○ The length of the final index is typically one-thirtieth the size of the book (Resnikoff and Dolby 1972, p. 10).

PERMISSIONS

12.43   This section does not give an exhaustive discussion of permissions. My purpose is to alert authors to their responsibilities in common situations. Most publishers routinely supply their authors with detailed information on permissions. For more information consult University of Chicago Press (1969, Chapter 4), Wagner (1976a,b,c), your publisher's guide, or the documents cited below.

Author's Responsibility

12.44 Obtaining permission to use someone else's work is usually the author's responsibility, although publishers will sometimes assist in this process. The fundamental principle governing the need for permissions is the doctrine of fair use. Its purpose is to allow normal quotation while requiring permission for the use of "substantial amounts" of an author's material.

> For example, one page of a 15-page article is usually a "substantial amount." So is one line of poetry. One page of a 600-page book may not be.

Usually you may quote up to 50 words of copyrighted prose without permission.

When Are Permissions Needed?

12.45 Material Taken from Copyrighted Documents. When using more than 50 words of copyrighted material from a single source, follow these guidelines:

○ If you are quoting from an article in a journal, check the journal's policy on permissions, sometimes published with *Instructions to Contributors* or on the page with the table of contents. Some permit quotation of up to 500 words without permission. Others require that you ask permission for any amount over 50 words. If you cannot find a statement of policy, write to the journal or to its sponsor and ask.
○ If you are quoting from a book, determine whether the publisher has signed the resolution on fair use sponsored by the Association of American University Presses.

If the publisher has signed the resolution you may quote without permission (1) if your work is a piece of original scholarship and not an anthology or book of readings; (2) your purpose is accurate citation of authority, criticism, review, or evaluation; (3) you do not use an entire unit, such as a complete poem, table, illustration, or chapter; (4) you give an accurate citation of source; and (5) you do not violate the doctrine of fair use (University of Chicago Press 1969, pp. 93–95).

○ If the publisher has not signed the resolution, ask permission for all quotations from a single source that total over 50 words.

○ Always ask permission to use tables, illustrations, and excerpts from poems or pieces of music.

○ When in doubt, seek advice from your publisher. If still in doubt, ask permission.

For further detail on the old copyright law, see Stedman (1967); for information on the new copyright law, which takes effect on January 1, 1978, see Wagner (1976a,b,c).

12.46 Material Taken from Unpublished Documents. Under the new copyright law, unpublished material is protected by common law. The protection is usually perpetual. Under the new copyright law, unpublished works are automatically protected by copyright beginning at the time the work is created (and *not* at the time of publication, as is the case with the old law; Wagner 1976a, p. 22). The new law makes mandatory deposit of the work with the Library of Congress but does not require registration (Wagner 1976a, p. 23). Regardless of the material's age or the amount you want to use,

○ Always request permission from the author or from the author's heirs.[2]

12.47 When, How, and What to Request.

○ Request a permission as soon as you know that you will need it. Some publishers will grant permission even if you have not found a publisher for your manuscript. Others will indicate their probable decision, but ask that you write again when a publisher has been found. Still others will not commit themselves until you have signed a contract. Never delay asking if you have signed a contract. *Some publishers will not begin production of a book until all permissions have been obtained.*

○ Request permission from both the publisher and the author. The publisher's name and address are normally located on the back of the title page of a book. For journals, information on publishers is usually printed with or near the table of contents.

○ If material you quote includes quotations from other—secondary—sources, obtain a separate permission (a "secondary permission") to quote the secondary source also.

12.48 In your letters requesting permission, specifically describe the material you want to use and the nature of your book.

○ For the material you want to use, give author's name; the title of the article, chapter, table or illustration; name of the journal or title of the book; year of original publication; name of publisher; name of copyright owner; and page number or inclusive pages.

○ For your book, give title (even if the title is tentative), the publisher (if you have signed a contract), the proposed date of publication, the intended use of the book, and estimated length. Indicate whether it will be part of a series.

○ Also specify the type of rights you are seeking. Permission may be granted exclusively or nonexclusively; and for United States publication, United States and Commonwealth publication, or world publication. The cost varies with the type granted.

For a sample letter, see Figure 12.2. Be prepared for some delays. Publishers normally respond promptly, but many authors do not. Locating the heirs of a deceased author can cause even more delays. Some publishers will grant permission by letter. Others will send you a form that you must fill out and return.

Dear Publisher [Author]:

I am requesting permission to quote 450 words from the following book:

John Author. "Chapter Eight." *Title of the Book.* City:
Publisher, 1956. Copyright held by John Author.

I want to quote from two sections in that chapter. On p. 250, I want to begin
quoting with the words "Beginning of quotation" in line 3 on that page. On p.
258, I want to quote the entire first complete paragraph on that page. For your
convenience I have attached copies of the pages in question and circled the
parts I want to quote.

My book is a monograph, titled *First Book.* My publisher is Book Company. The
proposed publication date is January 1978. The book will be part of the Scholarly Studies Series and will have approximately 210 pages.

I would like nonexclusive world publication rights.

I look forward to hearing from you at your earliest convenience.

Sincerely,

A. Monograph Writer

AMW/sec

enclosures

cc: John Author [Publisher]

Figure 12.2   A sample letter requesting permission.

12.49 What to Do with the Permissions You Receive.

○ Keep a master list of permissions you have requested. On that list note receipt of permission or rejection and the date on which you received each response. Also record the special conditions attached to each. For example, the publisher may request a certain form of acknowledgment, payment of a fee before publication, or a copy of your book when it is published. Some publishers give their authors a summary form designed for this purpose. If yours does not, use the form shown in Table 12.2.

○ Write a letter acknowledging receipt of permission, and accepting the conditions.

CAUTION. Note the exceptions stated in Section 12.50.

○ Keep a copy of your original letter, the response, and your acknowledgment in a file. Make duplicates for your publisher.

EXCEPTION. Some publishers prefer that you send them the originals.

○ If the permission requests a special kind of acknowledgment in the text or in the preface, place a copy of the letter with the manuscript.

○ NEVER send your only copy of a permission through the mails.

○ When acknowledging receipt of permission in your book, use the exact wording and placement specified by the publisher. If wording is not specified, when you use the material give complete bibliographic data in a note. Follow that information with a statement such as: "Used by permission of the author and the publisher."

The common places to acknowledge permission are:

○ For a borrowed illustration: in the legend. For example, see Figure 8.4.

Table 12.2 Summary Form for Information on Permissions

Source (Author's Name, Word from Title, and Date of Publication)	Date of Request	Response, Date		Location of Material in Manuscript	Rights	Fee			Special Conditions
		Author	Publisher			Amount	Date to Be Paid	Paid	
Smith, *Factors*, 1972	6/2/77	Yes 9/15/77	Yes 6/15/77	Table 4.3; quote on p. 85	Non-exclusive, world	$30	On publication		Acknowledge where used; "Used by permission of . . ."

○ For a borrowed table: in the source note (described in Section 3.19).

○ For a borrowed quotation, section, chapter: in a note, preferably to be printed as a footnote rather than as a note at the end of a chapter.

○ For many items taken from the same few sources: in the preface. With the individual items, cite source only.

12.50   How and When to Pay Fees.   Fees are usually the author's responsibility. See Section 16.14.

○ On each permission you receive, check for a fee and a payment date. Arrange for payments accordingly.

○ DO NOT AGREE to fees that stipulate a sliding payment based on sales of your book. Such agreements necessitate detailed accounting. They also give a potential competitor data on the success of your book. Also, do not agree to very high fees. In such cases, consult with your publisher before signing an agreement.

SUMMARY

12.51   In this chapter I discuss the difficulties of trying to write a book and suggest ways to cope with them (Sections 12.1 to 12.5). Then I explain how to choose an editorial style (12.6 to 12.9); how to type a manuscript (12.11 to 12.22); how to prepare the front matter (12.23 to 12.28), text (12.29 and 12.30), and back matter (12.31 to 12.42); and when and how to seek permissions (12.43 to 12.50).

NOTE TO CHAPTER 12

1.   Collecting notes separately at the end of each chapter does not necessarily mean that they will be printed that way. Sometimes notes are printed at the bottoms of the appropriate pages of text—that is, as *footnotes*.
2.   Under the new law a copyright will extend for the life of the author (or, in the case of joint authors, the last surviving author) plus 50 years (Wagner 1976a, p. 23).

CHAPTER THIRTEEN

Preparing Monographs, Textbooks, and Edited Collections

INTRODUCTION

13.1 Each type of book presents unique opportunities and difficulties.

MONOGRAPHS

Description of a Monograph

13.2 Monographs are scholarly books that concentrate on one aspect of science. Their authors are recognized authorities on the monographs' topics. Some monographs report research—for example, Althauser and Spivack's (1975) *The Unequal Elites.* Others are primarily theoretical—for example, Deutsch's (1963) *The Nerves of Government*; or methodological—for example Webb, Campbell, Schwartz, and Sechrest's (1966) *Unobtrusive Measures.* In a monograph, an author's viewpoint is as important as factual observations. Some authors establish a context largely in the literature (see Sections 2.13 and 2.14 and 2.25 to 2.28). Others also establish a context in a contemporary social concern. Although most monographs are written primarily for scholars, some are also used by students, and a few have even become popular with the general public—for example, Riesman's (1950) *The Lonely Crowd.*

Monograph or Articles?

13.3 If you want to write a monograph,

○ First ask yourself whether the topic requires such extended discussion that even a series of articles is impractical. If not, you may find the articles a more practical endeavor.

Since the late 1960s many publishers—even university presses—have been rejecting monographs with valuable content (and, sometimes, even well written) solely because the publishers cannot sell enough copies to meet costs and earn a profit. Contrary to popular belief, library purchases alone do not enable publishers to recover basic costs.

○ Also consider the factors that motivate you to write.

Monographs are much longer than articles and must be written for a somewhat less specialized audience. Willing publishers are hard to find. Advances and grants for manuscript preparation are virtually nonexistent. Royalties are small. Professional advancement and the approval of colleagues are often delayed until the book is published and reviews of it have appeared in journals. If you need a motivation to write other than a belief in the intrinsic value of your work, you probably will be unable to complete a monograph.

13.4 To help you determine the value of a monograph,

○ Write a test prospectus following the instructions in Chapter 15.

Think about the manuscript from the perspective of readers and publishers. Some monographs can have limited use as textbooks or trade books if their authors plan for it in advance. For example, a study of American voting behavior with a readability level of 16 or 17 (see Sections 5.65 to 5.68) might be useful in some college classes if rewritten at a lower level. As a useful byproduct, the book will also be easier for nonstudents to read.

Organization of a Monograph

13.5 Because it is lengthier than an article, a monograph permits wider scope and greater depth of topic. For example, books organized following the data-analysis outline (see Sections 2.24 to 2.40) may have a 10-page introductory chapter instead of a 100-word abstract; a 50-page chapter on prior research and theory instead of a 4-page section; and several chapters of findings and discussion. Not the least of an author's difficulties is choosing which of several possible outlines best fits the subject matter. For example, results and discussion can be organized in any of several ways (see Sections 2.36 to 2.39). Making a choice that fits 200 pages is harder than making a choice that fits the 10 or 20 pages of discussion in an article. The variety of organizational possibilities prohibits much generalization.

○ For general assistance in organization and writing, see Chapters 2 to 6 in this book.
○ For more specific assistance, read books on topics similar to yours. Authors of books on similar topics have generally solved similar problems.
○ When the manuscript is done, evaluate it using the criteria in section 9.21–9.22. Also check the accuracy of your documentation and calculations.

Monographs Based on Doctoral Dissertations

13.6 If you are trying to write a monograph based on your doctoral dissertation, read Holmes (1974, 1975). The following are among her useful suggestions.

○ Remember that the readership has changed. The book is for people who are interested in your topic. The thesis was for a committee whose purpose was to decide whether you knew enough to be awarded a Ph.D.
○ Discard summaries and warnings of what is coming, excessive cross-references, apologetic openings to chapters, and all but the most necessary tables.
○ Avoid repetitive statements, often signaled by an introductory *i.e.* or *that is*. Rewrite the first statement and the repetition as one statement.
○ Delete all quotations except those that add concreteness or

that make a necessary point in fewer words than you can write yourself.

○ Discard footnotes on side issues. Keep only notes that explain a point.

○ Discard material that is peripheral to your topic. Save it for later articles if you wish.

○ Reduce the bibliography to what a reader would need.

○ Reduce lists of items. Weave into the text the items you need to keep.

○ Reduce the number and size of headings and subheadings. In general three levels of headings, all short and topical, are adequate. See Section 5.6 for help in preparing headings.

13.7　Holmes also suggests what to do with what you have left:

○ Completely rewrite the introduction with the reader, and not the thesis committee, in mind. The final draft should be much shorter than the introduction to the thesis.

○ Make abstractions understandable. Use allegories, metaphors, and examples.

○ Rewrite beginnings and endings of chapters and sections.

Menzel, Jones, and Boyd (1961, p. 127) advise against rewriting. Ultimately, you may save time if you simply write a new manuscript on the same topic.

TEXTBOOKS

Definitions and Descriptions

13.8　Unlike monographs, most textbooks are written for nonprofessionals, and authors usually do not write them to obtain professional advancement. A *basic book* synthesizes the knowledge of an entire discipline or specialty and is often the only textbook required for a course. Basic books are most commonly used in introductory courses, but some specialized courses, such as general social theory, social problems, and sociology of religion, also use them. A *nonbasic book* is one of several required for a course. Such books have lower sales levels because students often prefer to share books, to read copies that have been placed on library reserve, or to buy the books secondhand. Some publishers classify *college-level textbooks* as either *introductory*—for first courses in a discipline or specialty—or *intermediate*—for more advanced courses. The market for the latter is smaller than that for the former, and sales depend more heavily on the author's reputation. Nevertheless, some intermediate basic books, while producing a smaller absolute profit than the introductory basic, actually yield a larger profit relative to investment.

13.9 Most textbooks are written for specific courses, such as introductory economics or advanced conversational analysis, at specific types of schools—for example, introductory economics at small, high-quality liberal arts colleges or psychology of religion at large state universities. The reason for specificity is that students' needs differ. For example, many students at junior colleges take only one course in the social and behavioral sciences. Freshmen and sophomores at large state universities may take two or three such courses. Also, the students' backgrounds and basic skills differ.

Markets for Textbooks

13.10 The major markets for textbooks are created by elementary schools, public scecondary schools, private secondary schools, freshman and sophomore courses (at large universities and at smaller schools of varying quality), junior college courses, junior-senior courses (for majors and for nonmajors), graduate courses, and adult and vocational education courses. In general, the largest market is at the elementary school level. The size of market steadily decreases through the graduate-school level. The demand for books in adult and vocational education courses varies with the subject.

13.11 Most publishing companies keep computerized records on markets. For each course they know:

- ☐ How many are taught at each type of institution.
- ☐ How many students are enrolled in each section of each course at each institution.
- ☐ Whether the recent trend has been rising, falling, or stable enrollment.
- ☐ How often the course is taught, and whether more than one section is taught each term.
- ☐ Who teaches each of the courses.
- ☐ Who is using what textbooks.
- ☐ What are the limitations of existing textbooks.

Some of this information is taken from college catalogs. Some is reported by traveling salespeople, and some is taken from the completed, returned questionnaires that often accompany examination copies of textbooks. These data, updated annually, enable publishers to determine when a new textbook is needed, how many copies it might sell in each of its first three years, and who a potential author might be.

Publishers' Assistance to Authors

13.12 The common assumption is that all books are originally conceived and written (or edited) by the person whose name appears on the title page as "author." Such is not always the case.

13.13 Managed Books. Publishers sometimes plan in detail a textbook for a specific course. Then they seek a qualified scholar, often one who has taught the course for a long time, who will accept the following proposal:

- ☐ If you will do the necessary research, outline the chapters in detail, and read and correct the chapters as they are written, you can be the author and the publishing house will do the rest.

The chapters are often written by free-lance writers. Royalties are generally lower on managed books than on other types of textbook. See Section 16.5 for details.

13.14 Author-Assisted Books. Author-assisted books are written by the author, but with editorial assistance from the publishing company on one or more drafts before the final draft. The process is expensive, and most publishers will not use it for a book that is not expected to sell at least 25,000 copies a year (some require 50,000) during its first two or three years. Publishers justify the expenditure because the assisting editor enables the author to tailor the book carefully to its market.

13.15 A typical project might proceed as follows. The author signs a contract and is assigned an assisting editor, who then examines all books that will compete with the author's. For each book the editor notes features such as good and bad formats and illustrations, special topics, and successful student and teacher aids, and gives this information to the author. After each chapter is finished, the assisting editor criticizes it and may even rewrite it before returning it. Sometimes, to prevent repetition of general errors, the editor will criticize and return the first two or three chapters before the author does any further writing. After each chapter has been criticized once, the author redrafts the entire manuscript. The editor may then criticize and edit again, or send it directly to one or more referees in the author's discipline for substantive evaluations. Afterward, the author writes a final draft which, if acceptable, then receives normal copy editing and is produced.

13.16 In-Depth Assistance. Some publishers offer in-depth editing on books that are not designed for large markets but can still be expected to have respectable sales—for example, intermediate basic books. In this process an in-house editor criticizes a complete copy of an author's final draft, noting weaknesses in writing and suggesting ways to correct them. The editor may also suggest changes in content to tailor the book more carefully to its market.

13.17 Professionally Written Books. There is a fine line between professionally written books and managed books. The fundamental difference is that the parties in the former type of project sign a contract as coauthors.

13.18 Author-Written Books. Author-written books receive little or no assistance from the publisher until the manuscript is submitted for production.

Unique Aspects of Writing a Textbook

13.19 First Steps. If you want to write a textbook,

○ Choose a specific course at a specific type of institution. In general, choose a course that you have taught.
○ Investigate students' needs, background, and skills.
○ Read the descriptions of author assistance (Sections 13.12 to 13.18) and consider your personal preferences. Note them in your prospectus (see Section 15.22).

For example, if you like research and outlining better than writing, you may prefer to work on a managed book. If you like writing but find revising difficult, you may prefer an author-assistance arrangement. If you like the give-and-take of coauthoring, you may like working with a professional writer. If you are considering author assistance, you may want to talk with the assisting editor before you sign a contract. Relations between authors and critics are seldom easy (see Section 6.8). Since the success of a book may depend on how well an editor can help you translate your thoughts into clear writing, compatibility is important.

○ Read Sections 13.20 to 13.25.
○ When the manuscript is done, evaluate it using the criteria in Section 9.23.

13.20 Organizational Problems. Most courses in the same subject require the same material. Only the order of topics, the emphases, and sometimes the integrating themes differ. In brief, textbooks are usually reorganized rather than organized. Organizational problems may arise if you have difficulty isolating and describing the basic assumptions that are necessary starting points for students. For help in solving this problem,

○ Read the first few chapters of textbooks that are similar to the one you plan.
○ Note the treatment of both general assumptions and assumptions specific to specific topics.
○ Let students read and criticize your chapters.

13.21 If you are writing a textbook for an introductory course in your discipline, you may experience difficulty when you write chapters on topics that are not in your special areas of knowledge. For help with this problem,

○ Read chapters on these topics in several textbooks.
○ Examine not only content but organization. Note which outlines seem most successful in conveying information.
○ Seek criticism of draft chapters from colleagues who specialize in those topics (see Sections 6.5 and 6.8 to 6.12). Redraft and then seek criticism from students.

13.22 The need to provide outlines, summaries, homework questions, and other aids to learning may also cause difficulty. To resolve such problems,

○ Read other textbooks.
○ Choose the kinds of aid you want to provide.
○ Be systematic. Include them at the same points in every chapter.
○ You may prefer to prepare no aids until you have written several or all chapters. At that point experiment with different aids and make a choice. Then draft the aids for all chapters at the same time. This procedure helps you give equal treatment to each aid in each chapter.

For example, you may decide to give outlines at the beginnings of chapters and summaries at the ends, or to highlight important points with bullets as I have done in this book. You may decide to turn your textbook into a teaching machine, in which a point made in one chapter is elaborated and repeated in subsequent chapters.

13.23 Writing and Readability. If students cannot read it easily, a textbook will not sell. To make your book readable,

○ Test readability as you write. See Sections 5.65 to 5.69 for help. If you decide to hire an expert, look for someone trained as a reading or remedial-reading teacher. Persons who evaluate textbooks for adoption by their schools are sometimes experts on readability.

○ Use simple, real-life examples. "A set of persons" might be followed by "for example, the Kiwanis Club of Xenia." "A subset" might be followed by "all lawyers in the Kiwanis Club of Xenia." You might even want to illustrate examples with your own cartoons.

○ Try drafting chapters from transcribed class lectures. See Section 4.34 for help.

○ Ask students to read the chapters and criticize your writing.

○ Use humor where possible, and short, catchy titles and subtitles.

○ Use simple graphs, charts, tables, and other illustrations. See Sections 3.4 to 3.21 for help.

13.24 Related Products. Most textbooks come with aids such as workbooks, teacher's guides, instructional tape cassettes, and computer cards.

○ Decide what aids your book needs and whether you want to prepare them yourself.

○ Mention them in your prospectus. See Section 15.21.

13.25 Permissions. Permissions to use other authors' material, published or unpublished, are usually costly. They can also be hard to obtain. Yet textbooks require many illustrations, and you may want to quote at length from one or more other authors' works. To keep expense and difficulties to a minimum,

○ First read Sections 12.43 to 12.50 and follow the instructions there when you need to seek a permission.
○ Quote directly as little as possible. Instead, summarize.
○ Whenever possible, supply your own photographs and draw your own illustrations.
○ For information on treatment of permissions in contracts, see Sections 16.14 and 16.29.

EDITED COLLECTIONS OF ORIGINAL CHAPTERS

Description

13.26   Edited collections of original chapters explicate a general theme. For example, *Sociological Methodology* (published annually by the American Sociological Association) is composed of chapters that either expand old methodologies or describe new ones.

Editorial Style

13.27   Follow instructions in Chapter 12 EXCEPT:

○ Collect bibliographies or lists of references at the ends of chapters, or separately at the end of the book.
○ Do not interalphabetize at the end of the book.

Coherence of Chapters

13.28   To achieve coherence,

○ Choose contributions with a common substantive, methodological, or theoretical theme.
○ Group similar chapters into parts, or arrange all chapters in a logical sequence.

○ Write an introductory essay.
○ Similar writing style in all chapters is not necessary, but you may want to edit so that key terms are always used in the same way by all authors. See Sections 5.19 to 5.21 for help.

Management of Editorial Tasks

13.29   The editor of a collection must be a skilled negotiator as well as a competent editor. Not all contributors will give you complete chapters by the date you need them. Some contributors will object to every editorial change you make as if their very lives depended on the original. To minimize such difficulties,

○ Make clear to all contributors at the outset that your decisions are final.
○ In letters to the contributors and in either letters of agreement (Section 16.39) or in the contract you sign with a publisher, state that failure to meet scheduled deadlines may cause you to drop the offending author's chapter from the book. (Be certain you have chosen enough contributions that loss of one or two will not damage the volume.)
○ When you need to make editorial changes to which an author objects, balance the objections against possible effects on the book as a whole and on other authors. For example, when an author wants to include a longer chapter than you had planned, other authors may have to reduce the length of their chapters to make space for the longer one.
○ Choose a single editorial style (see Sections 12.6 to 12.9) and require that all authors follow it.
○ Require that contributors proofread the galley and page proofs of their own chapters unless they are out of the country or physically unable to do so. Have them follow the instructions in Section 11.32. Require that corrected chapters be returned to you by a specific date, and state that chapters not returned will be presumed correct as they stand.
○ Index the volume yourself. Do not ask contributors to help. For instructions see Sections 12.34 to 12.42.

13.30 Expect to spend some time doing such small but necessary tasks as completing references for one or two of your least organized contributors. You may want to hire a part-time editor to relieve you of these details and to edit the manuscript for you.

EDITED CONFERENCE (SYMPOSIUM) PROCEEDINGS

General Instructions

13.31 Conference (symposium) volumes usually include papers given at conferences and transcribed discussion of the papers. Since it is not usually financially possible to publish all of the papers given at a conference, the editor must make choices. To avoid undue pressure from conferees and resentment from those whose manuscripts are not accepted,

○ Ask one or two referees to read and rank all the manuscripts. Or, have each manuscript read and evaluated separately; then rank them yourself.
○ Choose an editorial style for the book. See Sections 12.6 to 12.9 for help.
○ Make a preliminary choice that includes two or three more manuscripts than you want to include in the book.
○ Then request that authors revise the manuscripts in light of the referees' criticisms. Supply detailed instructions on editorial style and request that the resubmitted manuscripts follow that style. Ask that the revised manuscripts be returned to you by a specific date.
○ Make a final choice of manuscripts.
○ Read the suggestions in Sections 13.27 to 13.30.

13.32 When you notify contributors of your final choices,

○ Describe your procedure for handling manuscripts from this point on. For example: edit manuscripts for consistency and brevity; retype and return to authors for checking; edit and retype discussion; return to authors and other participants in the conference for checking; type final manuscript; send completed manuscript to publisher.

○ Assign dates to each step so that authors know your deadlines. State that failure to meet deadlines may cause you to drop the offending author's chapter. See Section 13.29.

○ If you have not yet found a publisher for the volume, set a policy on whether contributors may publish their chapters in other ways, for example as journal articles.

13.33 Because the market for conference volumes is usually small, you may not be offered a contract until after the final draft has been completed and referees have evaluated it. Understandably, authors dislike taking a chance that the volume will not find a publisher. You can deal with this problem in one of two ways:

○ Tell contributors that you will withdraw from the volume any manuscript that is accepted for publication elsewhere.

○ Or, require that prior publications be with publishers who will give the author written permission to republish the article in the volume at no charge.

In some instances, prior publication of chapters as articles will reduce sales of a conference volume.

Instructions for Editing a Transcript

13.34 When you edit a transcript of discussion,

○ Delete material that is unintelligible, irrelevant, or only tangentially relevant. You may eventually eliminate as much as two-thirds of the initial transcript.

○ Work at a large table. Until you are through cutting, you will often be working with several sections simultaneously.

○ Organize the discussion of each chapter and have a clean draft typed.

○ Then edit the revised discussion. Keep it clear, somewhat

conversational, and faithful to the speakers' intentions. As you work, check the revised chapters to be certain that criticisms by speakers are still valid.

○ Type separately the discussion of each chapter. Title the first page of each "Discussion of Chapter _____."

○ For ease of identification, precede each speaker's comments with his or her last name, typed in capital letters and followed by a colon. Triple-space between the end of one speaker's comments and the beginning of the next. Double-space the rest of the discussion.

○ For each reference a speaker makes to another chapter or to discussion of another chapter, prepare a 3 × 5 card that notes the location of the reference and the chapter or discussion to which the speaker refers. File by location of the reference. When the manuscript is complete, having the file will help you to complete cross-references.

○ Ask the speakers involved to read the edited discussion and notify you of either approval or suggested changes. Set a deadline for a response.

Possible Financial Assistance

13.35   The sponsors of a conference sometimes publish the proceedings themselves, in which case they pay all costs. If not, the sponsors sometimes assist the editor by paying for some of the expenses, such as typing and editing, or even by paying the eventual publisher a subvention to help defray publication costs.

EDITED ANTHOLOGIES

Description

13.36   Anthologies are collections of previously published articles and chapters. Sometimes the editor is the author of the documents. More often the collection includes the work of many authors, plus an interpretive chapter by the editor. Anthologies require some organization but little writing. Because most of the chapters have been previously published, the amount of work involved in editing an anthology seems small.

Fundamental Problems

13.37 Nevertheless, before you begin an anthology, consider the following facts:

☐ Permission costs are high and may be as high as $15,000 for one volume. Sometimes copyright holders request a percentage of royalties rather than a flat fee in exchange for a permission. See Section 12.50.

☐ The market for anthologies is usually too narrow to permit a low retail price. High prices reduce the market even more.

☐ Anthologies rarely confer professional status on their editors.

☐ Unless the anthology is to accompany a successful basic book (described in Section 13.8), publishers may not be interested.

EDITED BIBLIOGRAPHIES

Description

13.38 Bibliographies list documents pertinent to a limited topic. Two examples are Hare's (1962) bibliography on small-group research and Weinberg and Bell's (1972) on male homosexuality.

Instructions for Achieving Coherence

13.39 To achieve coherence,

○ Divide the entries into categories and subcategories. Treat the categories as chapters. Use the subcategories to title sections of chapters.

○ For suggestions on organization look at the divisions of

subject matter used by abstract services. Also examine the topical divisions in textbooks on your topic.

○ Regardless of the organization you choose, expect some overlap in categories. Most documents have primary relevance to one category but also secondary relevance to other categories.

You may treat overlap in either of two ways: list all articles in every section to which they are relevant (see, e.g., Irvine et al. 1973) or only in the section of primary relevance (see, e.g., Armer 1975). If you choose the latter course, provide a separate index that lists, by chapter and section, all documents with secondary relevance.

Instructions for Achieving Consistency

13.40 To achieve consistency,

○ Choose an editorial style. See Sections 12.6 to 12.9 for help. As you collect documents, record bibliographic data in that style. Doing so will help your typist when you prepare the manuscript.

○ If you annotate, in each annotation give the same information in the same order.

For a *research report* summarize briefly the problem, the method used for study, and the main results (see Sections 2.24 to 2.39). For a *theoretical* or *methodological document,* summarize the problem, the theory or method, and its chief implication or uses (Sections 2.41 and 2.42). For a review article summarize the concepts used, specific problems that need study, appropriate methods for research, and predictions for the future (Section 9.18 describes these elements).

Instructions for Permissions

13.41 To avoid unnecessary expense,

○ Write your own annotations.
○ If you take annotations from another source, read the

copyright statement for the conditions under which you must request permission for use. When in doubt, ask for permission. See Sections 12.43 to 12.50 for help.

Bibliographic information (see Section 3.36) may be used without permission.

Instructions for Preparing Indexes

13.42   To make indexing easier than it is with most books,

○ Number each entry, either by chapter (as I numbered the paragraphs in this book) or sequentially beginning with 1 from the first entry through the last. Doing so allows you to identify location of information by entry number instead of by page number.

○ Ask a computer consultant about indexing programs available at your institution. They can make indexing easier and eliminate many sources of error. See also Section 12.29.

○ Also ask about programs for editing and correcting text, described in Section 12.29. If they are available, consider typing and correcting the manuscript on a terminal. When you are through, the computer should be able to produce indexes for you. See discussion in Section 12.34.

○ For general instructions on indexing, see Sections 12.34 to 12.42.

SUMMARY

13.43   In this chapter I first discuss the special problems that affect authors of monographs (Sections 13.2 to 13.7). I then describe textbooks and textbook markets (13.8 to 13.11), publishers' assistance to textbook authors (13.12 to 13.18), and unique aspects of writing textbooks (13.19 to 13.25). I next discuss unique aspects of editing collections of original chapters (13.26 to 13.30), editing conference (symposium) volumes (13.31 to 13.35), editing anthologies (13.36 and 13.37), and editing bibliographies (13.38 to 13.42).

Part Four

PUBLISHERS, PROSPECTUSES, AND CONTRACTS; THE FORTHCOMING BOOK

CHAPTER FOURTEEN

How to Choose Possible Publishers for a Book Manuscript

INTRODUCTION

The Cost-Profit Squeeze

14.1 In recent years, rising inflation has intensified the squeeze between publishers' costs and profits, causing higher book prices and an increasing reluctance, on the part of publishers, to publish even well-written monographs of obvious scholarly value. Scholars protest both results, yet on each book publishers must earn a profit at least equal to the rate of inflation or authors may eventually find themselves with no place to publish their books.

Publishers' Expenses

14.2 Consider a few facts. The money you pay for a book is divided four ways. The *discount*—the difference between a book's retail price and the amount of money the publisher receives for each sale—is a bookstore's profit. Discounts range from 20 to 50 percent of the retail price. They are generally lower on monographs and textbooks, and highest on tradebooks. A second part of the money is applied to a publisher's *general costs,* such as overhead (e.g., salaries, office rent) and taxes, that exist regardless of whether a given book is produced. A third part is applied to *editorial costs* such as manuscript reviewing, editing, art design, and redrawing of illustrations—everything done to a book before it can be manufactured. A fourth part is applied to *manufacturing costs*—typesetting (composition); paper, cover, and binding material; and binding the book. Taken together, editorial and manufacturing costs can range up to $10,000 on a monograph of 250 to 325 pages, and up to $125,000 on a textbook. The actual cost is determined by factors such as page size, number of pages, amount of artwork, amount of editing needed, and number of copies printed.

14.3 For more detail, consider the distribution of the typical dollar received by a publisher from the sale of a textbook (Addison n.d.): 32 cents is spent for manufacturing costs; 7 cents for editing; 17 cents for marketing (including advertising and givιng away free books); 19 cents for general costs; 16 cents for royalties; 4 cents for taxes. The remaining 5 cents is the publisher's profit. Because production runs on monographs are usually smaller than those on textbooks, the unit cost of production is usually higher on monographs. As a result, publishers offer lower royalties on monographs, and some even require a *subvention*—a fee to pay part or all of the production costs.

Profit and Quality

14.4 To maximize the likelihood that books signed will be both profitable and of high quality, publishers ask referees to evaluate each manuscript's quality and potential market. Book publishers choose, use, and evaluate referees in much the same way as journal editors do (see description in Sections 10.24 to 10.34). However, referees of books usually receive a modest fee for their services, sometimes take up to nine months to evaluate a single manuscript, evaluate salability as well as quality of writing and scholarship, and often know the name of the manuscript's author. As is the case with articles, authors are rarely told who refereed their manuscripts. To make the best use of referees, some editors keep detailed records. For example, they note each referee's discipline and specialty, how he or she thinks, how long he takes to return a manuscript, and how good the evaluations are. To some editors, knowing a referee's characteristics is even more important than knowing the author's.

General Suggestions for Authors

14.5 You can improve your chances of finding an interested publisher by submitting for consideration only manuscripts of high quality. The higher the quality, the more prestigious a publisher you can hope to attract. With monographs, quality is determined by factors such as originality of research design, size and quality of data base, quality of analysis, originality and soundness of general thinking, and implications of findings, theory, or method. You can estimate a monograph's quality from colleagues' critical comments. A textbook's quality (see

Sections 13.20 to 13.23) depends less on originality than on readability, appeal to intended users, and thoroughness. For help in improving your writing, see Chapters 2 to 6. Help in improving the substance of your writing is beyond the scope of this book.

14.6 To further improve your chances of finding an interested publisher,

○ Do some research on publishing companies. For instructions, read the rest of this chapter.[1]

○ Prepare a prospectus that describes your manuscript and lists its virtues. For instructions, see Chapter 15.

CATEGORIES OF PUBLISHER AND KINDS OF BOOK

14.7 Table 14.1 shows the general (somewhat simplified) categories of publisher cross-classified with the kinds of book each generally publishes. The noncommercial publishers are subsidized to varying degrees by their sponsoring universities and associations and are thus able to publish some high-quality monographs that have small markets. For a list of commercial publishers and university presses,

○ Consult *The Literary Marketplace* (*LMP*). This is a reference book, revised annually, that lists publishers with telephone numbers, addresses, and editors' names and titles.

14.8 Many publishers in the "Other" category are not part of book-publishing companies and offer no royalties. Among these publishers are associations, journals, and presses that publish both journals and monographs. For example:

> *Associations.* American Psychological Association, American Sociological Association (Rose Monograph Series), Australian Political Studies Association, Population Council, Society for Research in Child Development.

Table 14.1 Examples of Categories of Publisher and Kinds of Manuscript Preferred

Kinds of Manuscript Preferred[a]	Commercial Publishers		Noncommercial Publishers	
	Large	Small	University Press	Others
	McGraw-Hill Harper & Row Rand McNally	Winthrop Allyn & Bacon	Chicago Harvard Cambridge	Rose Monographs APA Monographs Scholars Press
Large-market textbook (described in Sections 13.8 and 13.9)	Yes	Yes	No	No
Other textbooks (Sections 13.8 and 13.9)	Yes	Yes	Sometimes	No
Monograph (Section 13.2)	No	No	Yes	Yes
Monograph with textbook or trade book uses (Section 13.2)	Usually not	Sometimes	Yes	No

[a]Includes both authored books and edited collections. Edited collections are described in Sections 13.26, 13.31, 13.36, and 13.38.

Journals. American Journal of Sociology, The Sociological Review.

Presses. The Journal Press (Genetic Psychology Monographs), Scholars Press (described in Section 10.21).

To locate publishers of this sort,

○ Look for advertisements in journals and in the newsletters of associations. Read articles in *Scholarly Publishing* (described in Section 10.35).

○ Consult Table 7.1, column 4, for journals that publish articles longer than 90 typed pages. Some of the longest articles are monographs.

CRITERIA FOR EVALUATING PUBLISHERS

The Need to Reduce an Initial List of Publishers

14.9 An initial list of possible publishers usually needs to be reduced. No author wants to be involved in simultaneous negotiations with more than three or four publishers, yet competition can result in a more satisfactory contract. When reducing a list, consider the following factors.

Restrictive Policies

14.10 Unlike the situation with journal articles (see Section 11.15), authors may often submit book manuscripts for evaluation to more than one publisher at a time. Most nonuniversity presses expect that an author is doing so. However, some publishers, usually noncommercial ones, require *exclusive review*, at least for a fixed period of time, for example 90 days. Also, some publishers, again primarily noncommercial presses, prefer not to sign monographs based on *material already published in journals*, particularly if the articles are in major journals and contain most of a manuscript's major points. The reason is that prior publication has made the knowledge available and may also reduce sales of the monograph. See also Section 15.29.

Reputation of the Publisher

14.11 From your colleagues,

○ Find out who has had good experiences with what publishers.

Ask about such matters as quality of copy editing, typesetting, and finished product. To minimize the effect of any one person's bias, ask several persons. Be sure you understand the reasons for each person's overall evaluation.

○ Ask specifically about the trustworthiness of editors who work with scholars in your subject area.

Contract agreements are sometimes made by telephone, and the contract may not arrive for a month or more. Also, many of the factors that ultimately make publishing a book a good or a bad experience cannot be written into a contract. It is virtually impossible to specify precisely "a lot of promotion" or "a good copy editor." With matters like these, an author is dependent on the editor's competence, permanence in the job, good will, interest in the book, and reputation for trustworthiness.

Specialties, Special Series, and Special Needs

14.12 To determine a publisher's specialties, special series, and special needs,

○ Examine the publisher's general catalog and list of current and forthcoming books both in your discipline and in related disciplines.

For example, the University of Chicago Press publishes a relatively large number of books on the sociology of science. Some publishers formalize their interest in a general area, for example urban sociology or comparative politics, by sponsoring a series of several books on different topics within the area. Also look for gaps in a list. For example, if a publisher has introductory books in sociology, psychology, and anthropology but none in economics, finding one may be a major priority.

Special Skills

14.13 Look for books that are technically similar to your manuscript. For example, if you have an exceptional number of complex figures and graphs, look for a company whose published books show skill in executing such illustrations. Also indicate this need in your prospectus. See Section 15.22 for instructions.

Size and Kind of Sales Staff

14.14 If you are writing a textbook, both size of sales staff and geographical distribution are important.

○ Ask what kind of sales staff each publisher has. For example, a publisher may employ some persons who specialize in selling textbooks and some who specialize in selling trade books.

○ Also ask how many salespeople are in each category and where they are located. For example, a publisher may have 50 people who sell textbooks and 75 who sell trade books. All may be scattered evenly throughout the United States and Europe, or they may be concentrated in the United States, east of the Mississippi River.

○ If you are talking with a subsidiary of a larger publisher, ask the same questions about the parent company. Then ask whether the parent company's staff routinely sells books that are part of the subsidiary's list.

○ Evaluate data on sales staff in terms of the anticipated market for your book.

If you have written a monograph, data on sales staff will probably be irrelevant. Monographs usually have a limited market that can be reached easily and effectively through direct-mail advertising and convention showings.

Location of Production Offices

14.15   If you want to work closely with your publisher,

○ Choose one whose production offices are geographically located near you.

In general, because of the difficulty and expense involved in mailing a manuscript back and forth, publishers located inside the continental United States are easier to work with than publishers whose offices are overseas.

PERSONS TO WRITE OR TALK TO ABOUT A MANUSCRIPT

In-House Editors; Advisory Editors

14.16   To begin developing publishers' interest in a manuscript,

○ Talk with the in-house economics, psychology (social- or behavioral-science, etc.) editors of the publishing houses in which you are interested.
○ Talk with the advisory editors.

Most editors attend a discipline's annual convention, and many of the in-house editors visit some universities and colleges every year. Conventions are usually busy times for editors. If you want to talk with an editor, write in advance, send a prospectus (see Chapter 15 for instructions), and request an appointment. If the editor sees potential in your manuscript, he or she may invite you to stop by the booth for a chat, or to join him for coffee, lunch, cocktails, or dinner, and further discussion.

14.17   Advisory editors are usually well-known, respected scholars. They act as liaisons between publishers and scholars, evaluate manuscripts, and sometimes perform editorial services.

14.18   Before you submit a manuscript to an editor,

○ Read and follow the instructions in Chapter 15.
○ Submit at least two copies of everything except the letter of submission.
○ Inquire every month or so if more than two months pass without a response.

In general, the more material you provide, the more detailed and useful a publisher's response is likely to be. Even if a manuscript is eventually rejected, you will still gain by having useful comments on which to base a revision.

Salespeople (Travelers)

14.19   A less direct but often effective approach is to talk with the book salespeople who visit most schools on a fairly regular basis. Many scholars think that these people (sometimes called "travelers") are interested only in sales, but that is a misconception. Some publishers pay salespeople a "discovery fee" for each book they find that their companies ultimately sign. Those that do not pay fees (and some of those that do) may still use "discoveries" as a criterion for evaluating sales effectiveness. Moreover, some salespeople aspire to editorial positions, and one way to achieve that ambition is to demonstrate an ability to spot a good manuscript and get it signed. If you want to talk with a salesperson,

○ Mention that fact to your book-publishing colleagues. Salespeople rarely visit departments without stopping to chat with their companies' authors, who in turn often refer them to their book-writing colleagues.

When you talk with salespeople, give each a copy of the prospectus.

Colleagues

14.20   Let colleagues read your manuscript as it progresses, or after it has been completed. Editors are rarely specialists in the disciplines for which they are responsible. They rely on trusted academic friends to tell them what others are writing and how good the manuscripts are. A colleague who likes a manuscript may recommend it to friends in publishing with no prompting from the author, who may not even know that the recommendation has been made until a publisher requests a copy for evaluation.

The End Results of Conversations

14.21   Sometimes, as when you are writing a textbook, your conversations with publishers together with your prospectus may prompt one or more to offer you a contract. If so,

○ See Chapter 16 for a description of contract terms and discussion of ways to choose among competing offers.

Most of the time, though, your goal is only to create interest. Some publishers look more favorably on a manuscript that does not arrive completely unannounced, or "over the transom" (Balkin 1974).

SUMMARY

14.22   In this chapter I first discuss the cost-profit squeeze in publishing, the publishers' attempts to maximize profit and quality, and some general ways in which authors can maximize their chances of finding an interested publisher (Sections 14.1 to 14.6). I then discuss categories of publishers and kinds of books (14.7 to 14.8), criteria for evaluating publishers (14.9 to 14.15), and persons to write or talk to about a manuscript (14.16 to 14.21).

NOTE TO CHAPTER 14

1.   Agents are generally *not* helpful to scholars looking for publishers. Agents charge a commission, often 10 percent of an author's royalties, and scholarly books usually earn too little in royalties to make an agent's effort worthwhile.

CHAPTER FIFTEEN

How to Prepare a Prospectus

INTRODUCTION

15.1 A good prospectus explains the nature and purpose of a manuscript and presents it to publishers and referees in the best possible light. Prepare a prospectus whenever you submit any kind of manuscript, complete or incomplete, to a publisher for possible publication. When you write a prospectus, remember that most publishers are businessmen, not academicians. They may use your prospectus to evaluate not only your manuscript but also your ability to think, write, and do business. Therefore,

○ View the manuscript from the publisher's perspective as well as from your own.

It does not demean a scholarly book if you take a realistic, businesslike approach to its virtues. Also, you may know better than a publisher some of the scholarly and pedagogical needs that the book will meet, and some of the deficiencies in published books that appear similar to it. If you conceal such practical knowledge, you may deprive yourself of an eventual contract, and a publisher of a book that would confer both modest financial success and intellectual respectability on his company. For a sample prospectus that illustrates the discussion below, see Appendix C.

MECHANICAL ASPECTS OF PREPARING A PROSPECTUS

Content, Organization, and Length

15.2 Body of the Prospectus. Table 15.1 lists topics in the body of a prospectus.

○ Discuss these topics in the order listed, following the instructions in Sections 15.5 to 15.22.

Table 15.1 Length of Sections in, and Attachments to, a Prospectus

Sections and Attachments	Monograph	Textbook
Body		
Rationale	1–2 paragraphs	2–4 paragraphs
Subject and scope	1–2 paragraphs	1–2 pages
Approach	1–2 paragraphs	1–2 pages
Grade level	1–2 sentences	2–4 sentences
Market	1–3 paragraphs	1–2 sentences
Physical characteristics	2–3 sentences	2–3 sentences
Competition	1–2 pages	2–50 pages
Schedule for completion	1 paragraph	1 paragraph
Author's qualifications	1–3 sentences	1–2 paragraphs
Related products	Usually not needed	1 paragraph per item
Special concerns	1 paragraph per item	1 paragraph per item
Attachments		
References for documents cited in the prospectus	1 page	1 page
Letter of submission	1 page	1 page
Curriculum vitae	Varies with author's experience	Varies with author's experience
Table of contents	1–3 pages	1–3 pages
Outlines[a]		
Of completed chapters	Topic outline: 3 levels of importance, 1–3 pages per chapter	Topic outline: 3 levels of importance, 1–3 pages per chapter
Of unwritten chapters	Combination outline: 4 levels of importance, 2–20 pages per chapter	Combination outline: 4 levels of importance, 2–20 pages per chapter
Completed chapters	No set length	No set length

Note. Lengths are estimates. Do not follow them rigidly.
[a]For descriptions of outlines and help in preparing them, see Sections 2.3 to 2.7.

○ Allot space to each topic following the guidelines in Table 15.1.

Overall, the prospectus should be as short as comprehensiveness will allow, and as carefully written as the manuscript. Particularly with monographs, if a publisher is not quickly convinced that a manuscript has value, he or she may return it without refereeing.

15.3   Attachments to the Body.   Table 15.1 lists attachments to the body.

○ Begin each attachment on a separate page. Also, begin the outline for each chapter on a separate page.
○ Prepare these items according to the instructions in Sections 15.23 to 15.30.
○ Determine length following the guidelines in Table 15.1.
○ Place the letter of submission and the curriculum vitae on top of the body.
○ Place all other items beneath the body, in the order shown in the table.
○ For a model of style, see Appendix C.

Editorial Style

15.4   There is no prescribed editorial style for prospectuses. Therefore, treat a prospectus as you would the manuscript for a short article. Follow the typing instructions in Sections 8.6 to 8.14. Also,

○ Type all items except the letter so that you can produce multiple copies easily.
○ Prepare a cover sheet as is shown in Appendix C.
○ For a manuscript with more than one author, treat the byline as shown in Figure 8.3.

○ For the body, use as center headings the items listed under "Body" in Table 15.1.

○ For headings, references, notes, tables, and illustrations, follow the editorial style you are using in the manuscript for the book.

○ Optional: single-space quotations and lists of documents, but double-space above and below each quotation and document. Incorporate tables and illustrations into the text rather than placing them on separate pages.

○ Optional: you may want to indent features you wish to emphasize, such as lists of unique characteristics or markets.

CONTENT OF A PROSPECTUS

Descriptions of the Manuscript's Content

15.5 For details on content, refer readers to the preface, table of contents, and introductory chapter.

15.6 Rationale. State your reason for writing the book and what you want it to accomplish. For a *monograph*,[1]

○ Describe specific theoretical, methodological, or substantive gaps in the knowledge of your specialty.

○ Explain how your manuscript fills one or more of these gaps.

For a *textbook*,

○ Describe the current status of substance, theory and methods, and the status of, and trends in, teaching methods.

○ Explain your manuscript's approach to all four factors.

15.7 Subject and Scope. For a *monograph*,

○ State the manuscript's topic and the topic's limits.

○ Highlight the innovations, expansions, and improvements that are unique to your manuscript.

For example, for a monograph based on research, you might state the topic studied, the population used, the research method and analytical techniques, the theoretical framework, and the significance and value of each of these items. Often you can take this statement directly from the introductory chapter. For a *textbook*,

○ Discuss topics traditionally taught.
○ If you have omitted certain traditional topics, explain why.
○ Highlight unique features. Mention innovation, expansion, and improvement not only on substance, theory and method, but also on teaching methods.

15.8 Approach to the Topic. For all manuscripts, state:

○ How you designed your book.
○ Why you designed it that way.

For some manuscripts, you may want to discuss approach simultaneously with subject and scope. For example, to explain a monograph's unique substance, theory, or method, you may have to state how you approached the research. If political beliefs have always been studied by survey methods and the unique feature of your monograph is that it reports a study of this topic using participant observation, the organization and theory of your monograph may well be different from those in earlier books. Your presentation may be based on content analysis of excerpts from conversation rather than on regression tables, path models, and charts.

15.9 For a textbook,

○ Also describe your teaching methods.

For example, you may have written a textbook within the framework of some general theoretical perspective, such as structural functionalism. You may have divided the chapters by topics, and discussed each topic within the framework of that theory. You may have arranged the chapters so that the most general are first, and each subsequent chapter not only repeats the general theoretical approach but also adds specific items to it. As a result, your manuscript will function as a teaching machine.

Grade Level and Readability

15.10   State the grade level for which your book's content is appropriate. The content of most monographs is appropriate for professional scientists. It may also be appropriate for graduate students and upper-level undergraduates. Authors of textbooks write for specific grade levels. For example introductory textbooks are usually planned for freshmen and sophomores in college. See Section 13.9 for details.

15.11   If you are writing a textbook,

○ Also state the manuscript's level of readability. See Sections 5.65 to 5.69 for a discussion of readability.

A textbook to teach fourth graders how Columbus discovered America should be written in words, sentences, and paragraphs that third graders could understand. A textbook for college freshmen should be written in words, sentences, and paragraphs at tenth- or eleventh-grade level. If you have used readability tests on your writing,

○ State which tests you used.
○ If you have hired an expert in readability to help you with your writing, state that fact also.

Readability level is less important for monographs than for textbooks. However, the monograph whose readability score is

lower than the grade level for which the content is intended
may attract a broader market than the author had anticipated.

Potential Market

15.12   A clear statement about intended market prevents misunderstanding. For example, suppose you are writing a prospectus for a monograph with some possible uses as a textbook
or trade book. For you, the monographic aspect is primary.
Whenever you have had to choose between writing for a professional audience and writing for students, you have chosen to
write for the professionals. If, in your eagerness to obtain a
contract, you make textbook use seem as important as monographic use, the publisher may sign the manuscript primarily as
a textbook and plan editing and marketing accordingly. There-
after, at every stage of production, the publisher's purposes
may run counter to yours. The resulting struggle can produce a
book that pleases neither of you. Since techniques for marketing textbooks differ from those for marketing monographs,
further struggles may follow publication. Such struggles embit-
ter both parties, yet all too often the problem is not that either
party wanted to take advantage of the other. Rather, the author
did not fully appreciate the effect that the prospectus would
have. Such situations produce unhappy, and widely discussed,
stories about difficult authors and difficult publishers. Often,
neither party ever wants to work with the other ever again even
though, on a different book, the two might meet each other's
needs perfectly.

15.13   When stating potential market, balance honesty and
skepticism with thoroughness. Exaggeration can hurt your argument. So can omission of a possible market. For a textbook,

○ State the market by categories of students and types of
   schools (described in Sections 13.10 and 13.11).

For example, the potential market for an introductory textbook
in sociology might be all students at large state universities who

are taking introductory sociology. For such a statement, you need not estimate the size of the market.

15.14   If you have written a monograph,

○ Estimate the size of the potential market.
○ Consider these potential purchasers: libraries, professionals, graduate students, and upper-level undergraduates interested in your discipline or specialty.

For example, to document the market for his monograph, one sociologist checked the American Sociological Association's membership directory for the number of persons who listed, as one of their specialties, one of the specialties on which his book provided relevant information: for example, political sociology, 650. He also listed the specialties in related disciplines whose practitioners might be interested. He did not claim that all such persons would buy the book, only that they constituted a potential market. He then listed the courses for which the book might provide supplementary reading material. He also stated that some college and university libraries would buy copies because the book discussed topics important to several specialties. Finally, he listed published journal articles that had reported data from the research on which the manuscript was based. He discussed the relationship of the articles to the manuscript and showed that the articles would help sales of the book.

Physical Characteristics of the Manuscript

15.15   First, give type pitch and width of margins.

○ Then list the proposed or actual length of text, notes, and references or bibliography.
○ Also list the number of tables and illustrations.

For example: the manuscript is typed in elite type with margins of $1\frac{1}{2}$ inches. There are 250 pages of text, 25 pages of notes, and

20 pages of bibliography. There are 40 tables, 15 figures, and no photographs.

○ If the manuscript has been completed, make exact statements.
○ If not, make estimates; check them against existing books that are similar to yours.

Competition with Published Books

15.16 Competition is a more important consideration for textbooks than for monographs. By definition, a monograph presents an intellectual advance. Strictly speaking, then, it should have no competition. However, for a monograph,

○ Describe published books that are similar. In text, for each book give author's name, book's title, publisher, and date. See Appendix C for examples.
○ List differences between the manuscript and published books.

Sometimes you may eliminate this section by incorporating comparisons into discussion of rationale or of subject and scope.

15.17   For a textbook,

○ Compare the manuscript with all competing books on common substantive, theoretical, methodological, and pedagogical features. Note unique features of your manuscript.
○ In text, for each book give author's name, book's title, publisher, and date. See Appendix C for examples.

EXCEPTION. If you discuss more than 15 competing books, you may prefer to prepare a separate list of books and attach it to the text. In text, refer to the books by author's name and publication date only, as I do in this book (Chapter 8 excepted).

Schedule for Completion of the Manuscript

15.18   When preparing a schedule,

○ Give completion dates for first draft, second draft, . . . final draft.
○ State what work has been completed.
○ Make realistic estimates for work that has not been completed. Unrealistically short estimates may convince a publisher that you do not appreciate the difficulty of writing a book.

Author's Qualifications

15.19   For a monograph,

○ Attach a copy of your curriculum vitae. See Section 15.28.
○ Refer to it briefly.
○ Mention any books on it that have been either a financial or a critical success.

Publishers also consider an author's reputation for reliability. Some publishers estimate that between 25 and 50 percent of all contracts signed are never fulfilled by the publication of books. A few contracts are canceled by the publisher, but far more are "canceled" by the author's failure to write the book. An author who has performed reliably in the past is a better risk than one who has not. Therefore,

○ If you have completed previous manuscripts on schedule, mention that fact.

15.20   For a textbook,

○ Follow the instructions in Section 15.19.
○ Mention prior teaching experience, and at what kinds of school, in the course for which you are writing the book.
○ List the teaching aids you have developed for the course.

Related Products

15.21 *Monograph* authors normally omit this item. *Textbooks* are usually accompanied by teachers' manuals, student guides or workbooks, audiovisual aids, computer cards, and other related products.

○ List the items that should accompany your book.
○ Describe their length and nature. For example, "The student guide should be 100 pages long and should have workbook pages for the student to complete." Or, "It should contain only outlines and study helps."
○ State whether you wish to prepare the items yourself, or have someone else do them.

Special Concerns

15.22 Some authors have special concerns. For example, a manuscript may entail an unusual amount of artwork, or an author may need assistance in obtaining permissions.

○ List and describe special considerations so that prospective publishers can take them into consideration.

ATTACHMENTS TO THE BODY

List of Documents Cited

15.23 Include a list of documents cited in the body of the prospectus.

○ Cite as few documents as possible.
○ Omit the list if you cite no documents, or if the only ones are in your discussion of competition (described in Sections 15.16 and 15.17).

Table of Contents

15.24 Include a table of contents. Figure 12.1 shows a sample format.

Outlines for Chapters

15.25 For a completed manuscript, keep outlines brief.

○ Follow the guidelines in Table 15.1.
○ For help in preparing outlines, see Chapter 2, especially Sections 2.3 to 2.7.
○ For examples of a topic outline, see Sections 2.31 to 2.35 and the outlines at the beginnings of my chapters. Section 9.21 shows a combination outline.
○ Precede the outline for each unwritten chapter with a paragraph or two briefly describing the strategies, emphasis, theoretical framework, and data.

Completed Chapters

15.26 For a monograph, most publishers prefer that authors submit a complete manuscript for evaluation. A few want only a prospectus and two or three chapters. To find out who wants how much,

○ Write in advance and inquire.
○ Choose sample chapters that have been thoroughly revised and that show both your writing style and the manuscript's content. For example, for a research-based monograph you might send the introduction, a theory chapter, and a chapter of analysis.

15.27 For a textbook, submit chapters for evaluation before the manuscript is complete.

○ In general, choose the introduction, the chapter that sets the framework for the rest of the book (if that chapter is not the introduction), and two or three chapters that are typical of all others. In many textbooks, these last are topic-oriented chapters.

○ Revise the chapters carefully so that they reflect the book's content and your writing style.

Curriculum Vitae

15.28 Attach your most recent curriculum vitae.

Letter of Submission

15.29 Publishers dislike duplicated, form letters addressed to "Social (or Behavioral) Science Editor" or "College Department," with only the publisher's name and address typed in. *The Literary Marketplace—LMP*; revised annually and available at most library reference desks—lists all publishers with addresses, telephone numbers, preferred types of manuscript, and (often) names of editors in each major area.

○ Use *LMP* to help you direct a manuscript to the proper person. It will probably be handled more carefully as a result (Balkin 1974).

In a letter of submission,

○ Request that your manuscript be evaluated for possible publication.

○ State why you chose that publishing company. (For help in choosing, see Chapter 14.) For example, it publishes many books in econometrics and your manuscript is an advance in that specialty.

○ If you are submitting copies of the manuscript to more than one publisher, say so. Some companies have exclusive-review policies. You need not list the other publishers.

○ Optional but appreciated by some publishers: list possible referees. Omit persons who have read the manuscript in draft. State briefly your reason for choosing each person.

A personally addressed letter and mention of the factors affecting your choice tell an in-house editor that you have made a thoughtful choice of publishers.

15.30 Authors often ask whether they should simply mail completed manuscripts to publishers or write first, sending just a prospectus and inquiring about interest. Publishers are evenly divided on this point. Some authors resolve this dilemma by sending the prospectus and two or three chapters when they write the first letter.

SUMMARY

15.31 This chapter first discusses the mechanical aspects of preparing a prospectus—the organization of sections, the necessary attachments, the typing style, and the overall length (Sections 15.2 to 15.4). I then discuss the content of each section in the body of the prospectus (15.5 to 15.22) and in the attachments (15.23 to 15.30).

NOTE TO CHAPTER 15

1. I do not discuss trade books in detail. Subsequent references to monographs include scholarly edited collections; to textbooks, anthologies.

CHAPTER SIXTEEN

How to Negotiate a Contract and Choose a Publisher

INTRODUCTION

16.1   If you receive a contract offer from a publisher,

○ Notify other publishers evaluating the manuscript. They de-
serve the courtesy of time to make a competing offer. You
need not say who has made the first offer. Never tell a
publisher that you have received a firm offer unless such is
actually the case. Some authors think that such action will
speed evaluation, but it may backfire and cause the publisher to return the manuscript to you without further evaluation.
○ Set a date three weeks or so into the future, by which time
you expect to have heard from any publisher who wants to
make a competing offer.
○ Examine all offers carefully. Even if you have only one offer
and expect no more, which is usually the case with a monograph, it is still not wise to sign a contract before you understand it completely.

16.2   This chapter discusses various contract provisions and
suggests criteria for dealing with and choosing among publishers. Sometimes the type of book—trade book, textbook, or

monograph—affects not only the range of choices but also the type of choice you will prefer. If no qualifications are made, the comments apply to all types of books. Information is partly taken from Baumol and Heim (1967), Franklin (1967), Stedman (1967), Henry (1974), Barber (1975), and Wagner (1976a,b,c).

FINANCIAL TERMS

Payment for the Book

16.3   Standard financial arrangements take four forms: royalties, sale of rights, stock options, and subsidies. Of these four, the first is the most common. Financial agreements are easiest when a book has only one author. When a book has more than one author,

○ State in the contract exactly what payment each author will receive. For example, you and a coauthor may agree on 15 percent royalties, 7½ apiece.

○ If you are editing a collection (described in Sections 13.26 to 13.35) or are writing a chapter in a collection, state not only total royalties but the editor's share and each author's share. For example, the contract may call for 10 percent royalties. The editor will receive 3 percent for writing a chapter and managing the project. The remaining 7 percent will be divided equally among the authors.

16.4   Different Kinds of Royalties.   Publishers use many different terms to describe royalties. From one publisher to the next, the same term may mean different things. Thus it is important that authors know the basic kinds of arrangement. Fundamentally, a royalty is a percentage of a price. The price may be:

☐ A *list (retail) price,* or what you pay a bookstore for a book.
☐ A *list price minus discounts* to the bookstore (discounts are described in Section 14.2). Sometimes called gross proceeds,

net proceeds, net price, wholesale price, or publisher's dollar receipts.

☐ *A list price minus discounts to bookstores and other expenses,* as from books returned to the publisher. Sometimes called net proceeds.

The important point is not the difference in words, but in what they mean. Therefore,

○ When you negotiate a contract, keep asking the publisher to describe the characteristics of the price on which royalties are based until you are certain you know which of the three kinds it is.

○ For a trade book, which is sold to the general public, insist on a royalty based on a percentage of the retail price.

16.5 Common royalties on domestic sales of the first printing of books are as follows.

☐ For hardcover managed books (described in Section 13.13), between 3 and 10 percent of the publisher's dollar receipts.

☐ For hardcover textbooks (Sections 13.8 to 13.11), between 10 and 20 percent of the publisher's dollar receipts.

☐ On hardcover trade books, 10 percent of the retail price.

☐ On paperback books, $7\frac{1}{2}$ to 10 percent of the publisher's dollar receipts.

Some common complexities:

☐ On nondomestic sales of any book, royalties can range from 10 percent (a common figure) to 50 percent. In general, the higher the foreign royalty percentage, the poorer the publisher's foreign sales potential.

☐ On any sales of any books, some publishers offer sliding royalties, or "steps." For example, 10 percent of publisher's dollar receipts on sales of the first 5000 copies, $12\frac{1}{2}$ on the next 5000, 15 on the next, and 18 on all subsequent sales of an edition.

Authors sometimes wonder why royalties are not higher. The answer is that expenses and taxes can take up to 85 percent of the dollars a publisher receives from selling a book (see Sections 14.2 and 14.3). Only 15 percent may remain to be split between the author's royalties and the publisher's profits.

16.6   When negotiating royalties,

○ Ask publishers to estimate the projected retail price.
○ Ask them to estimate the discount, if any, and any other expenses that may be deducted before your royalties are calculated.
○ Ask publishers to estimate projected sales in each of the book's first three years of publication.
○ Ask whether the book will be published in hardcover, paperback, or both. Negotiate royalties for each.
○ Ask about royalties on nondomestic sales and estimates of nondomestic sales. Also ask whether Canadian sales are classed as domestic or foreign, and how well the publisher expects the book to sell in Canada.

With this information you can compare offers by multiplying the estimated price on which the royalty is based times the percentage times the number of estimated sales:

Price $\times$ % $\times$ number of sales = estimated royalties   [12.1]

Some publishers may be unwilling to estimate prices and number of sales. To obtain them may require all the bargaining skill you possess. Remember that the figures are only estimates. They may not be the same as the actual price at publication and the actual number of sales.

16.7   Sale-of-Rights Agreements.   A sale-of-rights agreement is self-defining. In return for a fixed sum, the author assigns to a publisher the copyright and all other rights and interests in a book or part of a book. Managed textbooks (see Section 13.13) are sometimes paid for in this way. The author usually loses control over the uses to which his or her material and name will be put. For example, revised editions may be issued that still use his name but are not prepared by him.

16.8 Stock Options. Stock options are usually given only by small or new publishers. The assigning of stock rather than royalties makes the contract a risk-sharing, profit-sharing arrangement.

16.9 Subsidy Agreements. Sometimes authors agree to pay publishers a subvention, or subsidy, to cover all or part of a book's publishing costs. Such arrangements are most common with the so-called vanity presses (and publishing with these presses rarely does any scholar any professional good), but authors sometimes make them with other publishers, particularly university presses. Occasionally, particularly with some noncommercial publishers (see Section 14.8), authors choose to waive royalties or pay a subvention to enable publication of a scholarly manuscript whose intellectual value is established but whose potential market is so small as to prohibit any other publishing arrangement. Occasionally the institution supporting an author's research will pay the subvention, which can amount to thousands of dollars. With a nonvanity publisher, a subvention cannot buy acceptance of a manuscript. The opportunity to pay a subvention is offered only after a manuscript has been refereed and judged worthy of publication.

Other Financial Arrangements

16.10 Grants. Many publishers will offer an outright, nonrefundable grant of money to cover the expenses of preparing and mailing a manuscript. If authors do not spend the money (perhaps their departments provide free editing, typing, photocopying, and mailing), it is theirs to keep. Grants are rarely offered for monographs. Some publishers offer a flat amount. Others will agree to pay typing bills for one, two, or three drafts. To determine the size of grant you need, calculate your probable expenses. Include:

○ Mailing costs.

○ Typing expenses, based on the number of drafts, number of pages, and price per page of typing.

○ Costs of reproducing the manuscript.

16.11 Advances. Advances are not outright grants. The author receives money, but the amount is charged against royalties. Thus advances lengthen the time, after publication, before an author begins to receive royalty checks. Sometimes, as with trade books, publishers offer *advances for competitive reasons.* In such cases,

○ Remember that the advance has no effect on the amount of royalties you receive from a given contract. The only difference is that you receive some of the book's earnings earlier than you otherwise would.

Sometimes a publisher offers an advance to *free an author to write.* For example, a publisher might offer an advance that equaled a professor's summer salary. The advance enables the author to write rather than to teach or do research, and thus complete the book sooner. If the book in question is a large-market textbook, such an arrangement may be advantageous to both the author and the publisher. Occasionally a publisher will offer an advance to *show good faith in a project.*

16.12 Depending on its purpose and on estimated sales of the book in question, an advance can range in size from $100 to several thousand dollars and is usually refundable if the contract is dissolved before the book has been published. As a general rule,

○ Try to obtain an advance. On a monograph, do not expect to receive one.

○ Request an advance that is close to one of these two figures: amount of royalties expected from sales of the first printing (Barber 1975) or amount from sales during the first 12 months. Be reasonable. You do not want to discourage a publisher by requesting too large an advance.

○ Negotiate times for payment of an advance. The common options are partial or complete payment: on signing; when the manuscript is sent in for final review; when the publisher accepts the manuscript and puts it into production; when the manuscript is published.

16.13 Subsidiary Rights. Reprints, lengthy citations, and translations of part or all of an author's work can bring additional income. In general, subsidiary rights are most important for authors of trade books. Be certain the contract:

○ Specifies the income you will receive from different kinds of subsidiary use. On domestic use, a 50-50 split between author and publisher is common. On foreign use 75-25, favoring the author (Barber 1975, p. 62), is common.

○ Requires the publisher to notify you of requests to use part or all of your book.

○ Requires that those seeking to use part or all of your book obtain your permission as well as that of the publisher.

16.14 Payment for Permissions. If you use published or unpublished work that belongs to another author, you may need to receive permission and pay a fee. Sections 12.43 to 12.50 describe when to seek permission, how and when to ask, and when to pay fees. Your contract should specify who will pay for what permissions. Four arrangements are possible:

☐ Publisher pays for permissions outright.

☐ Publisher pays permission fees and charges the amount against the author's royalties.

☐ The publisher and the author split permission costs. Author's portion is charged against royalties.

☐ Author pays for permissions in cash, usually at time of publication.

As a general rule,

○ Avoid the fourth option. The second is most common.

○ Pay particular attention to this part of the contract if you are using substantial quantities of previously published material, for example in an anthology (described in Sections 13.36 and 13.37).

○ If you have one or more coauthors, specify the division of costs to each account.

16.15 Payment for Corrections in Proofs. Most contracts state the amount of corrections an author will be allowed to make in galley and page proofs before the publisher will begin charging the cost of those changes against royalties, or requesting direct payment before publication. This clause is to prevent authors from making extensive, last-minute revisions.

☐ The normal allowance is between 5 and 15 percent of the cost of setting the manuscript in type, and is usually sufficient to cover minor changes.

Sections 11.32 and 11.33 describe the effects of corrections in galley and page proofs.

16.16 As a general rule, on scholarly books and textbooks financial arrangements are less important than other matters. In the long run, authors usually benefit more from the promotions, pay raises, and prestige that follow publication of a high-quality book than they do from royalties. However, if you expect the book to sell well,

○ Take your contract to a lawyer or accountant before signing so that future receipt of payments can be structured in the most profitable way possible.

Whatever financial arrangements are made, contracts are ordinarily written so that the publisher assumes all financial risks. Even if your book's sales never cover charges to your account, you need not reimburse the publisher if the book is later removed from print unless the contract requires it—a very rare situation.

"IN STYLE, FORM, AND CONTENT"

Meaning of the Clause

16.17 Contracts usually contain a clause that explicitly exempts the publisher from any commitment to publish, particularly when the contract has been signed prior to completion of the manuscript. This clause reads,

> The author shall deliver to the publisher a manuscript [tentatively] entitled _____, consisting of approximately __ words [pages] on [date] in style, form, and content acceptable to the publisher.

The fundamental problem for authors is that the meaning of *acceptable* is not precisely defined. Also, *acceptable* may mean one thing on Monday and another by Friday (Barber 1975, p. 61).

16.18 Legitimate Rejection. Acceptable *style* is frequently the publisher's editorial style (discussed in Sections 12.6 to 12.9). *Form* usually means that the publisher wants clean copy. Handwritten manuscripts are unacceptable. *Content* has several meanings. Examples of unacceptable content are: (1) The author and the publisher contracted for a textbook on developmental psychology but the author wrote a handbook on child-rearing. (2) Both agreed on approximately 100,000 words, but the author wrote 350,000 instead. (3) The author signed on the basis of an exciting-looking outline and prospectus, but the execution leaves much to be desired. Rejections on this basis are almost always accompanied by two or three referees' concurring opinions. (4) The author contracted to write an introductory text. The result was an upper-level textbook, or worse, a graduate-level monograph.

16.19 Questionable Rejection. There are also questionable reasons. Among these, stated from the publisher's perspective, are: (1) "Times are tough. The manuscript is what we contracted for, but now we can't afford to publish it." To guard against such an event,

○ Check into a publisher's financial condition before signing a contract. Instructions are in Section 16.55.

(2) "The market has changed since we signed the contract." (3) "Higher management has ruled that all books published must realize an income of $500,000 in the first year of publication." (4) "You missed your delivery date by a week (and, no, we have no record of the previous editor's having agreed to this delay)." (5) "Your royalties are too high to make the book profitable. Now if you want to accept lower royalties . . . ."

16.20　Most of the time the publisher's lack of an obligation to publish causes no difficulties. Reputable publishers generally do not sign books they do not intend to publish. However, a publishing company may change managing editors between the time an author signs a contract and the date the final manuscript is submitted. Furthermore, as the book market has tightened, policies have been reappraised. If a final manuscript does not appear profitable, some publishers will try to break the contract with the author by calling the manuscript unacceptable. For example, William Morrow and Company broke a contract with William Safire on that basis (Barber 1975, p. 61).

Protection for Authors

16.21　To protect yourself,

○ Include in the contract a date by which either the book will have been published or the manuscript will have been returned to you. Set a date 12 to 16 months after the publisher receives an acceptable manuscript.
○ Request a grant to cover expenses (see Section 16.10), an advance against royalties (16.11 and 16.12), or both. Specify that the advance will be nonrefundable if the publisher has not published the book by the specified date. The money you receive is both part payment for the investment of your

time and an investment of cash that may increase the company's interest in publishing your book with all due speed.

CAUTION.   Do not insist that a date be unconditional. Sometimes a publisher experiences legitimate delays, such as paper shortages, transportation strikes, and other acts of God. The publisher will probably want to include a clause that protects the company against such events.

OTHER CLAUSES

Right of First Refusal

16.22   A "first refusal" clause obligates you to submit a second (or subsequent) book to your first publisher for consideration before submitting it to anyone else. If the company decides that it wants to publish the second book, it can make an offer without competition from other publishers. Only if the publisher rejects the manuscript or you refuse the offer can you submit the new manuscript elsewhere. This situation may put you in a bad competitive position on future manuscripts. Also, if the company dallies in evaluating the manuscript because it holds this advantage, the manuscript may become dated. Some publishers use a modified version of this clause: they require right of first refusal, but agree to exercise this right within a specified period of time, such as 90 days. After this period the author may submit the manuscript to any other publisher, and any offer made by the first publisher may have to compete with other offers.

16.23   Publishers have been most anxious to retain this clause in contracts for trade books. They advertise such books heavily, and are naturally reluctant to have another publisher benefit from the sales of a sequel or of a second book by the same author. On contracts for monographs, most publishers will remove the clause if the author requests that it be removed. Some authors who have been unable to have such clauses removed and who have also been unhappy with their publishers have solved the problem by producing a notably unsatisfactory manuscript and submitting that as the next book. This practice fulfills the letter of the contract, and the authors are then free to submit the next manuscript wherever they wish. Fortunately, this practice is seldom needed.

Copyright Responsibility

16.24 Securing a copyright and placing an appropriate copyright mark on a book is the publisher's responsibility. Under the old law (see Section 12.45), American copyrights may be obtained for 28 years. They may be renewed during their final year for one additional 28-year period. After 56 years at most, then, a book copyrighted only in the United States enters the public domain. After January 1, 1978, copyright will be issued for the life of an author plus an additional 50 years (see Sections 12.45 and 12.46). Not all copyright provisions are the same. If your book is to be published in countries other than the United States, your publisher should also obtain copyrights for those countries. The copyright clause normally states that the publisher agrees to apply, pay for, and renew copyright on the author's book. As a general rule,

○ Ask that the publisher take out the copyright in your name rather than the company's. See also Section 16.31.

Payment and Accounting

16.25 The payment and accounting clause states the publisher's accounting policies and the dates on which royalty reports and payments are issued to authors. For example, some publishers report semiannually; others, annually.

Related Work

16.26 To protect sales, most contracts contain a clause that restricts use of a manuscript to citations by the author in other scholarly work. If you want to publish elsewhere substantial portions of a book manuscript, perhaps as an article in a journal,

○ Request a waiver of the restriction on publishing and include in the contract a statement of what you want to publish
and where.

See also Section 14.10.

Arbitration

16.27 Some contracts have an arbitration clause that states
who has final authority in event of a dispute between author
and publisher. For example,

> All disputes shall be settled by arbitration in [city, state]
> in accordance with the rules of the [arbitration associa-
> tion] then obtaining, and judgment upon the award may
> be entered in any court having jurisdiction thereof.

Number of Complimentary Copies

16.28 Most publishers give an author between 6 and 20 free
copies of the book at publication. If you need more than a
publisher normally offers, perhaps for colleagues who have
done critical reading for you or for other publishers who have
granted permission for you to use portions of published works,

○ Either request sufficient copies to cover these needs or include in the contract a statement that the publisher will
supply copies directly to the specified parties. Sometimes a
publisher will include only the general agreement and ask
that you list in a letter of agreement (Section 16.37) the names
of parties to receive books.

Responsibility for Obtaining Permissions

16.29 Contracts should state who will obtain permissions and
who will pay for them. Different arrangements for payment are
described in Section 16.14. In general, publishers expect authors to obtain their own permissions (for help, see Sections
12.43 to 12.50), but some publishers will assist in difficult
cases,[1] as when an author is out of the country or when a

copyright owner is requesting unusually high fees or making unusual demands. If you request assistance,

○ Supply the publisher with copies of all your correspondence with the copyright holders. See Section 12.49.

Revision Rights

16.30 This clause often seems meaningless to authors at the time a contract is signed. Subsequent editions of a book are usually far from the thoughts of authors who are glad just to have a contract. The publisher usually reserves the right to decide if and when a book needs revision. Difficulties arise if the publisher wants revisions more often than the author does, or if the contract does not give the author some control over those revisions. As a rule,

○ State in the contract that in the event you do not want to write a requested revision, the publisher may select, subject to mutual consent, some other person(s) to make the revisions on terms satisfactory to all contracting parties.
○ Another option: state that any revision prepared by others during the author's lifetime shall be subject to review by the author.
○ Include in the contract ways to settle both financial arrangements, such as royalty splits between author and reviser, and textual differences in the event that the contracting parties disagree.

This clause is particularly important to authors of textbooks and editors of bibliographies.

Reversion Rights and Remaindering (Out of Print)

16.31 Before signing a contract,

○ Make sure it contains a clause requiring the publisher to notify you within a specified period of time if the book is to go out of print.

○ Also make certain that the rights revert to you without charge, and that you will be told when the remaining copies of the book are to be disposed of, or *remaindered*.

This clause is usually most important to authors of monographs. It protects them from having their books go out of print without warning and allows them to regain rights to their books without having to pay a fee to the original publisher.

Warranty and Indemnity

16.32   When you sign a contract, you must guarantee that the manuscript is original and that you own all parts of it. If any substantial portion (see Sections 12.45 and 12.46) has been published elsewhere,

○ Obtain permission from the publisher and the author and include a copy of the permission with the contract. For instructions, see Sections 12.47 to 12.50.
○ Include notice of the original copyright somewhere in the book, normally on the copyright page, on the first page of the reprinted material, or in the acknowledgments.

Ordinarily, in the social and behavioral sciences, journals permit authors to reprint at no charge material from their articles in subsequent books that they either write or edit. See also Section 16.26.

16.33   The warranty and indemnity clause usually also states that the publisher can hold the author liable in full for legal expenses and damage awards, if any, resulting from publication of the book.

○ To protect yourself, delete warranties against "obscene or scandalous" material. Also delete such sweeping language as "otherwise unlawful" (see Barber 1975, p. 61).
○ If possible, include a clause that requires the publisher to notify you of any legal action against your book, allows you to prepare your own defense or a joint defense with the

publisher, and limits your liabilities to an amount related to the book's income. Liabilities should not be payable until court action has been completed, or you have agreed to an out-of-court settlement (see Barber 1975, p. 62).

Related Products

16.34 Sometimes—usually in contracts for textbooks—it is necessary to specify what related products, such as teachers' guides and student workbooks, will be published with the book (see Section 13.24).

○ Specify the aids and who will prepare them.
○ If someone other than you is to prepare them, specify the amount of payment. Also state whether payment will be made by the publisher, by you, or by the publisher but charged to your royalties.

Miscellaneous Clauses

16.35 Some clauses are rarely used, and only by a few publishers. Among these are:

☐ Permission for a publisher to cancel a contract if the author leaves the teaching profession before the manuscript has been set in type. Sometimes invoked if a high school textbook is involved.
☐ Guaranteed insurance, for the author's and the publisher's expenses and earnings, should either the manuscript or bound copies of the book be destroyed by fire or other natural causes.

Order of Signatures

16.36 When you sign a contract with one or more coauthors,

○ Sign in the order in which you want names to appear on the title page. First author should sign first, second author second, and so forth.

○ Sections 6.18 and 6.19 describe different orders of names and
   what the orders mean.

LETTERS OF AGREEMENT

16.37   Some matters cannot be put into a contract. To formalize
them, publishers and authors often exchange letters of agreement in addition to the formal contract. The following items are
among those often included in such letters.

Printing, Price, Binding

16.38   Not all books have justified right and left margins. Publishers sometimes omit justifying the right-hand margin of
pages to save money on typesetting costs. Some publishers
photoreproduce typed tables. Others have entire manuscripts
typed and photoreproduced. Pages with unjustified right
margins—whether typeset or photoreproduced—have even
margins on the left side but not on the right. If you want to
know about printing, price, and binding,

○ Ask the publisher to show you a book that the company has
   published and that looks as your book will probably look.
○ Ask about estimated price.
○ Include the answers in a letter of agreement.

Expect tentative rather than definite answers. Your goal is to
find mutually acceptable guidelines. On prices, for example,
inflation has made prediction, even for a point only nine
months into the future, very tentative.

Division of Responsibilities

16.39   If you are working with a coauthor or editing a collection,

○ Include in a letter of agreement a statement of the authors'
   division of responsibilities. For example, the first author

might be responsible for checking the edited manuscript; the second, for proofreading.

○ For edited collections, state the penalties for failure to meet deadlines. For suggested penalties, see Section 13.29.

GUIDELINES FOR NEGOTIATING WITH BOOK PUBLISHERS

Preparation for Negotiation

16.40 Before entering negotiations with a publisher, and periodically during them,

○ Examine your wishes for your manuscript, and rank them in order of importance. For help, see Sections 14.9 to 14.15.

Satisfactory negotiations are fostered by honesty, personal pleasantness, and thoughtful preparation. Some misunderstandings between authors and publishers are caused largely by a lack of thoughtful preparation and ranking of preferences. For an example, see Section 15.12. Some misunderstandings occur because authors do not understand one or more clauses. If you have any questions,

○ Ask them of your prospective publisher. Keep asking until you understand. Publishers dislike misunderstandings as much as authors do, and they know that authors tell colleagues about their displeasure.
○ If you have legal questions, consult with a lawyer.
○ Never sign a contract until everything in it is clear and acceptable to you.

Limits of Publishers' Authority

16.41 When a publisher makes an offer to you,

○ Ask him or her to describe the limits of his authority. In many cases, verbal offers mean something like: "This is what I'd like to offer. What is your reaction? If you approve, I'll submit a draft contract to [e.g., the board of trustees, vice president]. Then I'll let you know whether they approve, disapprove, or want to offer different terms."

○ Do not cut off negotiations with other publishers until you have a firm, approved offer in writing.

Contracts Signed Before Completion of a Manuscript

16.42 Particularly with textbooks and trade books, authors sometimes sign contracts before the manuscript has been completed. If you sign a contract before completion,

○ Be realistic in estimating a completion date.
○ Be certain you and the editor agree on content and writing style. See Section 16.45 for details.
○ Choose a publisher in whom you have confidence. You will be working together for quite a long period of time.
○ If you find yourself unable to complete the manuscript, ask the publisher to execute a termination agreement to dissolve the contract.
○ Return any advances you have received.

Letters That Confirm Telephone Conversations

16.43 Negotiations usually occur partly by letter and partly by telephone. After any telephone call, during negotiations and throughout your relationship with a publisher,

○ Write a letter stating the topics discussed and the agreements reached.

There are two reasons for such letters: they constitute a written record, and misunderstandings come to light immediately.

CRITERIA FOR CHOOSING THE BEST PUBLISHER

16.44 If you receive more than one offer of a contract, you will have to decide which publisher is best for your manuscript.

○ First examine your wishes for the manuscript (Section 16.40) and compare the different offers with your preferences.
○ Then evaluate the publishers on the factors discussed in Sections 16.45 to 16.55.

Take your time. You will have to work with this publisher for the next year or two, and you will have to live with the terms of the contract for the rest of your life, or until the book has been allowed to go out of print. The week or two before you sign a contract is your last chance to make certain that the contract and the publishers are as satisfactory as possible for you. The course that negotiations have taken often indicates the kind of relationship that you will have with the publishing company while the book is being produced. Most authors come to the end of a careful evaluation with a sense that one specific publisher is clearly the best one for the manuscript.

Content and Style

16.45 You and your publisher should agree on the content and writing style of the manuscript. If you are signing a contract before the manuscript has been completed,

○ Delay signing until the publisher has seen sufficient chapters and outlines that you can both agree on extent of coverage and writing style.

For example, if you are writing an introductory textbook, you will have to write in a somewhat informal style with a readability level around 10 or 11 (described in Sections 5.65 to 5.69). If you cannot do so, you and your publisher may want to agree on some form of author assistance. Different kinds are discussed in Sections 13.13 to 13.17. You should also agree on whether to plan the book for one or two semesters of use, or for some other length of time.

Publisher's Interest

16.46 To evaluate a publisher's interest,

○ Examine the contract offer and then use your intuition.

For example, most publishers will telephone frequently if they are strongly interested or will accept collect calls from authors with questions. With a potentially very successful book, some editors send a salesperson to wine and dine an author. Others come themselves. Some react enthusiastically to questions and suggestions. Others resent them. Some have read the manuscript and like it (although for some, failure to read only indicates that they are not scholars). Some draw up proposed production and marketing plans with no prompting from an author.

Marketing Plans

16.47 Authors of textbooks and trade books should pay special attention to a publisher's plans for marketing a book. Ask a publisher questions like the following:

> Will the book appear in paperback, hardcover, or both?
> Will it be part of a series?
> What level of sales do you anticipate? Why?
> What is the potential market? What research have you done on the market?
> How do you plan to reach the market?
> Have you published books like mine before? Have you sold them using similar strategies? Were the strategies successful?
> How will my book fit your total list?
> Do you plan related projects for the future?

16.48 Evaluating marketing plans can raise one of the most difficult questions an author has to answer: Which of two or more different, competing plans is best, or more accurate for the intended market? When clear differences exist, how much should be attributed to a publisher's personal characteristics and how much to genuine differences in companies' abilities to market a given book? Suppose you have written a handbook such as this one. One publisher might propose printing it as an inexpensive paperback and giving away many copies to promote sales. He or she projects sales of between 9000 and 10,000 copies during the first year of publication. A second publisher might plan a quality hardcover book, with very few giveaways, and project sales of 4000 copies per year. Still a third publisher might project 3000 sales the first year, and a fourth, 5000; the third and fourth also plan hardcover production.

16.49 Initially, recall that royalties on paperbacks are lower than royalties on hardcover books. Even with a projected sale of 10,000, the lower prices and royalties probably mean that between the first publisher and the rest, there will not be a substantial difference in amount of royalties ultimately received. In questioning the publishers, you may learn that the first publisher's list includes several similar handbooks, each marketed in the manner proposed for your book. In addition, sales figures relative to the potential market bear out the projected sales for your book.

16.50 In examining the second publisher's offer, you may discover that quality, hardcover books are a mark of pride with that company. Also, the list of publications is strong in the substantive areas whose practitioners are most likely to be interested in your book. Third, the list also includes other handbooks on writing that have been marketed successfully, and in the manner proposed for your handbook. Clearly, your book will receive reasonable exposure to appropriate audiences simply by being listed in brochures that the company already prepares. You would expect fewer sales with a higher price, so the second publisher's sales estimate does not seem out of line with the first publisher's.

16.51 On the surface, the two remaining publishers appear similar to the second. Both prefer quality, hardcover publications. However, investigation shows that while the third publishing house has as strong a list as the second publisher in related substantive areas, it has published no handbooks. Under this circumstance, it seems reasonable to expect that, as is the case, the third publisher's estimate will be lower than that of the second. As between the second and the third publishers, then, the second would probably be your choice.

16.52 Further examination discloses that the fourth publisher's list is substantially the same as the third publisher's. When you ask, the fourth publisher produces no supporting evidence for the estimate that differs from that produced by the second and the third. You may next discover, on asking questions of colleagues who have published with that company, that that managing editor's estimates are almost invariably higher than those of other editors. If you are able to check estimates with actual sales (authors receive annual or semiannual accountings of sales), you may discover that sometimes the estimates are accurate; other times they are not. It may be that this editor takes high figures from estimates by the marketing department rather than low figures. He may have unusual sales ability, or he may only be hoping to persuade you to sign with his company. However, since his company has never published a handbook, his optimism on your book may not be justified. This discovery will probably encourage you to narrow your choice to publishers one and two. You will probably choose between them on the basis of some factor other than dollar amount of royalties received, since dollar receipts from either, at least for the first year, may not be very different. If you value wide distribution, you will probably choose the first publisher.

16.53 The example is oversimplified. However, the important point is to understand possible differences and how to evaluate them.

Rapport with a Publisher

16.54 On a personal basis, with which publisher would you most like to work? To most authors, rapport is not as important as the other factors just noted. It becomes important only if all other factors are equal or nearly so.

Financial Stability

16.55 Check financial stability by examining *Standard and Poor's* ratings of the publishing companies (and of their owners, if any are subsidiaries of larger companies). When a publishing company fails, its contractees can suffer. Even if the company is purchased by one or more other publishers, the policies of the new publishers will probably differ from those of the failed company. If a company appears financially unstable, discuss this fact with the publisher before you sign a contract.

WHAT TO DO AFTER THE DECISION

16.56 After you reach a verbal agreement with one publisher, a month or so may elapse before you receive an official contract. During the interim, many authors prefer not to notify the other publishers with whom they have been dealing. However, if one of the other publishers calls while you are waiting, be honest about your situation. When you have signed a contract,

○ Send a courteous letter to the other companies so that they will welcome future manuscripts from you.

If you wish, indicate the factors that caused the decision. For example, the author of the handbook discussed in Sections 16.48 to 16.52 might want to tell the second publisher that he values wide distribution. Giving a reason lets rejected publishers know that you still value their interest and good will.

SUMMARY

16.57   In this chapter I first discuss financial terms in contracts (Sections 16.3 to 16.16); acceptable style, form, and content (16.17 to 16.21); and other clauses in contracts (16.22 to 16.36). I then discuss letters of agreement (16.37 to 16.39), guidelines for negotiating with a publisher (16.40 to 16.43), criteria for choosing the best publisher for a manuscript (16.44 to 16.55), and what to do after making a final choice (16.56).

NOTE TO CHAPTER 16

1. Seeking permissions takes considerable secretarial time. Also, some publishers believe that an author can obtain permissions at less cost than can a publisher acting for him.

CHAPTER SEVENTEEN

After Signing the Contract and Before Publication

FINAL PREPARATION, PROOFREADING, AND MAILING

Instructions for Final Preparation

17.1 After you have signed a contract, prepare the manuscript for submission to the publisher for acceptance and production.

○ Revise it carefully. For instructions, see Chapter 5.
○ Prepare it in proper editorial style. For instructions, see Sections 12.6 to 12.9.
○ Follow the rules for typing in Sections 12.10 to 12.22.
○ Prepare front matter according to instructions in Sections 12.23 to 12.28.
○ Prepare back matter following the instructions in Sections 12.31 to 12.33.
○ Obtain and organize permissions following the instructions in Sections 12.43 to 12.50.
○ Follow the instructions in Figure 17.1.

Proper preparation can save production time. If you have questions, ask your publisher.

Instructions for Proofreading

17.2 After the manuscript has been typed, proofread it.

○ Look for typographical errors. See Section 8.84.
○ Proofread out loud. Use the technique described in Section 11.32. See also Section 11.28, instruction 6.
○ Type corrections neatly. Section 12.30 gives instructions.

Instructions for Wrapping and Mailing

17.3 When the manuscript is complete—including all front matter, chapters, tables, illustrations, list of references, notes, back matter (except the index; see Section 12.41), and permissions,

1. *Contents.*   Include foreword and preface; all part, chapter, and appendix titles; and glossary, bibliography, and index. Titles should be exactly as they are shown on part and title pages.
2. *List of illustrations.*   Include all illustrations. Titles should be exactly as they are shown on the illustrations.
3. *List of tables.*   Include all tables. Titles should be exactly as they are on the tables.
4. *Notes.*   Check each text-reference number in every chapter with the list of notes for that chapter. You should have a number in text for every note. Also check correspondence between notes and text. It is easy to skip notes or mix them up.
5. *Part and chapter titles and all levels of headings.*   At each level, titles and headings should follow the same editorial style. For help, see Section 12.18.
6. *Documentation.*   Each document cited should be listed in the bibliography. The citation should be complete and should agree with information in the bibliographic entry. Look particularly for omissions of dates and pages and for typographical errors on dates and on volume and page numbers.
7. *Cross-references.*   Check accuracy. In revising, you may have deleted or rearranged some sections.
8. *Read the entire manuscript* as you would a novel. You will usually find a few more spelling, punctuation, and typographical errors, and a few sentences that do not read smoothly.

Figure 17.1   Checklist for final manuscript of a book.

○ Make at least two clear xerographic copies.

○ Check the sequence of page numbers in each copy to be certain no page is missing.

○ Securely pack the original and one copy for mailing. Never send an incomplete manuscript unless the publisher explicitly tells you to do so.

○ For each copy, arrange the pages as follows: front matter, text, references, permissions. Tie in a bundle. In a separate bundle tie the illustrations, with the list of illustrations on top. If your publisher wants the tables separate from the manuscript (see Section 12.15), tie them in a separate bundle with the list of tables on top. Leave no edges of pages sticking out.

○ USE NO CLIPS OR STAPLES.

○ DO NOT BIND IN BINDERS.

○ In a sturdy cardboard box, place one copy of the manuscript on top of the other. For bulky manuscripts, use one box for each copy. Place the tables on the bottom (if separate from the manuscript), the illustrations next, and the rest on top. Some authors also wrap the pages in plastic to prevent water damage.

○ Wrap the box in heavy paper, seal tightly, tie with stout cord, and address to the editor with whom you negotiated the contract.

○ Send the parcel third class or special fourth class. Insure it for the cost of reproducing the manuscript (in case of loss). If speed is important, send it first class.

○ Send photographs separately. Mark the package "Photographs. Do not bend." Insure these for the cost of replacement.

○ Write a separate letter telling the managing editor the date on which you mailed the manuscript. Ask him to notify you when he receives it. Alternative procedures: either certify the parcel and request a return receipt, or place a self-addressed postcard on top of the manuscript with a request that it be dated and mailed immediately.

○ Keep a complete copy of everything you send to the publisher.

FINAL EVALUATION

17.4 Unless the manuscript was completed at the time the contract was signed, the publisher will probably seek a final evaluation of its content and writing style. After the review, you may receive the manuscript and suggestions for revision. (If no changes are suggested, the publisher may put it into production without returning it.) The suggestions often point out obscurities in writing, small inaccuracies in data or method, and so forth. It is in your interest to remove or correct these, because the ultimate worth of the book will be measured not only by its scientific contribution to the literature but also by its scholarship. Some authors consider this evaluation so important that they mention it in their contracts or letters of agreement, and even request readers by name.

○ For help in using the suggestions, see Sections 6.8 to 6.10.
○ Prepare the manuscript again, following instructions in Sections 17.1 and 17.2. Mail it following the instructions in Section 17.3.
○ Write a letter to the managing editor. Request that he notify you when he puts the manuscript into production. Also request a production schedule.

THE PROCESS OF PRODUCTION

The Production Schedule

17.5 The production schedule lists your book's anticipated progress from manuscript to published book. It may include any of the following items (different items are omitted by different publishers):

☐ Date on which you will be sent the edited typescript and tables for checking (usually $1\frac{1}{2}$ to 6 months after the manuscript was put into production).
☐ Date on which you will be sent galley proofs (described in Section 11.32).
☐ Date on which you will be sent page proofs (described in Section 11.33).
☐ Dates on which you will receive edited illustrations and proofs for illustrations.
☐ Dates by which you must have returned checked typescript, galley proofs, page proofs, and proofs of illustrations.
☐ Date by which the publisher must have your index on hand.
☐ Unless you make other arrangements, most publishers require that all items be back in their offices NO LATER THAN

10 to 14 days from the date on which they were mailed to you.

To reduce the pressure of time, some publishers send edited manuscript, galleys, and page proofs in small batches that are easier to complete in a short period of time. Usually this material is sent back and forth by first-class mail, and occasionally by special delivery, since parcel post or fourth-class mail does not have the speed that is necessary.

17.6 Production schedules reflect careful planning based on marketing needs, printers' blocks of free time, availability of appropriate copy editors, and numerous other factors. Once prepared, a production schedule is hard to change. If you delay returning any item by even a day, you may set production back a month or more and thus upset the advertising schedule and raise the publisher's unit cost on the book. Equally important, the book may not receive the attention originally planned for it. For example, a production editor may have to complete both your book and someone else's simultaneously, when the schedule for the publishing cycle originally called for only one. Following the production schedule to the absolute letter is not just a matter of making the publisher happy, although authors who respect schedules make a publisher more anxious to sign them again. The important matter is what is best for the book.

○ If at any time you find yourself unable to meet the schedule, let your managing editor know *as soon as possible*, because the schedule will have to be reset immediately.

The Edited Manuscript

17.7 Checking and Responding to Comments. Some publishers do not send authors the edited manuscript. If you are given the opportunity, check the edited manuscript carefully. Any potential change that you overlook may have to be changed in the galleys or in page proofs, at substantial cost to either you, the publisher, or both. See discussion of the allowance for corrections in Section 16.15. To help you find errors,

○ Read the manuscript out loud to yourself.

○ Look particularly for editorial changes that have unintentionally changed your meaning, for example, insertion of a comma that has changed a restrictive clause to a descriptive one. For examples, see Sections 5.42 and 5.43.

○ If you make changes, use a pencil that is a different color from the editor's.

○ In general, do not make a change simply because the editor's phrasing does not appeal to you. Editors usually know more about grammar and writing than authors do. You may have made an error and not recognized it. For help in responding to editorial comments, see Sections 6.11 and 6.12.

○ Respond to all queries written by the editor.

Some editors write queries on small, colored slips of paper, attached to the backs of the typed pages at the point where the question occurs, and folded over onto the front. Others write them in the margins of the manuscript. Queries indicate that something is wrong with the writing, but the editor needs more information before making corrections. If at all possible,

○ Answer all queries on either the query slip or the manuscript page, in a different color of pen or pencil.

For a general question that requires a lengthy answer, you may need to answer either on a separate piece of paper, placed in the manuscript at the point where the question arose, or in your covering letter to the editorial supervisor when you return the manuscript. If you choose the latter option, mention the page and line number on which the question arose.

17.8 If you have questions or comments that are not direct responses to the copy editor's queries, include them in your covering letter when you return the manuscript.

17.9 Mailing the Checked Manuscript. When you are ready to mail the manuscript back to the publisher,

○ Follow the procedure in Section 17.3. Place the covering letter on top.
○ Because the editing and checking represent valuable commitments of time, register or certify the parcel, and send it first class. Either procedure permits tracing the parcel if it is lost.

If at any point you encounter a problem that must be solved before you can proceed, call your editorial supervisor immediately and resolve it. Any other method of communication is likely to delay the production schedule.

Galley and Page Proofs

17.10   Some publishers will send you both galley and page proofs of text, tables, and illustrations. Most commonly, though, you will receive one or the other, but not both.

○ Follow the publisher's instructions for proofreading. Use the publisher's set of proofreader's marks. Both will be either attached to the proofs or included in the publisher's manual for authors (described in Sections 12.6 to 12.8).
○ In the absence of instructions from the publisher, follow the instructions in Sections 11.32 and 11.33, and use the proofreader's marks in Figure 11.1.
○ If possible, schedule proofreading in blocks of time no longer than 2 hours, with at least a 15-minute break between blocks. Proofreading is mentally tedious, and especially tiring on the person reading out loud.

Preparation of the Index

17.11   Although much of the indexing can be done earlier (see Sections 12.34 to 12.40), page numbers and final typing must usually be delayed until you have page proofs.

○ For instructions on final preparation of the index, see Sections 12.41 and 12.42.

MARKETING PLANS

The Marketing Questionnaire

17.12 Shortly after the manuscript has been put into production, you will receive a marketing questionnaire from the publisher. The questionnaire's purpose is to guarantee that the publisher sells the book in the most effective way possible. Some authors find the questionnaire irritating. Having just finished the book, they want to forget it for a time. Often they also feel that they are only repeating information already in the book's preface, introductory chapter, and prospectus. What authors do not realize is that the repetition, on the form, is the only way to guarantee that the publisher will reach all possible readers.

17.13 When completing the questionnaire,

○ Take the viewpoint of a critic writing a favorable book review for a journal. Describe the book's background, prerequisites, goals, and success in meeting those goals. Emphasize the book's strong points and compare it with previously published books.

○ Use your prospectus (Sections 15.6 to 15.14, 15.16, 15.17, 15.19, and 15.20), the preface (Section 12.28), the table of contents (12.25), and the introductory chapter as resources. For example, the first part of a prospectus (Sections 15.6 to 15.9) usually contains information that relates to a question such as: "Please describe in one paragraph exactly what your book is about. What is there about your selection, organization, or treatment of the subject . . . that makes your book important, different, and stimulating?"

Your answer to that question may appear later, somewhat edited, on the inside flap of the book's jacket.

○ To answer other questions, do some research. For example, many publishers ask: "In which [six] journals or newsletters should your book be advertised?" (The number varies.)

To answer a question like this, think not only of journals and associations in your own discipline but also of those in related specialties that are part of other disciplines. Answer each question as carefully and fully as possible.

17.14 If you have suggestions not elicited by the questionnaire,

○ Make them either in the "Additional Comments" section (some publishers provide one) or in a covering letter.

Some ideas may be inappropriate or excessively expensive, but others may ultimately benefit both you and the publisher.

Publishers' Use of Questionnaires

17.15 On the basis of the questionnaire, the manuscript, and other information, the publisher's marketing department plans promotional activities such as advertisements in appropriate journals; brochures for direct mailing to special groups— scholars in the book's specialty area or members of a particular association (one expense of advertising is purchasing such lists); display of the book at appropriate conventions; review copies mailed to crucial journals; descriptions of the book in catalogs distributed to bookstores and to the public at conventions; advance promotion in brochures for bookstores, and publicity releases to other media such as professional societies and alumni organizations that have regular publications. Some companies send advertising copy to authors for approval. Others do not. Regardless of policy, your book will receive the most careful and efficient promotion that the publisher can afford for that book. No publisher wants a book to lose money needlessly. The advertising effort will diminish over time unless the book is unusually successful. Nevertheless, it will continue to be listed in a publisher's catalog until the book goes out of print.

AFTER PUBLICATION

17.16 After the book is published, keep a list of errors as you find them. Periodically, send them to the publisher. Some can be corrected in later printings if the book is successful enough to warrant them. Whatever the book's success, critical or financial, take pride in the fact that you finished it. Few scholars succeed in that task.

SUMMARY

17.17 In this chapter I first give instructions for final preparation and mailing of a manuscript (Sections 17.1 to 17.3). I then discuss the final review (17.4), the process of production (17.5 to 17.11), marketing plans (17.12 to 17.15), and what to do after publication (17.16).

Journals: Exclusions and Supplements

EXCLUSIONS

A.1 In Table 7.1 I listed only journals that I could examine. Most were shelved in the Indiana University Library's current periodicals reading room. My basic source of information was 1973, 1974, and 1975 issues of the journals. I included only journals that appeared to offer 10 or more opportunities per year for social and behavioral scientists to publish refereed, unsolicited articles written in English. I excluded unrefereed journals for the reasons noted in Section 10.24. I excluded journals without an open submission policy because their editors chose articles on the basis of factors in addition to quality of article and appropriateness of topic. For example, *The Annals of Economic and Social Measurement* usually publishes only articles that have been presented previously as papers at conferences of the National Bureau of Economic Research. As a result, publication in *The Annals* is usually possible only for those who have given papers at conferences.

A.2 I also omitted most journals that published only articles by authors, or on topics, severly limited by geographical area.

Table A.1   Supplementary List of Journals[a]

Academy of Management J.[r]
Acta Criminologica[r]
Administration in Mental Health[r]
Administrative Science Rev.[r]
Am. Academy of Political and Social Science
Armed Forces and Society
Behavioral and Social Science Teacher
Berkeley J. of Sociology[r]
Catalyst[r] (social science theory)[b]
Change Magazine
Clinical Social Work J.[r]
Community College Social Science Q.[r]
Cornell J. of Social Relations
Counseling and Values
Criminal Justice and Behavior (correctional psychology)[b]
Current Sociology[r]
Curriculum Bull.
Cycles[r] (fluctuating social phenomena)[b]
Day Care and Early Education[r]
Ethnic Studies
Family Planning Perspectives[r]
Federal Probation[r] (criminal justice and policy)[b]
Georgia Social Science J.[r]
Gerontologist[r]
Green Revolution: Perspectives on Living[r]
Group Psychotherapy and Psychodrama[r]
Health Services Research
Hospital Administration[r]

Human Resource Management[r]
Indian J. of Social Research[r]
Industrial Marketing Management
International Development Rev.[r]
International J. of the Addictions[r]
International J. of Clinical and Experimental Hypnosis
International J. of Ethnic Studies[r]
International J. of Offender Therapy and Comparative Criminology
International J. of the Sociology of Language
International Labour Rev.
International Studies in Sociology and Social Theory
International Social Science J.
International Social Science Rev.
J. of the Am. Geriatrics Society
J. of the Association for the Study of Perception
J. of Applied Rehabilitation Counseling
J. of Autism and Childhood Schizophrenia
J. of Business
J. of Community Health
J. of Community Psychology
J. of Consumer Affairs[r]
J. of Consumer Research
J. of Emotional Education[r]
J. of Employment Counseling
J. of Homosexuality[r]

Table A.1 *(Continued)*

J. of Individual Psychology	Planning Outlook (land-use
J. of Phenomenological	planning)[b]
Psychology	Political Science Rev.
J. of Secondary Education	Political Scientist
J. of Social and Behavioral	Population and Development
Sciences	Rev.
J. of Social Psychology[r]	Population Rev.[r]
J. of Socio-Economic Planning	Q. Rev. of Economics and
Sciences[r]	Business
J. of Sociology and Social	Religious Humanism[r]
Welfare	Research on Consumer
J. of Thought[r]	Behavior[r]
Kansas J. of Sociology[r]	Rev. of Public Data Use[r]
Liberal Education (general	Rev. of Social Theory[r]
education)[b]	Social Action[r] (developing
Midwestern J. of Language and	areas)[b]
Folklore	Social Biology
Negro Educational Rev.	Sociological Practice (theory and
New Scholar: A J. of Graduate	applied work)[b]
Studies in the Social Sciences[r]	Sociological Symposium[r]
Ontario Psychologist	Southern Speech
Operations Research	Communication J.[r]
(economics, statistics)[b]	Technology Assessment[r]
Organizational Behavior and	Transportation
Human Performance (applied	Urban and Social Change Rev.[r]
psychology)[b]	Viewpoints (education)[b]
Perception and Psychophysics	War/Peace Report[r]
Personnel[r]	Wisconsin Sociologist[r]
Personnel Administrator[r]	

[a]Abbreviations: Am. = American; Bull. = Bulletin; J. = Journal; Q. = Quarterly; Rev. = Review. Superscript "r" = information listed in Rhoades (1974).

[b]Parenthesized comment indicates preferred topics. On all other journals, the journal's name is an adequate indicator.

For example, I eliminated *Africa, Africa Today, African Social Research, African Studies, African Studies Review, Amerasia Journal, Asian Survey, Indian Historian, Philippine Sociological Review, Psychologia (Japan), Rhodesian Journal of Economics, Rural Africa, South African Journal of Economics, South Asian Review,* and *Studies in African Linguistics.* Many of these journals are easy for interested scientists to locate because the name of the country or area is the first word of the journal's name. Also, many libraries catalog such journals by geographical area.

A.3 Finally, I omitted journal-type books, such as *Sociological Methodology,* that publish only one issue annually; and journals that publish only book reviews, translations or digests of articles, or articles by authors with non-American affiliations.

SUPPLEMENTS

Additional Journals

A.4 Table A.1 lists some journals not included in Table 7.1. Some were suggested by reviewers who read drafts of this book. Others were listed in collections such as Rhoades (1974). Because most were not available in the Indiana University library, I could not determine whether they met the criteria for inclusion that I applied to journals listed in Table 7.1. Further information on these journals, including addresses, may be found in the most recent editions of the *Directory of Publishing Opportunities, Ulrich's International Periodicals Directory,* or Rhoades (1974).

Indexes and Abstracting Services

A.5 Indexes and abstracting services list the names of journals whose articles they include. You may find the following indexes and abstracting services useful.

ABC Political Science
Abstracts for Social Workers
Abstracts in Anthropology
Abstracts on Criminology and Penology
African Abstracts (now defunct—1973)
America: History and Life
Child Development Abstracts and Bibliography
CIJE Abstracts
Current Contents
Exceptional Child Education Abstracts
International Political Science Abstracts
Journal of Economic Literature
Language & Learning Behavior Abstracts
Mental Retardation Abstracts
Poverty and Human Resources Abstracts
Psychological Abstracts
Sage Public Administration Abstracts
Sage Urban Studies Abstracts
Social Sciences Citation Index
Sociological Abstracts
Sociology of Education Abstracts
Statistical Theory and Method Abstracts
Universal Reference System

APPENDIX B

Suggestions for Class Papers, Dissertations, Proposals for Research Grants, Progress Reports, and Oral Presentations

B.1 This book is about writing for publication. Many of my suggestions hold for all kinds of writing. In this appendix I give a few cautions and suggestions for types of manuscript that you do not necessarily intend to publish.

CLASS PAPERS AND DISSERTATIONS

B.2 The content of class papers and dissertations may differ from that of manuscripts for publication. You may need:

- An introduction that constitutes more than 10 percent of your manuscript.
- Detailed explanations of the importance of each document you cite.
- Explicit statement, and explanation, of assumptions.

○ Detailed explanations of methods, even if well described in previous publications.
○ A detailed summary at the end.

You may also be forbidden to seek critical help from fellow students. The reason for these differences is that you are showing your knowledge of a topic, much as you would on an examination. On other aspects of writing, follow the guidelines given in Part I. You may also want to read Bart and Frankel (1971), *The Student Sociologist's Handbook;* and Lester (1971), *Writing Research Papers.*

B.3   With respect to editorial style, you may be required to:

○ Type tables and illustrations into the body of the text.
○ Type notes at the bottoms of pages on which they occur.
○ Single-space notes, list of references, and bibliographies.
○ Single-space blocked, indented quotations.

Always ask your instructor or dissertation supervisor what style guide you should follow. Many prefer Turabian (1973), *A Manual for Writers of Term Papers, Theses, and Dissertations*, which is available in paperback.

PROPOSALS FOR RESEARCH GRANTS

B.4   When writing a proposal for a research grant, you will probably need:

○ An introduction that explains in detail each hypothesis you want to test, and why.
○ A very detailed, step-by-step, month-by-month explanation of method and analytical techniques.
○ A section that explains the results you expect, and why.
○ A detailed budget.
○ A detailed timetable.

On other aspects of writing, follow the guidelines in Chapters 2 to 6, especially Sections 2.3 and 2.11. For more information on grants see White (1975), *Grants: How to Find Out about Them and What to Do Next.* For editorial style and format, follow the instructions of the agency to which you are applying. After you have done the research, you may be able to use information in the proposal as the basis for the introduction, method, and discussion sections of journal articles.

PROGRESS REPORTS

B.5 For progress reports to sponsoring agencies on research grants and contracts, be specific and pay particular attention to practical results:

○ How far along is your investigation?
○ Exactly what work have you done?
○ How much work remains?
○ How much money have you spent, and for what?
○ Justify outlay in terms of results, or explain why when the results do not give justification.

For other aspects of writing, follow the guidelines in Part I and the instructions from your agency. Also consult Mathes and Stevenson (1976), *Designing Technical Reports.* If your original proposal has been sufficiently specific, you may be able to base part of your report on answers to questions raised in the proposal.

ORAL PRESENTATIONS

B.6 For an oral presentation,

○ Concentrate on one main idea. Delete most details rather than trying to summarize them.

○ Use a written text. Plan on approximately 10 typed pages (250 words per page) for a 20-minute presentation.

○ Mark places at which you wish to show slides or write on the blackboard.

○ If possible, put data in tabular form and reproduce for distribution. This technique allows you to omit detail from your oral presentation.

○ Do not read the text. Speak it to your audience. Try speaking from abbreviated note cards even though you have the text. If interrupted, mark your place on text or cards.

○ If you use visual aids, test the equipment beforehand in the room where you will speak. You should be able to read each illustration from the farthest point in the room.

○ Rehearse to be sure your speech flows smoothly. Speech for an oral presentation is different from the written speech of a journal article.

○ Ask a few colleagues to listen to a dress rehearsal, or deliver the talk as part of a class lecture.

Most commonly, you will find the talk too long and the wording somewhat awkward. For suggestions to reduce length, consult Sections 5.56 to 5.62.

A Sample Prospectus
for a Monograph

This prospectus is unpublished and is used by permission of its author.

PROSPECTUS FOR

Power, Social Structure, and Advice in American Science

The United States Federal Science Advisory System from 1950 to 1972

NICHOLAS C. MULLINS
Indiana University

Draft. August 1975. Do not cite or quote without permission.

403

RATIONALE, SUBJECT, AND SCOPE

This book reports on a study of the federal science advising system. Detailed knowledge of this system is important because the United States federal government asks scientists for advice on many topics. Some topics are purely technical, while others affect federal policy. For example, scientists are presently being asked to suggest and investigate ways to produce energy that do not use oil. Scientists also advise on matters that directly affect all scientists, such as the need to support the training of more scientists, or to provide funds for building research laboratories.

Scientists are called together in committees to provide information and judgments on specific topics; subsequently the committees adjourn or are disbanded. The advisory system is important to science because the committees' evaluations affect resources for research and training. The system is probably less important to government, but it still affects decisions on policy. Detailed analysis of advising is also important for another reason. The advisory system has often been accused, on the basis of little evidence, of being an elite. My data answer this accusation, and my analysis shows why controversy has persisted.

My population is the entire universe of advisers (over 30,000 persons) who served in the federal science advisory system (NAS/NRC, NIH, NSF, and DOD) between 1950 and 1972. I use structural theory as a framework, and structuralist analytic techniques. Most of the data are membership lists taken from annual reports. The result is an analysis different from any previous analysis of organizations in general or of scientific organizations in particular. For the first time, we can examine the entire deep structure of science advising. No longer need we depend only on organizational charts (though I use some of those) or on unsystematic interview data for a picture of science advising and its effects.

This book will become a standard reference on the federal science advising system. It contains data not available elsewhere. Interpretations of those data will have to be taken

into account by all future students of science advising, power
and influence in science, social stratification in science, sociology of knowledge, social structure, and elites generally, and
their behavior.

MARKET

This book will interest (1) participants in the advisory system,
(2) managers and staff of advising systems, (3) organizational
sociologists, (4) sociologists of science, (5) political scientists,
and (6) sociological theorists. Some present and former advisers
(my study included over 30,000 advisers) may want to know
more about the organizations they advise; they may also want
to know how their experience compares with my analysis.
Managers and staff of advising systems (there are approximately 1000 such persons, in a group covering health, defense,
agriculture, energy, and many basic science areas) may want to
learn more about their organizations, see what has been good
and bad, and have a guide for correcting poor practices.

Sociologists specializing in organizations (approximately 500
in the United States) will be interested in my methodology.
Sociologists of science (approximately 200 in the United States
and 200 overseas) will be interested in my substantive findings.
Political scientists will be interested in my findings on elites
and on the relationship of advising to politics. Sociological
theorists (about 500) will be interested in my structuralist approach to organizational theory.

The book may have limited use (largely as reference-room
reading) in graduate and upper-level undergraduate courses in
social organization, social theory, and sociology of science.
Most likely, only students planning to specialize in one of the
specialties named above would purchase it.

COMPETITION

My book has no direct competition. The recent books that
discuss similar topics, but from much different perspectives
and with more limited data, are listed below (most recent first).

Boffey, Philip. 1975. *Brain Bank of America*. McGraw-Hill.

Von Hippel, Frank and Joel Primack. 1974. *Advice and Dissent*. Basic Books.

Salomon, J. J. 1973. *Science and Politics*. MIT Press.

Schooler, Dean. 1971. *Science, Scientists and Public Policy*. Free Press.

Brooks, Harvey. 1968. *The Government of Science*. MIT Press.

Price, Don K. 1965. *The Scientific Estate*. Harvard University Press. 1963 (reissue of 1953). *Science and Government*. Oxford.

The recent, steady flow of high-quality books on science policy implies that a market for such books exists. Boffey studied the NRC by doing case studies of NRC activities. His focus was the NRC as an agency that affects public policy (e.g., on environmental affairs and food additives) but is not either a policymaking body or an organization open to change through political elections. Von Hippel and Primack also did case studies, but on several different agencies, and make arguments similar to Boffey's. Both books make strong objections to current practices, and both argue for alternative institutions to help balance current institutions. Schooler's is a more scholarly version of Von Hippel and Primack's book. He analyzed specific decisions on policy and showed whether scientific input affected them. The book is dry, with very few surprises.

Salomon outlines science policy by placing science in a general, societal framework. He sometimes uses data, but his focus is on general issues. Brooks and Price are both wise men, writing only from their personal experiences. The books by Salomon, Brooks, and Price have important insights, but all are essays rather than studies.

PHYSICAL CHARACTERISTICS

My book has two parts. The first part describes the history, formal structure, and general functions of the NAS/NRC, NIH, and NSF. The second part is sociological analysis of the first part. In Part II I examine crucial aspects of advising and give a clear picture of the total system and of advisers' characteristics.

The manuscript, prepared in elite type, has 11 chapters (including an introduction) plus a preface, a methodological appendix, and a glossary of acronyms (without which casual reading would be difficult). The chapters average 40 typed pages in length. Part I has 151 text pages. Chapter 6 has 40 pages of text. Chapters 1 to 6 also have 27 tables and 13 figures. Chapters 7 to 11 will have approximately 200 pages of text, 20 tables, and 5 figures. The typed lines are 6 inches long. The top and bottom margins are approximately $1\frac{1}{4}$ inches. Overall estimates, including appendix: 440 text pages, 49 tables, and 19 figures. There will be no photographs.

The manuscript will follow *A Manual of Style*'s natural science requirements.

AUTHOR'S QUALIFICATIONS

I have a reputation in the sociology of science and in social theory, which should aid in selling the book. I have also been a reliable and cooperative author of previous books. My vita is attached.

SCHEDULE FOR COMPLETION

Chapters 1 to 6 are done.
Chapter 7: January 30, 1976.
Chapter 8: February 1.
Chapter 9: February 20.
Chapter 10: March 5.
Chapter 11: March 20.
Appendix: April 1.
Glossary: April 10.
Bibliography: April 20.

APPENDIX D

A Guide for Typists

D.1 If you are typing an article,

○ Read Sections 8.1 to 8.5 and the general instructions in Sections 8.6 to 8.17.

○ Instructions on use of numbers are in Section 5.53.

○ If you need instructions for a specific part of an article, look in the outline at the beginning of Chapter 8. Each part of an article is treated in a separate major section. Cover sheets are discussed in the third major section; abstracts in the fourth, and so forth.

○ When typing tables, use Figure 3.1 (from Chapter 3) and the instructions in Sections 8.60 to 8.68 as a guide.

○ If possible, obtain a copy of the journal to which the author will submit the article, or copies of pages that show headings, subheadings, tables, illustrations, notes, and documentation. Also request a copy of the journal's editorial style sheet. Use the examples to guide you when instructions are ambiguous. However, also note the cautions in Section 8.3.

○ When you return the manuscript, ask the author to tell you about any recurrent errors in the typing. Knowing them may improve your typing on the next article.

D.2   If you are typing a manuscript for a book,

○ Read the general instructions in Sections 12.10 to 12.22. Instructions for capitalization are in Section 8.13; for use of numbers, in 5.53.
○ Use Figure 3.1 (Chapter 3) as a guide for preparing tables.
○ Obtain a copy of the publisher's style manual. Most publishers supply them free to authors when they sign contracts. If the author has not signed a contract, ask which editorial style you should follow. Agree on formats for tables, illustrations, headings, subheadings, chapter beginnings, notes, and documentation. If the author is using one of the styles commonly used by journals, use the guidelines in Chapter 8.
○ When you return the manuscript, ask the author to tell you about any recurrent errors in the typing. Knowing them may improve your typing on subsequent manuscripts.

Bibliography

Abelson, P. H. 1974. Troublesome portents for scientific journals. *Science* **186**:693.

Addison, H. J. n.d. Books and bucks: The economics of college textbook publishing. New York: Association of American Publishers, Inc.

Addison-Wesley Publishing Company, Inc. 1965. *A guide for authors*. Reading, Mass.: Addison-Wesley.

Althauser, R. P., and Spivack, S. S. 1975. *The unequal elites*. New York: Wiley-Interscience.

American Psychological Association. 1974. *Publication manual of the American Psychological Association*. 2d ed. Washington, D.C.: American Psychological Association.

American Psychologist. 1974. Summary report of journal operations for 1973. *American Psychologist* **29**:474.

————. 1975. Summary report of journal operations for 1974. *American Psychologist* **30**:619.

American Sociological Review. Notice to contributors. Rev. 1975. *American Sociological Review* **40**:inside front cover.

Armer, M. 1975. *African social psychology: A review and annotated bibliography*. African Bibliography Series, Vol. 2. New York: Africana Publishing Company.

Backman, C. W. 1972. Report of the editor of *Sociometry*. *The American Sociologist* (August):26.

Balkin, R. 1974. On submitting a proposal to a publisher. *Sociological Inquiry* **44**:65–72.

Barber, V. 1975. How to negotiate a publishing contract. *Change* (April):61–63.

Bart, P., and Frankel, L. 1971. *The student sociologist's handbook*. Cambridge, Mass.: Schenkman.

411

Bartlett, J. 1968. *Familiar quotations: A collection of passages, phrases, and proverbs traced to their sources in ancient and modern literature.* 14th ed., rev. and enlarged, ed. E. B. Morrison. Boston: Little, Brown and Co.

Baumol, W. J., and Heim, P. 1967. On contracting with publishers: Or what every author should know. *A.A.U.P. Bulletin* (Spring):30–46.

Bernstein, T. M. 1965. *The careful writer: A modern guide to English usage.* New York: Atheneum.

Bidwell, C. E. 1974. From the editors. *American Journal of Sociology* **79**:1071–1072.

Blanchard, D. C. 1974. References and unreferences. *Science* **185**:1003.

Bunnett, J. F. 1975. Journal reviews. *Science* **189**:1045.

Cole, J. R., and S. Cole. 1973. *Social stratification in science.* Chicago: University of Chicago Press.

Corbett, E. P. J. 1973. *The little English handbook: Choices and conventions.* New York: Wiley.

Cutright, P. 1974. The civilian earnings of white and black draftees and non-veterans. *American Sociological Review* **39**:317–327.

Dale, E., and Chall, J. S. 1948. A formula for predicting readability. *Educational Research Bulletin* **27**:11–20, 28.

Davis, J. A., and Jacobs, A. M. 1968. Tabular presentation. *International encyclopedia of the social sciences.* New York: The Macmillan Company and The Free Press.

DeBakey, L., ed. 1976. *The scientific journal: Editorial policies and practices.* St. Louis: C. V. Mosby Company.

Denzin, N. K. 1969. Symbolic interactionism and ethnomethodology: A proposed synthesis. *American Sociological Review* **34**:922–934.

Deutsch, K. W. 1963. *The nerves of government: Models of political communication and control.* London: Free Press of Glencoe.

The directory of publishing opportunities. 2d ed. Chicago: Marquis Academic Media.

Ewing, D. W. 1974. *Writing for results in business, government, and the professions.* New York: Wiley-Interscience.

Flesch, R. F. 1951. *How to test readability.* New York: Harper & Brothers.

———. 1974. *The art of readable writing.* New York: Harper & Row.

Fowler, H. W. 1965. *A dictionary of modern English usage.* 2d ed. Rev. by Sir Ernest Gowers. Oxford: Oxford University Press.

Frankenthaler, M. R. 1976. Utilizing the computer to prepare a manuscript. *Scholarly Publishing* **7**:61–68.

Franklin, M. A. 1967. Another look at publishing contracts: The indemnity provision. *A.A.U.P. Bulletin* (Autumn):275–277.

Freeman, H. W. 1972. Report of the editor of the *Journal of Health and Social Behavior. The American Sociologist* (August):27.

Fry, E. 1968. A readability formula that saves time. *Journal of Reading* **11**:513–516, 575–578.

Garfield, E. 1975. Libraries need a copyright clearinghouse—ISI has one they can use. *Current Contents* (December 8):5–7.

Garvey, W. D., Lin, N., and Nelson, C. E. 1970. Communication in the physical and the social sciences. *Science* **170**:1166–1173.

Gilbart, H. n.d. Readability of college texts. St. Petersburg (Florida) Junior College, Clearwater Campus (mimeo).

Gunning, R. 1968. *The technique of clear writing.* Rev. ed. New York: McGraw-Hill.

Hare, A. P. 1962. *Handbook of small group research.* New York: Free Press.

Harper & Row. 1966. *Author's manual.* New York: Harper & Row.

Henry, N. L. 1974. Copyright: Its adequacy in technological societies. *Science* **186**:993–1004.

Hill, R. T. 1973. Report of the editor of *Sociometry. A.S.A. Footnotes* (August):13–14.

Hirsch, W., Kulley, A. M., and Efron, R. T. 1974. The gatekeeping process in scientific communication: Norms, practices, and content of book reviews in professional journals. Working paper #83, Institute for the Study of Social Change, Department of Sociology and Anthropology, Purdue University (September, mimeo).

Holmes, O. 1974. Thesis to book: What to get rid of. Parts I and II. *Scholarly Publishing* **5**:339–349; **6**:40–50.

———. 1975. Thesis to book: What to do with what is left. *Scholarly Publishing* **6**:165–176.

Houghton Mifflin Company College Department. 1974. *A guide to publishing.* Boston: Houghton Mifflin.

Irvine, S. H., Sanders, J. T., and Klingelhofer, E. L. 1973. *Human behavior in Africa: A bibliography of psychological and related writings.* Westport, Conn.: Greenwood Press (for the African Bibliographic Center).

Jackson, J. J. 1973. Report of the editor of the *Journal of Health and Social Behavior. A.S.A. Footnotes* (August):14.

———. 1974. Report of the editor of the *Journal of Health and Social Behavior. A.S.A. Footnotes* (August):13–14.

———. 1975. Report of the editor of the *Journal of Health and Social Behavior. A.S.A. Footnotes* (August):13.

Jakobovits, L. A., and Osgood, C. E. 1967. Connotations of twenty psychological journals to their professional readers. *American Psychologist* **22**:792–800.

1961-. Journal citation reports. In *SCI.* Philadelphia: Institute for Scientific Information.

Journal of the American Statistical Association. n.d. *JASA* style sheet. Washington, D.C.: American Statistical Association.

Kachergis, J. 1976. New technology, new solutions. *Scholarly Publishing* **7**:157–160.

Kitsuse, J. 1975. Report of the editor of *Sociology of Education*. *A.S.A. Footnotes* (August):13.

Knoke, D. 1974. A causal synthesis of sociological and psychological models of American voting behavior. *Social Forces* **53**:92–101.

Kuhn, T. S. 1970. *The structure of scientific revolutions*. Rev. ed. Chicago: University of Chicago Press.

Labovitz, S., and Hagedorn, R. 1971. *Introduction to social research*. New York: McGraw-Hill.

Lester, J. D. 1971. *Writing research papers; a complete guide*. Rev. ed. Glenview, Ill.: Scott, Foresman.

Lin, N. 1974. Stratification of the formal communication system in American sociology. *The American Sociologist* **9**:199–206.

Linton, M. 1972. *A simplified style manual; for the preparation of journal articles in psychology, social sciences, education, and literature*. New York: Appleton-Century-Crofts.

Literary market place. Published annually. New York: R. R. Bowker Co.

McCartney, J. L. 1972. The editor's page. *The Sociological Quarterly* **13**:430.

———. 1973a. Publish or perish. *The Sociological Quarterly* **14**:450, 600.

———. 1973b. Manuscript reviewing. *The Sociological Quarterly* **14**:290, 440–444.

———. 1973c. Preparing manuscripts. *The Sociological Quarterly* **14**:2, 144.

———. 1973d. Selecting reviewers. *The Sociological Quarterly* **14**:146, 287–288.

———. 1974. Simultaneous submission of manuscripts. *The Sociological Quarterly* **15**:163, 315–317.

———. 1975. The responsibilities of reviewers. *The Sociological Quarterly* **16**:434, 437, 478, 499, 521, 533.

McGraw-Hill Book Company. n.d. *Guidelines for equal treatment of the sexes in McGraw-Hill Book Company publications*. New York: McGraw-Hill, Public Information and Publicity Department.

McLaughlin, G. H. 1969. SMOG grading—a new readability formula. *Journal of Reading* **12**:639–646.

Manning, R. 1975. Thurble's fabulous word machine. *The Atlantic* **235** (6):67–69.

Mathes, J. C., and Stevenson, D. W. 1976. *Designing technical reports: Writing for audiences in organizations*. Indianapolis: Bobbs-Merrill.

Mayhew, L. 1974. Report of the editor of *The American Sociologist*. *A.S.A. Footnotes* (August):13.

———. 1975. Report of the editor of *The American Sociologist*. *A.S.A. Footnotes* (August):13.

Menzel, D. H., Jones, H. M., and Boyd, L. G. 1961. *Writing a technical paper*. New York: McGraw-Hill.

Merton, R. K. 1961. Singletons and multiples in scientific discovery. *Proceedings of the American Philosophical Society* **105** (October): 470–486.

Miles, J. A., Jr. 1976. Knowing the score at Scholars Press. *Scholarly Publishing* **7**:221–234.

Miller, D. C. 1970. *Handbook of research design and social measurement.* 2d ed. New York: David McKay. 3d ed.: 1977.

Mitchell, J. H. 1968. *Writing for professional and technical journals.* New York: Wiley.

Modern Language Association of America. 1970. *The MLA style sheet.* 2d ed. New York: Modern Language Association.

Nature (editorial). 1971. Who will referee the referees? *Nature* **230**:3.

Newman, E. H. 1974. *Strictly speaking. Will America be the death of English?* Indianapolis: Bobbs-Merrill.

Nisbet, J. P. 1974. Editing the journal. *British Journal of Educational Psychology* **44** (November):221–223.

O'Connor, M., and Woodford, F. P. 1975. *Writing scientific papers in English; An ELSE-Ciba Foundation guide for authors.* The Hague: Elsevier.

Oromaner, M. J. 1970. A note on analytical properties and prestige of sociology departments. *The American Sociologist* **5**:240–252.

Orwell, G. 1950. Politics and the English language. In *Shooting an elephant*, pp. 77–92. New York: Harcourt, Brace.

1933. *The Oxford English dictionary.* Oxford: At the Clarendon Press.

Parsons, T. 1949 (first published in 1937). *The structure of social action.* Glencoe, Ill.: Free Press.

Perrin, P. G. 1972. *Writer's guide and index to English.* 5th ed. Rev. by W. R. Ebbitt. Glenview, Ill.: Scott, Foresman.

Pescosolido, J., and Gervase, C. 1971. *Reading expectancy and readability.* Dubuque, Iowa: Kendall/Hunt.

Pirsig, R. M. 1974. *Zen and the art of motorcycle maintenance: An inquiry into values.* New York: Bantam.

Polanyi, M. 1946. *Science, faith and society.* Chicago: University of Chicago Press.

Pope, W. 1973. Classic on classic: Parsons' interpretation of Durkheim. *American Sociological Review* **38**:399–415.

Price, D. de S. 1964. Ethics of scientific publication. *Science* **144**: 655–657.

Resnikoff, H. L., and Dolby, J. L. 1972. *Access: A study of information storage and retrieval with emphasis on library information systems.* Washington, D.C.: U.S. Department of Health, Education, and Welfare (Office of Education, Bureau of Research).

Rhoades, L. J. 1974. *The author's guide to selected journals.* ASA Professional Information Series. Washington, D.C.: American Sociological Association.

Riesman, D. 1950. *The lonely crowd.* New Haven: Yale University Press.

1962. *Roget's international thesaurus*. 3d ed. New York: Thomas Y. Crowell Co.

Sage Publications. n.d. *Journal editorial style*. Sage Publications. Beverly Hills, Calif.: Sage Publications.

Schwartz, B. 1975. Manuscript queues and editorial organization. In *Queuing and waiting: Studies in the social organization of access and delay*, pp. 63–87. Chicago: University of Chicago Press.

Selltiz, C., Jahoda, M., Deutsch, M., and Cook, S. W. 1961. The research report. In *Research methods in social relations*. Rev. ed., pp. 441–454. New York: Holt, Rinehart, and Winston.

Short, J. F., Jr. 1972. Report of the editor of the *American Sociological Review*. *The American Sociologist* (August):26.

———. 1973. Report of the editor of the *American Sociological Review*. *A.S.A. Footnotes* (August):13.

———. 1974. Report of the editor of the *American Sociological Review*. *A.S.A. Footnotes* (August):12–13.

Silverman, R. J., and Collins, E. L. 1975. *The "gatekeeper" role in educational journal publishing*. National Institute of Education Project Report #3-1104. Columbus, Ohio: The Ohio State University Research Foundation (May).

Smith, A. E. 1975. Comments on multiple submissions policy. *A.S.A. Footnotes* (May):2, 13.

Standard and Poor's register of corporations, directors, and executives. Published annually. New York: Standard and Poor's Corp.

Standing Committee on Publications of the British Psychological Society. 1971. *Suggestions to authors*. Rev. ed. London: Cambridge University Press.

Stedman, J. C. 1967. The copyright law revision: Its impact upon educational activities. *A.A.U.P. Bulletin* (Summer):126–132.

Strunk, W. Jr., and White, E. B. 1959. *The elements of style*. Rev. ed. New York: Macmillan.

1973. Submission guide for journals in general teacher education. *Teacher Education Forum* 1(11):1–27.

1951. *Thorndike-Barnhart comprehensive desk dictionary*. 1st ed. Garden City, N.Y.: Doubleday & Co.

Tichy, H. J. 1966. *Effective writing for managers, engineers, scientists*. New York: Wiley-Interscience.

Treiman, D. J., and Terrell, K. 1975. Sex and the process of status attainment: A comparison of working women and men. *American Sociological Review* 40:174–200.

Turabian, K. L. 1973. *A manual for writers of term papers, theses, and dissertations*. 4th ed. Chicago: University of Chicago Press.

1975–1976. *Ulrich's international periodicals directory*. 16th ed. New York: R. R. Bowker.

University of Chicago Press. 1969. *A manual of style*. 12th ed., rev. Chicago: University of Chicago Press.

Wagner, N. 1976. Scholars as publishers: A new paradigm. *Scholarly Publishing* 7:101–112.

Wagner, S. 1976a. S.22: Copyrighted 1976; Congress approves "monumental" bill. *Publishers Weekly* 210 (October 11):22–24.

———. 1976b. Copying and the copyright bill: Where the new revision stands on "fair use." *Publishers Weekly* 210 (October 18):28–30.

———. 1976c. Provisions of new copyright bill move U. S. closer to Berne Union. *Publishers Weekly* 210 (October 25):28,30.

Webb, E. J., Campbell, D. T., Schwartz, R. D. and Sechrest, L. 1966. *Unobtrusive measures: Nonreactive research in the social sciences.* Chicago: Rand McNally.

1972. *Webster's biographical dictionary.* Springfield, Mass.: G. & C. Merriam Co.

1975. *Webster's new collegiate dictionary.* Springfield, Mass.: G. & C. Merriam Co.

1973. *Webster's new dictionary of synonyms; a dictionary of discriminated synonyms with antonyms and analogous and contrasted words.* 1st ed. Springfield, Mass.: G. & C. Merriam Co.

1972. *Webster's new geographical dictionary.* Rev. ed. Springfield, Mass.: G. & C. Merriam Co.

1961. *Webster's third new international dictionary of the English language, unabridged.* 3d ed. Springfield, Mass.: G. & C. Merriam Co.

Weinberg, M. S., and Bell, A. P., eds. 1972. *Homosexuality: An annotated bibliography.* New York: Harper & Row.

White, H. C., Boorman, S. A., and Breiger, R. L. 1976. Social structure from multiple networks: I. Blockmodels of roles and positions. *American Journal of Sociology* 81:730–780.

White, V. P. *Grants: How to find out about them and what to do next.* New York: Plenum.

Wilson, E. K. 1974. An appeal to prospective *Social Forces* authors. Reprinted with permission in *The Sociological Quarterly* 15:2, 159.

Woodford, F. P., ed. 1968. *Scientific writing for graduate students: A manual on the teaching of scientific writing.* New York: Rockefeller University Press.

Zeisel, H. 1968. *Say it with figures.* 5th ed., rev. New York: Harper & Row.

Zelditch, M., Jr. 1975. Report of the editor of the *American Sociological Review.* *A.S.A. Footnotes* (August):12.

Ziman, J. M. 1968. *Public knowledge: The social dimension of science.* Cambridge: Cambridge University Press.

Zuckerman, H. A. 1968. Patterns of name ordering among authors of scientific papers: A study of social symbolism and its ambiguity. *American Journal of Sociology* 74:276–291.

———, and Merton, R. K. 1971. Patterns of evaluation in science: Institutionalisation, structure, and functions of the referee system. *Minerva* 9(1):66–100.

Index

Unless otherwise noted, references are to section numbers. Sections are numbered sequentially by chapter (5.1, 5.2, and so forth).